THE AMERICAN CIVIL LIBERTIES UNION

ORGANIZATIONS AND INTEREST GROUPS
(VOL. 3)

GARLAND REFERENCE LIBRARY
OF SOCIAL SCIENCE
(VOL. 743)

Organizations and Interest Groups
Series Editor: James S. Bowman

1. The General Accounting Office: An Annotated Bibliography
   Robert L. Hollings

2. Consultants and Consulting: Sources and Resources
   Donald Levitan

3. The American Civil Liberties Union: An Annotated Bibliography
   Samuel Walker

THE AMERICAN CIVIL LIBERTIES UNION
An Annotated Bibliography

Samuel Walker

GARLAND PUBLISHING, INC. • NEW YORK & LONDON
1992

© 1992 Samuel Walker
All rights reserved

Library of Congress Cataloging-in-Publication Data

Walker, Samuel, 1942–
   The American Civil Liberties Union : an annotated bibliography / Samuel Walker.
      p. cm. — (Organizations and interest groups; vol. 3) (Garland reference library of social science; vol. 743)
   Includes indexes.
   ISBN 0-8153-0047-6 (acid-free paper)
   1. American Civil Liberties Union—Bibliography. I. Title. II. Series. III. Series: Garland reference library of social science; v. 743.
KF4741.W35   1992
016.34273'085—dc20
[016.34730285]   91-46579
                                                                              CIP

Printed on acid-free, 250-year-life paper
Manufactured in the United States of America

Contents

SERIES FOREWORD	xi
FOREWORD	xiii
INTRODUCTION	xv
I. GENERAL WORKS	3
A. Descriptions of the ACLU	3
B. Official Policies	4
C. Periodicals	5
D. Reports	6
E. ACLU Handbooks	8
F. Collections of Essays	13
II. HISTORY OF THE ACLU	15
A. General ACLU History	15
B. Origins of the ACLU, 1914–1919	19
C. The 1920s	26
1. General	26
2. Amnesty for Political Prisoners	31
3. Federal Government, Illegal Actions of	32
4. Labor, Rights of	33
5. Sacco and Vanzetti Case	35
6. *Scopes* Case	36
7. Speech, Press, and Assembly, Freedom of	37
D. The 1930s	41
1. General	41
2. Academic Freedom	43
3. Aliens, Immigrants, Rights of	44
4. Civil Rights	45

5.	Communist–Related Issues	46
6.	Labor, Rights of	51
7.	Nazi-Related Issues	54
8.	Police Misconduct	55
9.	Religious Liberty	56
10.	Speech, Press, and Assembly, Freedom of	57
11.	Other Issues	59

E. World War II, 1940–1945   59
  1. General   59
  2. Academic Freedom   62
  3. Civil Rights   63
  4. Conscientious Objectors   65
  5. Japanese-Americans, Internment of   65
  6. Religious Liberty   68
  7. Speech, Press, and Assembly, Freedom of   69

F. The Cold War, 1945–1960   70
  1. General   70
  2. Academic Freedom   75
  3. Blacklisting   76
  4. Federal Bureau of Investigation   77
  5. Federal Loyalty Program   79
  6. Fifth Amendment   80
  7. House Un-American Activities Committee   80
  8. Loyalty Oaths   83
  9. The Smith Act   84
 10. Wiretapping   84
 11. Other Issues   85

G. Post-World War II America, 1945–1960   86
  1. General   86
  2. Civil Rights   88
  3. Due Process/Police Misconduct   89
  4. International Civil Liberties   90
  5. Labor, Rights of   91
  6. Religious Liberty   92
  7. Speech, Press, and Assembly, Freedom of   94

H. The 1960s and 1970s   98
  1. General   98

2. Academic Freedom	104
3. Civil Rights	107
4. Death Penalty	110
5. Due Process/Police Misconduct	111
6. Mentally Ill, Rights of the	115
7. National Security	116
8. Prisoners, Rights of	118
9. Privacy	119
10. Religious Liberty	123
11. Skokie	124
12. Speech, Press, and Assembly, Freedom of	128
13. Vietnam War	131
14. Watergate	135
15. Women, Rights of	136
16. Other Issues	138

III. CONTEMPORARY CIVIL LIBERTIES ISSUES, 1980–1991 — 141

A. The ACLU — 141
  1. General — 141
  2. 1988 Presidential Election, ACLU Role in — 148
  3. Bork, Robert, Nomination to the Supreme Court, ACLU Role in — 149

B. Freedom of Belief, Expression, and Association — 150
  1. Censorship, General — 150
  2. Conscientious Objection to Military Service — 154
  3. Pornography — 155
  4. Racist/Sexist Speech/College Campus Speech Codes — 156
  5. Religious Liberty — 159

C. Due Process of Law/Crime/Police Misconduct — 163
  1. General — 163
  2. Police Misconduct — 166

D. Equal Protection — 169
  1. Race Discrimination — 169
  2. Women's Rights — 170

E. National Security — 172

F. Prisoners' Rights	178
G. Privacy	180
1. General	180
2. Lesbian and Gay People, Rights of	180
3. Reproductive Freedom	182
4. Right to Die	185
H. Other Civil Liberties Issues	185
1. Children, Parents, Families, Rights of	185
2. Economic Rights/The Poor/The Homeless	186
3. Employees, Rights of	187
4. Immigration	188
5. International Civil Liberties	189
IV. GENERAL CIVIL LIBERTIES ISSUES	**191**
A. Civil Liberties, Constitutional Law	191
B. Legal Role of ACLU and Other Public Interest Groups	195
C. Public Opinion about Civil Liberties	198
D. International Perspectives	200
V. INDIVIDUAL ACLU LEADERS	**203**
A. Roger Nash Baldwin	203
1. Books and Articles about	203
2. Books and Articles by	205
a. 1910–1919	205
b. 1920–1929	208
c. 1930–1939	211
d. 1940–1949	215
e. 1950–1981	219
3. Interviews with	222
4. Obituaries	223
B. Other ACLU Leaders	224

Contents

VI. RESOURCES	237
A. ACLU Offices	237
1. National Offices	237
2. ACLU Affiliate Offices	238
B. Archival Material	245
1. Records of the National ACLU	245
2. Records of ACLU Affiliates	246
3. Personal Papers of ACLU Leaders	250
4. Records of Other Organizations	258
NAME INDEX	261
SUBJECT INDEX	281

Series Foreword

The modern era is one of organizations, and as we approach the next century there is little evidence that the importance of institutions in society will diminish. As they have grown in scope and number so has material published by and about them. Yet managers, academicians and their students, and researchers do not have ready access to information about these significant social entities. In an increasingly complex world of organizations, more and more people need such data to assist in defining and solving problems.

The lack of a comprehensive information system has frustrated users, disseminators, and generators of knowledge; the documentation and control of the literature on organizations have been generally neglected. Indeed, major gaps in the development of the literature, the bibliographical structure of the field, have evolved

Garland Publishing, Inc., has inaugurated the present series as an authoritative guide to information sources on the subject. It seeks to consolidate published material on a wide variety of public, private, and non-profit organizations including: (a) federal agencies, Congressional committees, the judicial branch, and international bodies; (b) corporations, interest groups, trade unions, and consulting firms; as well as (c) professional associations, scientific societies, and educational institutions.

Each book will be compiled by one or more specialists in the area. The authors—practitioners and scholars—are selected in open competition from across the country. They design their work to include an introductory essay, a wide variety of bibliographic materials, and, where appropriate, an information resource section. Thus each contribution in the collection provides a systematic basis for managers and researchers to make informed judgments in the course of their work.

Since no single volume can adequately encompass such a broad, interdisciplinary subject, the series is intended as a continuous project that will incorporate new bodies of literature as needed. Its titles represent the initial building blocks in an operating information system for understanding organizations and society. As an open-ended endeavor, it is hoped that not only will the series serve to summarize knowledge in the field but also will contribute to its advancement.

This collection of book-length bibliographies is the product of considerable collaboration on the part of many people. Special appreciation is extended to the individual contributors in the series and to the anonymous reviewers of each of the volumes. Inquiries should be made to the Series Editor.

James S. Bowman
Department of Public Administration
Florida State University

Foreword

Since its founding after World War I, the American Civil Liberties Union has become an integral part of American society. Committed to upholding key elements of the Constitution, this relatively small group of individuals who are dedicated to the maintenance of the Bill of Rights has weathered criticism from both the right and the left as it has defended unpopular individuals and groups such as the Ku Klux Klan, Nazis, Jehovah's Witnesses, and Communists.

The history of the ACLU parallels the extension of civil rights and liberties in the United States. Not until the twentieth century were the freedoms enshrined in the Bill of Rights extended to protect citizens from actions by the states. The process by which these rights and liberties were incorporated through the Fourteenth Amendment has been long and piecemeal. Not until U.S. the Supreme Court under the leadership of Chief Justice Earl Warren were major advances made to uphold the freedoms of speech, press, religion, assembly and privacy, the due processes rights of defendants in criminal cases, and equal protection under the law. The ACLU has fought to uphold and extend these rights in the wake of attacks by groups intent on maintaining the status quo.

During his famous visit in 1831, Alexis de Tocqueville observed the propensity of Americans to join organizations concerned with the public interest. Political scientists have since developed a large literature about the role of interest groups in American politics. Most such organizations pursue their public policy objectives through lobbying activities in the legislative and executive branches of the national and state governments. The ACLU, however, is a prime example (another would be the NAACP) of a group that has sought to achieve its goals through the judicial system. By providing direct legal assistance to individuals and organizations, and through extensive use of the amicus brief, the ACLU has been a major force in upholding and advancing civil liberties and rights. The fact that this has been accomplished with the support of only a limited staff, volunteer attorneys, and a relatively small membership is a major achievement. In addition to litigation the ACLU has played an important role in educating the public about the crucial role of civil liberties.

With a total of 1454 entries spanning almost three quarters of a century, this annotated bibliography provides an important research tool for scholars, attorneys, and policy analysts. Samuel Walker has organized the work into six chapters: general works concerning the ACLU, the history of the organization, contemporary and related civil liberties issues, ACLU leaders, and resources to guide scholars.

The American Civil Liberties Union today faces a very different judicial environment than it did when the U.S. Supreme Court and district courts were more supportive of rights and liberties. No longer can the ACLU expect to win 80 percent of its cases, as it did during the years of the Warren Court. Yet the organization continues its basic thrust. In recent years it has been active with respect to new issues such as the death penalty, prisoners' rights, and privacy. Through almost three quarters of a century the ACLU has remained a distinctively American institution, a strong and dedicated defender of the Bill of Rights

George F. Cole
University of Connecticut

Introduction

The American Civil Liberties Union (ACLU) is a private non-profit organization devoted to the defense of individual rights. The ACLU provides free legal assistance to persons whose rights have been violated, engages in lobbying on behalf of laws to protect individual rights, and conducts a program of public education in support of civil liberties.

The ACLU and Civil Liberties

The ACLU defines civil liberties in terms of four broad areas: First Amendment rights; due process of law; equal protection of the law; and privacy.

First Amendment rights include freedom of speech, press, and assembly; separation of church and state; and the right to free expression of religion. The area of due process of law encompasses rights guaranteed by the Fourth, Fifth, Sixth, Eighth, and Fourteenth Amendments to the Constitution. These include but are not limited to freedom from unreasonable searches and seizures, protection against self-incrimination, and protection against cruel and unusual punishments.

The area of equal protection of the law includes freedom from discrimination. This incorporates the area popularly referred to as "civil rights," referring to equality for African-Americans. It also includes protection against any form of discrimination based on race, ethnicity, national origins, religion, sex, age, physical condition, or sexual preference. The area of privacy includes the right to reproductive freedom, such as the right to choose an abortion, access to contraceptives, and protection against intrusive surveillance and/or unreasonable collection of personal information by government agencies.

The distinguishing feature of the ACLU's program is its nonpartisan defense of civil liberties. Thus, it defends the free speech rights of a controversial group without endorsing the ideas that group advocates. It defends the right of a criminal suspect to a fair trial without reference to that person's guilt or innocence. The defense of the rights of unpopular groups has been the source of some of the greatest controversies in ACLU history. The ACLU has defended the rights of Communists, Nazis, the Ku Klux Klan, and other groups considered unpopular by most Americans.

ACLU History

The ACLU was founded in January, 1920. It was a continuation of the National Civil Liberties Bureau (NCLB), established in 1917 to defend the rights of conscientious objectors and to protest violations of freedom of speech, press, and assembly during World War I. Because of its defense of dissenters, the NCLB was spied on by the federal government and its leaders were nearly prosecuted for violating the Espionage Act.

At the time it was founded, the ACLU had about 1,000 members and informal working relationships with local organizations in a number of cities. In its first years, it concentrated on defending the First Amendment rights of labor union organizers, seeking amnesty for persons convicted during World War I, and protesting vigilante attacks against African-Americans, Socialists, and alleged radicals. The ACLU achieved national fame in 1925 when it represented John T. Scopes who challenged a Tennessee law prohibiting the teaching of evolution in the public schools. The Scopes "Monkey Trial" has been a symbol of the ACLU's commitment to the free expression of controversial ideas.

During the 1930s the ACLU expanded its program to include a more comprehensive attack on censorship, including restrictions on the distribution of contraceptives and the dissemination of information about birth control. It also defended the First Amendment rights of American Nazi groups, and was criticized by many liberals for doing so. During World War II the ACLU was the only national organization that provided legal assistance to the Japanese-Americans who were

Introduction

evacuated from the west coast and interned in government relocation centers.

The ACLU challenged the anti-Communist measures of the Cold War during the 1940s and 1950s. As a result it was attacked by right-wing groups as "un-American" and "pro-Communist." The Federal Bureau of Investigation conducted a massive campaign of secret and illegal spying on the organization. Also during the post-World War II years the ACLU stepped up its challenge to government censorship in the arts and its support of civil rights for African-Americans. The ACLU filed an amicus brief in the famous 1954 case of *Brown v. Board of Education*, which declared segregated schools unconstitutional, along with most of the other important civil rights cases before the Supreme Court. Meanwhile, the ACLU pressed for a strict separation of church and state, opposing religious activity in public schools and any form of government financial aid to private religious schools.

The ACLU underwent a significant change in the 1960s, both in terms of its program and its organizational structure. Its civil liberties program expanded to include many new issues, such as the rights of women, prisoners, children, the mentally ill, and other groups. It decided that the existing criminal abortion laws violated individual rights and that the death penalty was unconstitutional. During the Vietnam War, the ACLU defended the rights of anti-war protesters and persons facing arbitrary treatment by their draft boards. In 1970 the ACLU declared the Vietnam War itself unconstitutional because Congress had not made a formal declaration of war. In 1973 the ACLU called for the impeachment of President Richard Nixon on the grounds that his actions in the Watergate scandal violated constitutional rights.

Organizationally, the ACLU also changed in the 1960s. Membership increased from about 50,000 in the early 1960s to about 250,000 in the early 1970s. The number of ACLU affiliates increased from about 15 in the early 1960s to the point where there was a staffed affiliate in all but four states by the mid-1970s. Finally, the ACLU organized a series of "special projects" devoted to particular civil liberties issues. Each project was funded by grants from private foundations. This represented both a new means of organizing the work of the ACLU and an important new source of financial support.

Throughout its history, the ACLU's definition of civil liberties issues has continued to evolve. While the protection of free speech was the ACLU's primary goal at the time of its founding in 1920, its view of the First Amendment was somewhat limited by the standards of later years. In its first ten years, for example, it concentrated on the protection of political speech and did relatively little to fight censorship of artistic works. Until the 1950s the ACLU was uncertain about whether the First Amendment protected allegedly "obscene" works of art. Also, until the 1950s the ACLU did not believe that libel suits violated freedom of speech and, on occasion, filed libel suits against its own critics. In the 1950s the ACLU began to move toward an "absolutist" interpretation of First Amendment rights.

On a few issues, the ACLU has reversed its official policy. In the 1940s, for example, the ACLU opposed an Equal Rights Amendment to the U.S. Constitution to protect women's rights. In 1970 the ACLU reversed itself, endorsed the ERA, and created a Women's Rights Project. The ACLU initially supported hand gun control legislation. It later reversed itself, holding that there was no civil liberties rationale for gun control.

In short, the ACLU's position on various civil liberties issues changes over time, reflecting new emergence of new ideas, changed social and political circumstances, and new perspectives on old issues. Decisions about official ACLU policy are made by the national Board of Directors.

The ACLU's Legal Program

The ACLU has been involved in most of the important Supreme Court cases involving individual rights. One historian estimated that the ACLU was involved in about 80% of the recognized "landmark" cases decided by the Supreme Court since 1925. The ACLU's first important victory before the Court was the 1925 case of *Gitlow v. New York* in which the Court held that the Fourteenth Amendment to the U.S. Constitution incorporated the Bill of Rights and made them applicable to the states. The incorporation principle established the foundation for

Introduction

much of the development of civil liberties and civil rights law that followed over the next sixty-five years.

In the mid-1960s, at the high point of the "Warren Court" years, the ACLU often won as many as 80% of its cases before the Supreme Court. When the Court began to move in a more conservative direction in the 1970s, the ACLU's success rate declined, in some years to less than 50%. In response, the ACLU began to shift is priorities and placed more emphasis on legislative protection of civil liberties. The ACLU Washington office, which had only one staff person in the 1960s, expanded to include over twelve full-time professional lobbyists by the 1980s.

The ACLU legal program has traditionally relied on free legal assistance provided by volunteer "cooperating" attorneys. Until the early 1960s, for example, the national office of the ACLU employed a single legal director to coordinate its litigation program. By the 1970s, the vast majority of ACLU cases were handled by the ACLU affiliates rather than the national office. This included an estimated 4,000 to 5,000 cases a year, with about 1,000 active cases at any given moment. The ACLU appears before the U.S. Supreme Court more than any other organization, with the exception of the federal government.

Beginning in the mid-1960s the ACLU began to make greater use of paid staff attorneys. A few of the larger affiliates began to employ staff lawyers, while the ACLU Foundation developed a number of "special projects" devoted to particular civil liberties issues. These included the National Prison Project, the Reproductive Freedom Project, the Women's Rights Project, and others. Special projects are funded by grants from private foundations and employ a full-time professional staff.

Criticisms of the ACLU

Because of its controversial positions on civil liberties issues, the ACLU has always been the object of strong criticism. From the very beginning, conservative and right-wing groups accused the ACLU of being "un-American" or "pro-Communist" because it defended the rights of American Communists. At the same time, some left-wing groups argued that the ACLU failed to help the poor and the working class because its definition of civil liberties only served the interests of the middle class and the rich who were able to take advantage of freedom of speech and press.

When the ACLU began to take a stronger position on separation of church and state in the 1940s, it was accused of being "anti-religion" and "anti-Christian." Conservative and religious fundamentalist groups were particularly upset by the ACLU opposition to prayer in public schools and opposition to censorship of sexually-oriented material. Beginning in the 1930s, the ACLU developed serious conflicts with the Catholic Church. From that point through the 1960s the conflict centered upon the Catholic Church's opposition to birth control and its support for censorship of the movies. In the 1950s a new conflict arose over the ACLU opposition to public funds for parochial schools, which the Catholic Church began to seek. Then, in the late 1970s, conflict increasingly centered on the Catholic Church's opposition to abortion and the ACLU's position on reproductive freedom.

In the late 1930s, when public support for civil liberties began to grow, a new criticism of the ACLU appeared among some liberals and moderate conservatives. This criticism expressed general support for civil liberties, but argued that the ACLU pushed individual rights to a dangerous extreme. Some liberal critics, for example, argued in favor of freedom of the press but held that the First Amendment did not protect obscenity. Others argued that the ACLU pushed separation of church and state too far when it opposed the singing of Christmas carols in public schools.

The ACLU's opposition to the Vietnam War and its call for the impeachment of President Nixon in the Watergate scandal led to a new criticism. Neo-conservatives argued that the ACLU had abandoned its historic nonpartisan role and was now following a partisan liberal political agenda. In the 1980s neo-conservatives argued that the ACLU's extreme interpretation of individual rights undermined the communitarian values necessary for a healthy society.

At the same time, the ACLU faced criticism from the political left. Some leftists felt that the ACLU had not been vigorous enough in its opposition to the Cold War during the

Introduction

1950s. In the late 1980s, some liberals and leftists criticized the ACLU's policy of defending the rights of racists and other hate groups. These critics supported policies that would punish forms of expression that were offensive to racial minorities, women, gay and lesbian people, and other powerless groups.

Organizational Structure

Organizationally, the ACLU maintains a national office in New York City, a legislative office in Washington, D.C., and regional offices in Atlanta and Denver. There are also staffed affiliate offices in forty-six states and the District of Columbia. The ACLU is governed by a Board of Directors consisting of eighty-one members that meets four times a year. Fifty-one of the Board members are elected by their respective affiliates; thirty members are elected at-large.

The ACLU affiliates maintain a federated relationship with the national organization. All affiliates are bound by the official policies of the ACLU. Each affiliate is chartered as an independent organization and is governed by its own board of directors. Each affiliate is free to develop its own program, with its own priorities, consistent with the official policies of the national organization. Each affiliate is free to develop policies on civil liberties issues that are different from the national ACLU policy where the national organization has no official policy. It may also adopt a policy different from national ACLU policy, provided that its activities related to that issue are confined to its own geographic area.

Finances

The ACLU is financed by three sources of income. The annual dues paid by individual members constitute the primary source. In addition, members and other persons sympathetic to civil liberties make tax-deductible contributions to the ACLU Foundation. Finally, the ACLU Foundation receives grants from private foundations to support activities on specific civil liberties issues. The ACLU accepts no money from government sources.

Membership

Membership in the ACLU is open to anyone who supports civil liberties and the program of the ACLU. There is no test for membership. By 1991, the ACLU had a membership of between 275,000 and 300,000 persons.

A User's Guide to the Bibliography

The chapters of this annotated bibliography on the ACLU are organized in the following manner.

I. GENERAL WORKS. Chapter I is devoted to general works on the ACLU. This includes general descriptions of the organization, along with official policies and publications. The *Policy Guide of the American Civil Liberties Union* (#9) contains the official policies of the organization. The policy guide is updated on a regular basis and researchers should check with the ACLU national office (#1293) for new policies and possible revisions of old policies.

Section E of Chapter I includes the ACLU Handbook series (#27–#68). These books are part of the ACLU's public education program. Each volume contains a brief summary of the legal issues surrounding a particular area of civil liberties. They are written for the lay person and not the legal scholar. While the handbooks are official ACLU publications they do not necessarily reflect official ACLU policy. Thus, a handbook will summarize current law on an issue even though the ACLU takes a different position on that issue. New handbooks are published periodically and existing handbooks are revised and republished. Researchers should check with the ACLU national office for the current list of volumes.

Section F of Chapter I includes collections of essays that have been published under the imprimatur of the ACLU (#69–#71). Like the handbooks, these volumes contain general discussions of civil liberties issues written for the layperson rather than the legal scholar. While many of the essays are written by ACLU members or staff, they do not necessarily reflect official ACLU policy.

Introduction xxiii

II. HISTORY OF THE ACLU. Chapter II covers the history of the ACLU from 1920 to 1979. The material on the history of the ACLU is divided into eight major periods, reflecting distinct eras in American history. Each period is then subdivided according to subject matter.

Section A includes general works covering the entire history of the ACLU. Section B covers the founding of the ACLU from 1914 to January, 1920. This includes material on the history of the National Civil Liberties Bureau (NCLB), its parent organization, the American Union Against Militarism (AUAM), and the violations of civil liberties during World War I.

Section C of Chapter Two covers the first ten years of the history of the ACLU during the 1920s. This includes the famous Scopes "Monkey Trial" in which the ACLU challenged a Tennessee law banning the teaching of evolution. The Scopes case was the first case that brought the ACLU favorable national attention. Section D covers the history of the ACLU during the 1930s. Two of the most important subjects during this period were the ACLU's defense of the rights of American Nazi groups and the ACLU's response to anti-Communist hysteria in the late 1930s.

Section E covers the World War II years, from 1940 to 1945. This period includes the ACLU's role in the Japanese-American cases. The ACLU challenged the evacuation of the Japanese-Americans from the west coast of the United States and their internment in government relocation centers. This section also includes issues related to the rights of conscientious objectors and freedom of speech during war time.

The period between 1945 and 1960 is divided into two parts. Section F is devoted entirely to issues related to the Cold War. This includes material related to the federal loyalty program, the House Un-American Activities Committee, the enforcement of the Smith Act, and others. Section G is devoted to all other civil liberties issues during the 1945–1960 period. This includes civil rights, religious liberty, freedom of speech and press, and other issues.

The post-World War II years introduce a new problem concerning the use of this bibliography. Beginning with these years, the ACLU began to enjoy increasing success in the courts, winning many landmark cases in the Supreme Court. This exerted a major influence over the course of American law and many of the issues, separation of church and state, for example, became matters of great national controversy. As a result, there begins to be published an increasing number of articles and books on particular civil liberties issues without any specific reference to the ACLU. To cite one example, there are law review articles discussing court cases on separation of church and state that do not mention the ACLU, even though the cases under discussion were brought by the ACLU. For the most part, these items are not included in this bibliography. Anyone attempting in-depth research on a particular civil liberties issue will need to consult other reference guides. The *Index to Legal Periodicals* is an important source.

Section H of Chapter Two covers the decades of the 1960s and 1970s. Of particular interest are ACLU activities related to the civil rights movement, the Vietnam War, and the Watergate scandal, and the Skokie, Illinois incident (1977–1978) where the ACLU defended the rights of an American Nazi group to demonstrate in the predominantly Jewish community of Skokie, Illinois.

III. CONTEMPORARY CIVIL LIBERTIES ISSUES. Chapter III covers Contemporary Civil Liberties Issues, which includes the years 1980 to 1991. Items in this chapter are organized according to subject matter.

IV. RELATED CIVIL LIBERTIES ISSUES. Chapter IV is devoted to Related Civil Liberties Issues. This includes general works that do not deal directly with the ACLU but provide relevant background on constitutional law, the legal role of the ACLU and other advocacy groups, public opinion about civil liberties, and international civil liberties. The section on civil liberties and constitutional law is selective rather than comprehensive. It is designed to direct the researcher to a small list of items that will place the ACLU in a broader context. Researchers seeking more detailed material should consult the appropriate reference works in the fields of law and political science.

V. INDIVIDUAL ACLU LEADERS. Chapter V includes material on individual ACLU leaders. Section A is devoted to

Introduction

Roger Nash Baldwin (1884–1981). Baldwin was director of the National Civil Liberties Bureau, 1917–1919, the principal founder of the ACLU, and director of the organization from 1920 to 1950. Baldwin was the central figure in the history of the ACLU over its first thirty years and, consequently, an important figure in the development of civil liberties. He wrote extensively, publishing over 100 articles and books. During the period of his career as director of the ACLU, his writings are one of the principal sources on the organization and civil liberties issues. Many, but not all of his publications serve as statements of ACLU policy. Care must be exercised in using his published writings, however. Some of Baldwin's publications express his personal views which were not necessarily those of the organization. Researchers should take care to check Baldwin's published views against the official policies of the ACLU of the time.

Section B of Chapter V includes material by and about other ACLU leaders. This includes biographies, memoirs, and articles related to their civil liberties activities. Researchers should be advised of one major limitation on the material cited here. Many ACLU leaders wrote voluminously in their area of professional activity (law, literature, etc.). Published works by those individuals that do not bear on either the ACLU or civil liberties issues are not included here.

VI. RESOURCES. Chapter VI is a guide to resources for persons conducting more extensive research on the ACLU. Section A lists the current (1991) addresses and telephone numbers of all ACLU offices. These change periodically and the researcher may need to check for the current address and telephone number. The national office of the ACLU in New York City can provide the current address and telephone number of affiliates and chapters.

Section B lists the location of archival material on the ACLU and ACLU affiliates. The records of the national office of the ACLU are located in the Seeley G. Mudd Library at Princeton University (#1352). These records are extensive and very well indexed. Particularly in the early years of the organization (i.e., through the 1950s), they also contain valuable material on issues that the ACLU was involved in (e.g., civil rights, the labor movement, etc.) and other organizations that were also involved with these issues. The records of the ACLU affiliates present a more difficult problem for the researcher. The records of the ACLU affiliates (#1356–#1399) have been handled in an inconsistent fashion. Not all affiliates have saved all their records, especially for the early years. Some affiliates have deposited their records with a historical society or university archives. Other have retained their records in the affiliate office. Some of these are open to the researcher upon request. In some instances, portions of the records are closed to researchers in order to protect the privacy of clients and other persons seeking ACLU assistance. Researchers are advised to contact individual affiliates regarding the availability of the records.

Section C includes the personal papers of individuals who were active in the ACLU. As the annotations indicate, some of these records are presently closed to researchers. Anyone planning to do research in any of these archives is advised to contact the institution which holds the collection in advance in order to determine possible limitations on access or use. Section D includes the records of organizations that are relevant to the ACLU. In some cases this involves direct contact with the ACLU on one or more issues. In other cases it involves work on civil liberties issues but without any direct contact with the ACLU.

THE AMERICAN CIVIL LIBERTIES UNION

I. General Works

A. DESCRIPTIONS OF THE ACLU

1. "American Civil Liberties Union." *Public Interest Profiles, 1988–1989.* Washington: Congressional Quarterly, 1988. Pp. 122–127.

    Brief description of the ACLU as an organization: staff, budget, tax status, funding sources, etc.

2. Dorsen, Norman. "American Civil Liberties Union." *Encyclopedia of the American Constitution.* V. I. New York: Macmillan, 1986. P. 50.

    Brief description of the ACLU, written by then-President Norman Dorsen.

3. Dorsen, Norman. "The American Civil Liberties Union: An Institutional Analysis." *Tulane Lawyer* (Spring 1984): 6–14.

    Excellent short description and analysis of the mission, structure, and procedures of the ACLU by its then-president. Illustrates general points with examples of specific cases and controversies from ACLU history.

4. Dorsen, Norman. "Civil Liberties." *Encyclopedia of the American Constitution.* Vol. 1. New York: Macmillan, 1986. Pp. 263–270.

    Brief essay defining the nature of civil liberties under the American Constitution, by the then-president of the ACLU.

5. Glasser, Ira. *How To Celebrate the Constitution.* New York: ACLU, 1991.

Brief pamphlet on the role of constitutional rights in America by the Executive Director of the ACLU. Issued on the occasion of the 200th anniversary of the Bill of Rights.

6. Glasser, Ira. "We Are the Ignition For the Constitutional Engine." *Civil Liberties*, No. 362 (Fall 1987): 8.

Statement by ACLU Executive Director on the role of the ACLU in protecting civil liberties, on the occasion of the Bicentennial of the U. S. Constitution.

7. Leeds, Jeffrey T. "The A.C.L.U.: Impeccable Judgments or Tainted Policies?" *The New York Times Magazine* (September 10, 1989): 72–78.

Good description and analysis of the current policies and activities of the ACLU. Generally sympathetic to the ACLU, but presents the point of view of some of the major critics. Article prompted by the controversy over the ACLU in the 1988 presidential election.

8. Reitman, Alan. *What is the Biennial Conference?* New York: ACLU, nd.

Brief description of the structure and purpose of the ACLU Biennial Conference (see # 21). Issued to delegates at each conference. The conference meets every two years and has the power to initiate new policies for the organization.

B. OFFICIAL POLICIES

9. ACLU. *Policy Guide of the American Civil Liberties Union*. New York: ACLU, revised periodically.

Contains the official policies of the ACLU. Policies are organized into the following categories: freedom of belief, expression and association; due process of law; equality; privacy; and organizational policies. Updated

periodically. Published in looseleaf notebook form; revised periodically.
First published in 1966. Revised, 1967, 1971, 1972, 1976. The 1976 edition was published in book form (Lexington, MA: Lexington Books, 1976), followed by the *1977 Supplement to the American Civil Liberties Union Policy Guide* (Lexington: Lexington Books, 1978).

10. ACLU Affiliate Policies.

ACLU affiliates have the authority to develop their own policies where no national ACLU policy exists. Consult individual affiliates for policies. For addresses of affiliate offices, see #1298–#1351.

C. PERIODICALS

11. ACLU. *Civil Liberties.* (Quarterly)

The official newsletter of the ACLU. Contains news of important current ACLU cases, discussions of civil liberties issues, opinion pieces by ACLU leaders and others, letters to the ACLU.

12. ACLU. *Civil Liberties Alert.* (Five times a year)

Official newsletter of the ACLU Washington office. Contains information on civil liberties issues before Congress, ACLU lobbying activities, and voting records of members of Congress on key civil liberties issues.

13. ACLU. *Civil Liberties Review.* (1973–1978)

General interest magazine devoted to civil liberties issues. Ceased publication due to the ACLU's financial crisis in 1978.

14. ACLU and the Center for National Security Studies. *First Principles.* (Six times per year)

Official newsletter of the joint ACLU/CNSS project on national security issues.

15. ACLU. National Prison Project. *National Prison Project Journal.* (Quarterly)

    Official newsletter of the ACLU National Prison Project. Contains news of current court cases and articles on general issues related to prisoners' rights.

16. ACLU. Reproductive Freedom Project. *Reproductive Rights Update.* (Biweekly)

    Official newsletter of the ACLU Reproductive Freedom Project. Contains news of current court cases, legislation, and other activities related to reproductive rights.

17. ACLU. Mountain States Office. *Mountain States Observer.*

    Published periodically by the ACLU Mountain States Office in Denver. Covers activities of ACLU affiliates in the Great Plains and Mountain states.

18. National Coalition Against Censorship. *Censorship News.*

    Official publication of the National Coalition Against Censorship, of which the ACLU is a member. Contains news of current events related to censorship.

19. Affiliate Newsletters.

    Each ACLU affiliate publishes an official newsletter at least quarterly.

D. REPORTS

[NOTE: The ACLU and its affiliates publish many reports on particular civil liberties issues. For those items consult the appropriate time period and subject heading.]

20. ACLU. *Annual Report.* (Annually)

    The ACLU published an annual report every year from 1920 through the mid-1970s. The reports for the years 1920 through 1969 have been bound and

General Works

republished in book form (ACLU. *Annual Reports, 1920–1970.* New York: Arno Press, 1970). The annual reports for the early 1970s were published as inserts in *Civil Liberties,* the ACLU quarterly journal. No annual report was published for several years in the late 1970s and early 1980s, primarily because of financial constraints. An annual report was issued for several years in the late 1980s.

21. ACLU. Biennial Conference. *Report of the Biennial Conference.* (Biannually)

    Official report of the proceedings of the ACLU Biennial Conference. Includes summaries of debates at general meetings and recommendations for ACLU policy. The first Biennial Conference was held in 1954, and conferences have been held every two years except for a brief interruption in the late 1970s and early 1980s.

22. ACLU. *Briefing Papers.* New York: ACLU. (Periodically)

    Short pamphlets on selected topics. Papers include: "A History of the Bill of Rights," "The American Civil Liberties Union: Guardian of Liberty," "Freedom of Expression," "Racial Justice," "English Only," "Church and State," "Drug Testing in the Workplace," "Lie Detector Testing," "Reproductive Freedom: Rights of Minors," and others.

23. ACLU. Lesbian and Gay Rights Project. *Annual Report.*

    Annual report of the activities of the ACLU Lesbian and Gay Rights Project, established in 1986.

24. ACLU. Reproductive Freedom Project. *Annual Report.*

    Annual report of the ACLU Reproductive Freedom Project. Includes information on court cases, legislation, and public education activities of the project.

25. ACLU. Washington Office. *Civil Liberties in the 102nd Congress.* Washington, DC: ACLU, 1991.

Summary of civil liberties issues pending in the Congress. Describes bills pending, the relevant civil liberties issues, and the ACLU position on each bill. Issued annually.

26. ACLU. Women's Rights Project. *Annual Report*.

    Annual report of the activities of the ACLU Women's Rights Project. Includes material on court cases, legislation, and public education activities.

E. ACLU HANDBOOKS

[NOTE: The ACLU Handbooks are brief summaries of the state of the law on particular civil liberties issues. They do not represent official ACLU policy on these issues. The Handbooks series is edited by Norman Dorsen, Professor of Law, New York University. The first series of Handbooks was published by Bantam Books; the second series by Avon Books; they are currently published by Southern Illinois University Press. Many of the Handbooks have been revised and republished in second or third editions. Only the current edition is listed here. The Handbooks are listed below in alphabetical order according to topic (e.g., privacy, teachers).]

27. Carliner, David, Lucas Guttentag, Arthur Helton, and Wade Henderson. *The Rights of Aliens and Refugees*. 2nd ed., revised. Carbondale: Southern Illinois University Press, 1990.

    First edition published as *The Rights of Aliens*.

28. Carliner, David. *Los Derechos De Los Extranjeros*. Chicago: The Roger Baldwin Foundation, 1977.

    Spanish language version of Carliner, *The Rights of Aliens*.

29. Norwick, Kenneth P., Jerry Simon Chasen, and Henry R. Kaufman. *The Rights of Authors and Artists*. New York: Avon Books, 1984.

    [Revised edition. Carbondale: Southern Illinois University Press, in preparation].

30. Neuborne, Burt and Arthur Eisenberg. *The Rights of Candidates and Voters*. Second edition, revised. New York: Avon Books, 1980.

31. Stark, James and Howard Goldstein. *The Rights of Crime Victims*. Carbondale: Southern Illinois University Press, 1985.

32. Robertson, John A. *The Rights of the Critically Ill*. New York: Bantam Books, 1983.

33. Annas, George and Barbara Katz. *The Rights of Doctors, Nurses, and Allied Health Professionals*. New York: Avon Books, 1981.

34. Outen, Wayne N., Noah A. Kinigstein, and Lisa Lipman. *The Rights of Employees*. New York: Avon Books, 1984.

    [Second edition, revised. Carbondale: Southern Illinois Press, in preparation].

35. Rudenstine, David. *The Rights of Ex-Offenders*. New York: Avon Books, 1979.

36. Guggenheim, Martin, Patricia Hennessey, and Marcia Lowry. *The Rights of Families*. Second edition, revised. Carbondale: Southern Illinois University Press, in preparation.

    [Formerly *The Rights of Parents*].

37. Stoddard, Thomas, E. Carrington Bogan, Charles Lister, John Rupp, and Marilyn Haft. *The Rights of Gay People*. Second edition, revised. Carbondale: Southern Illinois University Press, 1983.

[Third edition in preparation].

38. O'Neil, Robert. *The Rights of Government Employees*. New York: Avon Books 1978.

    [Revised edition, to be published as *The Rights of Public Employees*, in preparation].

39. Marwick, Christine M. *Your Right to Government Information*. New York: Bantam Books, 1985.

40. Larry Gostin, William Rubenstein, Ruth Eisenberg. *The Rights of People Who Are HIV Positive*. Carbondale: Southern Illinois University Press, in preparation.

    [Formerly included as part of *The Rights of the Physically Handicapped*].

41. Pevar, Stephen L. *The Rights of Indians and Tribes*. New York: Bantam Books, 1983.

    [Revised edition in preparation].

42. Gillers, Stephen. *The Rights of Lawyers and Clients*. New York: Avon Books, 1979.

43. Ennis, Bruce J. and Richard D. Emery. *The Rights of Mental Patients*. Revised Edition. New York: Avon Books, 1978.

44. Levy, Rob, Len Rubenstein, and Larry Gostin. *The Rights of the Mentally Disabled*. Carbondale: Southern Illinois University Press, in preparation.

    [Formerly *The Rights of the Mentally Ill and the Mentally Retarded*].

45. Friedman, Paul R. *The Rights of Mentally Retarded Persons*. New York: Avon Books, 1978.

    [Revised edition to be published as *The Rights of the Mentally Disabled*.]

46. Rivkin, Robert and Barton F. Stichman. *The Rights of Military Personnel*. New York: Avon Books, 1981.

General Works 11

[Formerly *The Rights of Servicemen*.]

47. Brown, Robert. *The Rights of Older Persons*. Second edition, revised. Carbondale: Southern Illinois University Press, 1988.

48. Sussman, Alan and Martin Guggenheim. *The Rights of Parents*. New York: Avon Books, 1980.

   [Revised edition to be published as *The Rights of Families*.

49. Annas, George J. *The Rights of Patients*. Second edition, revised. Carbondale: Southern Illinois University Press, 1988

   [Revised edition of *The Rights of Hospital Patients*.]

50. Hull, Kent and Paul Hearnce. *The Rights of Physically Handicapped People*. New York: Avon Books, 1981.

51. Brancato, Gilda and Elliot E. Polebaum. *The Rights of Police Officers*. New York: Avon Books, 1981.

52. Law, Sylvia. *The Rights of the Poor*. New York: Bantam Books, 1974.

   [Second edition, revised, with Helen Hershkoff and Stephen Loffredo, in preparation. Carbondale: Southern Illinois University Press].

53. Rudovsky, David, Alvin J. Bronstein, Edward I. Koren, and Julia Cade. *The Rights of Prisoners*. Fourth edition, revised. Carbondale: Southern Illinois University Press, 1988.

54. Hayden, Trudy and Jack Novick. *Your Rights to Privacy*. New York: Avon Books, 1980.

55. Hendricks, Evan. *The Right to Privacy*. Carbondale: Southern Illinois University Press, 1990.

56. Goldberger, David, Joel Gora, Morton Halperin, and Gary Stern. *The Right to Protest*. Carbondale: Southern Illinois University Press, 1991.

57. O'Neil, Robert. *The Rights of Public Employees*. Carbondale: Southern Illinois University Press, in preparation.
   [Formerly *The Rights of Government Employees*].

58. Larson, E. Richard, Laughlin McDonald, John Powell. *The Rights of Racial Minorities*. Second edition, revised. Carbondale: Southern Illinois University Press, in preparation.

59. Gora, Joel M. *The Rights of Reporters*. New York: Avon Books, 1974.

60. Bernard, Mitchell, Ellen Levine, Stefan Presser, and Marianne Stecich. *The Rights of Single People*. New York: Bantam Books, 1985.

61. Levine, Alan, Eve Cary, and Janet Price. *The Rights of Students*. Third edition, revised. Carbondale: Southern Illinois University Press, 1988.

62. Rosengart, Oliver. *The Rights of Suspects*. New York: Avon Books, 1974.

63. Rubin, David, and Steven Greenhouse. *The Rights of Teachers*. Second edition, revised. Carbondale: Southern Illinois University Press, 1984.

64. Blumberg, Richard E. and James R. Grow. *The Rights of Tenants*. New York: Avon Books, 1978.

65. Summers, Clyde and Robert Rabin, *The Rights of Union Members*. New York: Avon Books, 1981.
   [Revised edition, in preparation, to be published as *The Rights of Employees and Union Members*.]

General Works 13

66. Addlestone, David, Fred Gross, and Susan Hewman. *The Rights of Veterans*. New York: Avon Books, 1978.

67. Ross, Susan Deller and Barcher, Ann. *The Rights of Women*. Second edition, revised. New York: Bantam Books, 1983. [Third edition in preparation].

68. Sussman, Alan and Martin Guggenheim. *The Rights of Young People*. Second edition, revised. Carbondale: Southern Illinois University Press, 1985.

F. COLLECTIONS OF ESSAYS

[Collections of essays on civil liberties issues. The points of view expressed by authors of particular essays do not necessarily reflect official ACLU policy, or ACLU policy at the time they were written.]

69. Dorsen, Norman, ed. *Our Endangered Rights: The ACLU Report on Civil Liberties Today*. New York: Pantheon Books, 1984.

    Collection of essays on civil liberties issues as of the mid-1980s. Includes essays on substantive civil liberties issues (e.g., race discrimination) and different avenues for protecting civil liberties (e.g., legislation, litigation).

70. Dorsen, Norman, ed. *The Rights of Americans: What They Are—What They Should Be*. New York: Pantheon Books, 1971.

    An extremely important collection of articles on different civil liberties issues at a crucial turning point in ACLU history. Includes articles on many of the new civil liberties issues that had begun to emerge in the late 1960s (e.g., prisoners' rights, the rights of mental patients, etc.). A total of thirty-one articles. Most of the articles are now out of date in terms of current law, but they are important as historical documents of the intellectual life of the

ACLU at an important turning point. The collection is edited by the future president of the ACLU.

71. Reitman, Alan, ed. *The Price of Liberty: Perspectives on Civil Liberties By Members of the ACLU.* New York: W. W. Norton, 1968.

Articles on privacy, the Cold War, religious liberty, censorship, police procedures, civil rights, and the rights of workers.

II. History of the ACLU

A. GENERAL ACLU HISTORY

72. Bean, Barton. *Pressure for Freedom: The American Civil Liberties Union.* Unpublished Ph.D. Dissertation, Cornell University, 1955.

    An extremely dated history of the ACLU through 1955. Contains some valuable detail but is very weak in terms of its analysis of substantive issues and its general interpretive framework.

73. Bernhard, Edgar, Ira Latimer, and Harvey O'Connor. *Pursuit of Freedom: A History of Civil Liberties in Illinois, 1987–1942.* Chicago: Chicago Civil Liberties Committee, 1942.

    A history of civil liberties in Illinois, with special focus on the activities of the ACLU affiliate in Chicago. Co-author Latimer was director of the affiliate from the late 1930s until it disaffiliated from the ACLU in 1945.

74. Donohue, William A. *The Politics of the American Civil Liberties Union.* New Brunswick, NJ: Transaction Books, 1985.

    A highly critical account of ACLU history by a conservative sociologist and prominent critic of the ACLU. The author accuses the ACLU of pursuing a left-liberal political agenda instead of a nonpartisan defense of civil liberties.

75. Ennis, Bruce. "ACLU: 60 Years of Volunteer Lawyers." *American Bar Association Journal,* 66 (September 1980): 1080–1083.

Article on the role of volunteer lawyers in ACLU history. Written by a former ACLU legal director. Cites examples of notable ACLU cases.

76. Epstein, Sam and Beryl Epstein. *Kids in Court: The ACLU Defends Their Rights.* New York: Four Winds Press, 1982.

    Discussion of ACLU cases involving the rights of children and students. Written for high school age audience.

77. Fechtmeier, Karl. "Defending the Bill of Rights: The ACLU Archives at CHS." *California History,* 58 (1979-1980, No. 4): 362-364.

    Brief description of the materials in the records of the ACLU of Northern California located at the California Historical Society.

78. Habenstreit, Barbara. *Eternal Vigilance: The American Civil Liberties Union in Action.* New York: Julian Messner, 1971.

    Account of some of the notable ACLU cases written for a high school audience.

79. Hall, Kermit L. *The Magic Mirror: Law in American History.* New York: Oxford University Press, 1989.

    General history of American law. Places the role of the ACLU and the development of civil liberties in a broad historical context.

80. Honig, Douglas and Laura Breener. *On Freedom's Frontier: The First Fifty Years of the American Civil Liberties Union in Washington State.* Seattle: ACLU of Washington, 1987.

    Short history of the activities of the ACLU affiliate in Washington state from 1937 to 1987. Illustrated.

81. Irons, Peter. *The Courage of Their Convictions.* New York: The Free Press, 1988.

    A series of case studies of famous civil liberties cases that resulted in landmark Supreme Court decisions. Interviews with individual plaintiffs in each case. The

ACLU was involved, directly or indirectly, in virtually all of the cases. Includes such famous cases as *Gobitis, Hirabayashi, Tinker, Hardwick,* and others.

82. Katz, Stanley N. "An Historical Perspective on Crises in Civil Liberties." Norman Dorsen, ed. *Our Endangered Rights.* New York: Pantheon Books, 1984. Pp. 311–324.

    Historical overview of the development of civil liberties in the United States. Places the history of the ACLU in a broader context.

83. Lamson, Peggy. *Roger Baldwin: Founder of the American Civil Liberties Union. A Portrait.* Boston: Houghton, Mifflin Co., 1976.

    An informal biography of the founder of the ACLU. Extremely episodic and based on little original research. In many respects more of an annotated interview rather than a full biography. Contains some colorful recollections by Baldwin on the history of the ACLU.

84. Markmann, Charles Lamm. *Noblest Cry: A History of the American Civil Liberties Union.* New York: St. Martin's Press, 1965.

    A dated and somewhat idiosyncratic history of the ACLU written by an amateur historian. The lack of footnotes makes it of little value as a reference work. Its value as history is also weakened by the topical, as opposed to chronological, arrangement of the chapters. Carries the story of the ACLU through the early 1960s.

85. Murphy, Paul L. "Dilemmas in Writing Civil Liberties History." *Civil Liberties Review,* V (May/June 1978): 16–22.

    Reflections of a noted historian who has written extensively on the ACLU (#109; #148) on the tensions between commitments to the cause of civil liberties and the professional obligations of a historian.

86. Popeo, Daniel J. *Not OUR America: The ACLU Exposed!* Washington, DC: Washington Legal Foundation, 1989.

A right-wing attack on the ACLU. Accuses the ACLU of having had Communist associations and of being out of the mainstream of contemporary American life.

87. Reitman, Alan, ed. *The Pulse of Freedom: American Liberties, 1920–1970s.* New York: Norton, 1975.

    An extremely valuable collection of essays on the history of civil liberties through the early 1970s by a group of noted historians. The primary focus is on civil liberties generally, rather than the ACLU as an organization. The quality of the individual chapters is very high.

88. Roche, John P. *The Quest for the Dream: The Development of Civil Rights and Human Relations in Modern America.* Chicago: Quadrangle Books, 1968.

    General history of the development of civil rights and civil liberties in the United States from the early 20th century through the 1960s. Includes references to the ACLU and other civil rights groups.

89. "Sixtieth Anniversary Issue." *Civil Liberties,* No. 334 (September 1980): 3–14.

    Special insert in ACLU newsletter featuring highlights of sixty years of ACLU history.

90. Taft, Clinton J. *Fifteen Years on Freedom's Front.* Los Angeles: ACLU of Southern California, 1939.

    History of the first fifteen years of the ACLU affiliate in Southern California, written by the then-executive director of the affiliate.

91. Walker, Samuel. "The American Civil Liberties Union." Kermit L. Hall, ed. *The Encyclopedia of the Supreme Court.* New York: Oxford University Press, in preparation.

    A brief description of the role and history of the ACLU.

92. Walker, Samuel. *In Defense of American Liberties: A History of the ACLU*. New York: Oxford University Press, 1990.

    Detailed scholarly history of the ACLU from its founding through 1988. Author argues that the ACLU has been extremely successful and has reshaped the American mainstream in a civil libertarian direction. Illustrated. Extensive footnotes.

B. ORIGINS OF THE ACLU, 1914-1919

[See also #1091, #1292.]

93. American Union Against Militarism. *Concerning Conscription*. New York: AUAM, April 1917.

    The first pamphlet issued by the AUAM regarding the new selective service bill being debated by Congress and the rights of conscientious objectors.

94. American Union Against Militarism. *Constitutional Rights in War-Time*. New York: AUAM, 1917. Second edition, July, 1917.

    One of the first pamphlets issued by the Civil Liberties Bureau of the AUAM regarding the different civil liberties issues raised by American entry into the war.

95. "A New Civil Liberties Union." *The Survey*, 43 (January 31, 1920): 480-481.

    Short article on the founding of the ACLU in a social work journal that was highly sympathetic to the ACLU.

96. Bourne, Randolph. "The War and the Intellectuals." *Seven Arts*, 2 (June 1917): 133-146. Reprinted in Randlolph Bourne. *War and The Intellectuals: Collected Essays, 1915-1919*. New York: Harper and Row, 1964.

    Classic criticism of liberal intellectuals who supported the war effort during World War I and refused to speak out against the violations of civil liberties.

Contains no specific references to the Civil Liberties Bureau, but is an important statement of the civil libertarian perspective.

97. Chafee, Zechariah, Jr. *Free Speech in the United States.* Cambridge, MA: Harvard University Press, 1941.

    The classic scholarly treatment of free speech issues from World War I through 1940. Exerted a major influence on the development of First Amendment doctrine through the 1960s. Detailed account of the World War I free speech cases. Greatly revised and expanded version of #98.

98. Chafee, Zechariah, Jr. *Freedom of Speech.* Cambridge, MA: Harvard University Press, 1920.

    Initial and much shorter version of #97. Extremely influential work on First Amendment doctrine during the 1920s and 1930s.

99. Chamberlain, Lawrence H. *Loyalty and Legislative Action: A Survey of Activity by the New York State Legislature, 1919–1949.* Ithaca, NY: Cornell University Press, 1951.

    Detailed scholarly history of anti-Communist activity by the New York state legislature. Includes a chapter on the Lusk Committee investigation (#119) which attacked the Civil Liberties Bureau for being Communist-influenced and which served as the source of many subsequent anti-Communist attacks on the ACLU.

100. "Civil Liberties in War Times." *The Survey,* 39 (November 3, 1917): 130–131.

     Brief article on the creation of the National Civil Liberties Bureau as an organization independent of its parent, the American Union Against Militarism.

101. "Civil Liberty Dead." *The Nation,* 107 (September 14, 1918): 282.

Article describing the violations of individual rights during the massive roundup of thousands of suspected draft dodgers in New York City in early September, 1918.

102. Jensen, Joan. *The Price of Vigilance.* Chicago: Rand McNally, 1968.

    Scholarly account of the suppression of dissent during World War I by private vigilantes. Special focus on the American Protective League which had the official support of the federal government.

103. Johnson, Donald. *The Challenge to American Freedoms: World War I and the Rise of the American Civil Liberties Union.* Lexington: University of Kentucky Press, 1963.

    A somewhat dated history of the founding of the ACLU during World War I. It has been superceded by the more recent and more detailed research by Murphy (#109) and Walker (#92).

104. Lane, Winthrop D. "The Strike at Fort Leavenworth." *The Survey,* 41 (February 15, 1919): 687–693.

    Account of a strike by conscientious objectors imprisoned at the Fort Leavenworth military base.

105. Lawrence, Thomas. "Eclipse of Liberty: Civil Liberties in the United States During the First World War." *Wayne Law Review,* 21 (1974): 33–112.

    Analysis of the violations of civil liberties during World War I, focusing on the most important Supreme Court cases.

106. Marchand, Roland. *The American Peace Movement and Social Reform, 1898–1918.* Princeton: Princeton University Press, 1972.

    Detailed scholarly account of American pacifism and social reform in the pre-World War I years. Particularly valuable for placing the founders of the ACLU in the context of broader social reform movements.

107. Milner, Lucille. *Education of an American Liberal: An Autobiography*. New York: Horizon, 1954.

   Autobiography of the secretary of the ACLU from 1920 to 1945. A vivid first-hand account of some aspects of the ACLU's early years. The author's interpretation is influenced by the fact that she quit the ACLU in a dispute over policy during World War II.

108. Mock, James R. *Censorship 1917*. Princeton: Princeton University Press, 1941.

   An analysis of the suppression of free speech during World War I, written on the eve of World War II.

109. Murphy, Paul L. *World War I and the Origin of Civil Liberties in the United States*. New York: Norton, 1979.

   Scholarly treatment of the emergence of civil liberties as a national issue during the World War I years. Emphasis primarily on the issue rather than on the ACLU as an organization.

110. Murray, Robert K. *Red Scare: A Study in National Hysteria, 1919–1920*. New York: McGraw-Hill, 1964.

   Detailed scholarly account of the violations of civil liberties in the "Red Scare" in 1919 and 1920 which culminated in the famous "Palmer Raids."

111. National Civil Liberties Bureau. *The Facts About Conscientious Objectors*. New York: NCLB, June, 1918.

   Analysis of the rights of conscientious objectors, based on the experience of the first year of selective service.

112. National Civil Liberties Bureau. *The Individual and the State*. New York: NCLB, 1918.

   Reprint of Roger Baldwin's speech to the judge upon being sentenced to prison for refusing to be inducted in the military. (See #1091).

113. National Civil Liberties Bureau. *Open Letter to the President.* New York: NCLB, 1918.

    Pamphlet criticizing the federal government's prosecution of the leaders of the Industrial Workers of the World (I.W.W.).

114. National Civil Liberties Bureau. *The Outrage on Rev. Herbert S. Bigelow.* New York: NCLB, 1918.

    Pamphlet on the mob attack on the Reverend Bigelow in Cincinnati. Good example of the vigilante violence during the war.

115. National Civil Liberties Bureau. *Some Aspects of the Constitutional Questions Involved in the Draft Act of May 18, 1917.* New York: NCLB, 1917.

    Legal memorandum on the unresolved questions regarding the rights of conscientious objectors.

116. National Civil Liberties Bureau. *The Truth About the I. W. W.* New York: NCLB, 1918.

    Pamphlet defending the I.W.W. in the face of government repression.

117. National Civil Liberties Bureau. *Wartime Prosecutions and Mob Violence.* New York: NCLB, 1918.

    Report on government prosecutions of critics of the war under the Espionage Act and vigilante violence against anti-war activists. Covers the period from mid-1917 to mid-1918.

118. Nelles, Walter. *A Liberal in Wartime: The Education of Albert DeSilver.* New York: Norton, 1940.

    A biography of Albert DeSilver, attorney who worked for the National Civil Liberties Bureau during World War I and then served as co-director of the ACLU from 1920 to 1924. A vivid account of the early years of the ACLU. The author served as one of the ACLU's most important cooperating attorneys for many years.

119. New York (State) Senate, Joint Legislative Committee Investigating Seditious Activities. *Revolutionary Radicalism.* 4 Vols. Albany: J. B. Lyon, 1920.

Investigation of the ACLU and other political groups by a New York state legislative investigating committee, 1919–1920, popularly known as the Lusk Committee. Accuses the ACLU of both serving the German cause during the war and of being allied with Communists and other radical movements. The original source for many of the subsequent right-wing attacks on the ACLU, and an extremely important document in that regard.

120. Peterson, H. C. and Gilbert C. Fite. *Opponents of War, 1917–1918.* Seattle: University of Washington Press, 1968.

Scholarly history of the opposition to American involvement in World War I and the suppression of dissent by the government. Very few direct references to the Civil Liberties Bureau, but good material on the suppression of civil liberties.

121. Polenberg, Richard. *Fighting Faiths: The Abrams Case, The Supreme Court, and Free Speech.* New York: Viking, 1987.

Detailed scholarly history of the *Abrams v. United States* (1919) case which produced a famous dissenting opinion by Justice Oliver Wendell Holmes on freedom of speech. Vivid account of the circumstances of the case and the individuals involved.

122. Preston, William, Jr. *Aliens and Dissenters: Federal Suppression of Radicals, 1903–1933.* Cambridge, MA: Harvard University Press, 1963.

Detailed scholarly study of the repression of dissent during World War I. Emphasizes anti-immigrant and anti-labor aspects of the hysteria. Covers both the pre-World War I and post-World War I years.

123. Sayre, John Nevin. "American War Prisoners." *Socialist Review,* 8 (January 1920): 81–84.

Description of the prison treatment of conscientious objectors and persons imprisoned for opposing the war.

124. Thomas, Norman. *The Conscientious Objector in America.* New York: B.W. Huebsch, 1923.

    Detailed account of the conscientious objector issue during World War I by a prominent pacifist and co-founder of the ACLU.

125. Thomas, Norman. "The Present Status of Conscientious Objectors." *The World Tomorrow*, 1 (1918): 287–288.

    Early report on the problems of conscientious objectors during the first year of selective service.

126. Thomas, Norman. "War's Heretics." *The Survey*, 38 (August 4, 1917): 391–394.

    Defense of free speech for dissenters. Pivotal document published during the first months of American involvement during World War I. An important early statement of the ACLU's views on free speech.

127. Villard, Oswald Garrison. "On Being in Jail." *The Nation*, 109 (August 2, 1919): 142–143.

    Article on Roger Baldwin's release from prison after being convicted of refusing to be drafted. Material on Baldwin's prison experience and plans for the future.

128. Walker, Samuel. "The Growth of Civil Liberties, 1900–1945." Raymond Arsenault, ed. *Crucible of Liberty: 200 Years of the Bill of Rights.* New York: The Free Press, 1991. Pp. 36–51.

    Interpretive survey of the history of the growth of civil liberties from 1890 to 1945. Special emphasis on the role of the ACLU. Based on material in #92.

C. THE 1920s

1. General

129. ACLU. *Annual Reports, 1921–1929.* New York: ACLU, 1921–1929. Reprinted: New York: Arno Press, 1970.

    Detailed accounts of both the ACLU's activities and violations of civil liberties. Extremely useful as a resource in identifying particular issues and events in the period.

130. ACLU. *Blue Coats and Reds.* New York: ACLU, 1929.

    Report on police repression of labor and radical meetings across the country.

131. ACLU. *Mob Violence in the United States.* New York: ACLU, 1923.

    Survey of violence against political radicals and black Americans by mobs led by the American Legion, the Ku Klux Klan, and other groups.

132. ACLU. *Old Fashioned Free Speech.* New York: ACLU, 1929.

    Collection of statements by famous Americans on behalf of free speech.

133. ACLU. *The Police and the Radicals: A Report on the Attitudes and Methods of the Police in Handling Radical Meetings in About 100 Cities.* New York: ACLU, 1920.

    National survey of the suppression of freedom of speech and assembly by the police in 100 cities.

134. American Defense Society. *What is the American Civil Liberties Union?* New York: American Defense Society, 1927.

    Pamphlet. Right-wing attack on the ACLU.

135. *Civil Liberty.* New York: H. W. Wilson, 1927.

    Debater's handbook with reprints of articles and bibliography on civil liberties issues. Compiled with the assistance of the ACLU staff.

136. Curti, Merle. "Subsidizing Radicalism: The American Fund For Public Service, 1921–1941." *Social Service Review*, 33 (September 1959): 277–295.

   Scholarly account of an early private foundation (popularly known as the "Garland Fund") that supported many ACLU causes in the 1920s. Roger Baldwin helped to create the Fund and largely controlled its operation.

137. DeSilver, Albert. "Backward and Forward." *The World Tomorrow*, 4 (April 1921): 117–118.

   Discussion of Supreme Court decision upholding Post Office censorship of Socialist newspaper in peacetime.

138. DeSilver, Albert. "The Ku Klux Klan." *The Nation*, 112 (September 14, 1921): 285–286. Reprinted: New York: ACLU, 1921.

   Report on violence against African-Americans by the Ku Klux Klan. Written by the co-director of the ACLU.

139. DeSilver, Albert. "The Lusk-Stevenson Report." *The Nation*, 112 (July 13, 1921): 38–40.

   Reponse to the New York State Senate investigation of radical groups which accused the Civil Liberties Bureau and the ACLU of being Communist-influenced (#119).

140. DeSilver, Albert. "Mr. Palmer Shudders." *The World Tomorrow*, 3 (March 1920): 74–75.

   Report on adverse public reaction to the Palmer Raids and growing opposition in Congress to a peacetime sedition law.

141. DeSilver, Albert. "On Civil Liberty: 1921." *The World Tomorrow*, 4 (December 1921): 361.

   Brief analysis of the state of civil liberties in 1921 by the co-director of the ACLU.

142. [Frankfurter, Felix]. "Can the Supreme Court Guarantee Toleration?" *The New Republic*, 43 (June 17, 1925): 85–87.

   Unsigned editorial written by Frankfurter commenting on the Supreme Court decision in *Pierce v. Society of Sisters*. Argues in favor of legislative rather than judicial protection of civil liberties. Revealing insight into the views of an important member of the ACLU and an indication of his future position on civil liberties as a Supreme Court justice.

143. Hapgood, Norman. *Professional Patriots*. New York: Albert and Charles Boni, 1927.

   Exposé of right-wing groups in the United States, emphasizing their connections to big business. Partially sponsored by the ACLU. Includes material on attacks on the ACLU.

144. Hays, Arthur Garfield. *Let Freedom Ring*. New York: Boni and Liveright, 1928. Revised edition, New York: Liveright, 1937.

   Lively first-hand account of some of the early ACLU cases by the ACLU general counsel who was directly involved in many of these cases. Includes sections on the *Scopes* case, Sacco and Vanzetti case, labor union struggles in West Virginia, Pennsylvania, New Jersey, and other famous cases.

145. Hays, Arthur Garfield. *Trial By Prejudice*. New York: Covici, Friede, 1933.

   Lively discussion of several famous political trials of the 1920s and 1930s by ACLU co-general counsel who was directly involved in some of these cases. Includes sections on the Scottsboro case, the Gastonia strike, the *Angelo Herndon* case, and others.

146. *Law and Freedom Bulletin* (1921–1928).

   Legal periodical analyzing current civil liberties cases. Edited by Walter Nelles, ACLU cooperating attorney, and Carol Weiss King, important civil liberties attorney of the period. Distributed by the ACLU.

147. Layton, Edwin. "The Better America Federation." *Pacific Historical Review*, 30 (May 1961): 137–147.

    Scholarly study of one of the leading right-wing organizations in the 1920s which frequently attacked the ACLU.

148. Murphy, Paul L. "Communities in Conflict." Alan Reitman, ed. *The Pulse of Freedom*. New York: Norton, 1975. Pp.1–39.

    An excellent brief account of civil liberties issues in the 1920s. The article summarizes the material in the author's *The Meaning of Freedom of Speech* (#149).

149. Murphy, Paul L. *The Meaning of Freedom of Speech*. Westport, CT: Greenwood Press, 1972.

    A detailed scholarly study of civil liberties during the 1920s, with primary emphasis on labor issues. Although not a history of the ACLU per se, it provides rich detail on many of the ACLU's major campaigns during the period. Author argues that by 1931 public attitudes in the United States had shifted in the direction of greater tolerance for unpopular groups and ideas.

150. Murphy, Paul L. "Sources and Nature of Intolerance in the 1920s." *Journal of American History*, 51 (June 1964): 60–76.

    Analysis of the nature of intolerance in the United States during the 1920s. Early statement of themes developed at greater length in #148.

151. Nelles, Walter. "The Legality of the Left-Wing Doctrines." *The World Tomorrow*, 3 (January 1920): 28

    Analysis of the conviction of Benjamin Gitlow under the New York criminal anarchy law for possession of the *Left Wing Manifesto*. Written by the attorney who handled many NCLB and ACLU cases in the early years. The case eventually resulted in a landmark Supreme Court decision (see #152; #213).

152. Nelles, Walter. *Seeing Red: Civil Liberty and Law Since the Armistice.* New York: ACLU, 1920.

    Pamphlet by an attorney who handled many important cases for the Civil Liberties Bureau and the ACLU analyzing court decisions and the status of civil liberties between November 1918 and 1920.

153. Pickens, William. *Lynching and Debt-Slavery.* New York: ACLU, 1921.

    ACLU-sponsored report on vigilante violence against African-Americans and the problem of exploitation of African-American farm workers by white land owners. Author was a Field Secretary for the NAACP.

154. Pollak, Louis H. "Advocating Civil Liberties: A Young Lawyer Before the Old Court." *Harvard Civil Rights—Civil Liberties Law Review,* 17 (Spring 1982): 1–30.

    Extremely valuable biographical sketch of attorney Walter Pollak who argued four landmark cases before the Supreme Court in the 1920s and 1930s on behalf of the ACLU. The most important case was *Gitlow* (1925). Written by his son, then a U.S. District Court judge.

155. "Relief For Radicals." *The Survey,* 44 (September 15, 1920): 701.

    Brief article on Roger Baldwin's plans to create a League for Mutual Aid as an "offshoot" of the ACLU. The League was designed to provide direct financial assistance to radicals. It was one of several organizations Baldwin created in 1920–1921. There is no evidence that the League was ever formally established.

156. Sinclair, Upton. "Upton Sinclair's Arrest." *The New Republic,* 35 (July 11, 1923): 180.

First-hand account of the arrest of the noted author which led to the creation of the ACLU affiliate in Southern California (see #159).

157. Thomas, Norman. "Where are the Prewar Radicals?" *The Survey*, 55 (February 1, 1926): 563.

    Contribution to symposium on the collapse of radicalism in the 1920s. Interesting insights into the thinking of a leading member of the ACLU in the period.

158. Whitney, Richard M. *Reds in America*. New York: The Beckwith Press, 1924.

    Right-wing attack on social reform movements, including the ACLU, accusing them of being Communist-influenced.

159. Zanger, Martin. "Politics of Confrontation: Upton Sinclair and the Launching of the ACLU in Southern California." *Pacific History Review*, 28 (November 1969): 383–406.

    A scholarly account of the founding of the ACLU affiliate in Southern California in 1923. Emphasizes role of the affiliate in the defense of I.W.W. members. Vivid account of the suppression of First Amendment rights at the local level.

2. Amnesty for Political Prisoners

160. ACLU. *Amnesty for Political Prisoners*. New York: ACLU, 1920.

    Pamphlet arguing ACLU case for amnesty for persons convicted under the Espionage Act during World War I.

161. ACLU. *Restore the Rights of Citizenship to the 1,500 Espionage Act Victims!* New York: ACLU, 1928.

    Call for restoring the citizenship of persons convicted under the Espionage Act during World War I.

162. ACLU. *Set the Political Prisoners Free.* New York: ACLU, 1922.

Discussion of the amnesty issue as of 1922.

163. "Amnesty and the Civil Liberties Union." *The Nation,* 118 (March 26, 1924): 346.

Discussion of the issue of amnesty for persons convicted under the Espionage Act during World War I. Focuses on the role of the ACLU and the split between those advocating amnesty and those willing to accept pardons.

3. Federal Government, Illegal Actions of

164. ACLU. *The Nationwide Spy System Centering in the Department of Justice.* New York: ACLU, 1924.

ACLU report attacking the illegal tactics used by U.S. Department of Justice against radicals during the 1920s.

165. National Popular Government League and the ACLU. *Report Upon the Illegal Practices of the United States Department of Justice.* Washington, DC: NPGL, 1920.

A detailed exposé of illegal actions by the U.S. Justice Department during the "Palmer Raids" of 1920. Co-sponsored by the ACLU. Provides rich detail on the violations of individual rights in various cities.

166. Williams, David. "Failed Reform: FBI Political Surveillance, 1924–1936." *First Principles,* 7 (September/October 1981): 1–4.

Scholarly analysis of the reform of the FBI by Attorney General Harlan Fiske Stone in 1924. Argues that reform failed to end government spying.

167. Williams, David. "The Federal Bureau of Investigation and its Critics, 1919–1921: The Origins of Federal Political

Surveillance." *Journal of American History*, 68 (December 1981): 560–579.

Scholarly historical treatment of government spying on the ACLU and other political groups, 1919–1921.

168. Williams, David. "They Never Stopped Watching US: FBI Political Surveillance, 1924–1936." *UCLA Historical Journal*, 2 (1981): 5–28.

Scholarly analysis of FBI spying on the ACLU and other groups, 1924–1936.

4. Labor, Rights of

[See also #1121.]

169. ACLU. *The Denial of Civil Liberties in the Coal Fields*. New York: ACLU, 1921.

ACLU report on the denial of freedom of speech and assembly in the coal mining areas of West Virginia and Pennsylvania.

170. ACLU. *The Shame of Pennsylvania*. New York: ACLU, 1928.

Report on suppression of labor union activity in Pennsylvania, the worst in any state according to the ACLU.

171. ACLU. *State Police in Relation to Labor and Civil Liberty*. New York: ACLU, 1924.

Short pamphlet on the role of state police forces in denying freedom of speech and assembly to labor union organizers. Particular emphasis on Pennsylvania.

172. ACLU. *The War on the Colorado Miners*. New York: ACLU, 1928.

Short report on anti-labor union activity in Colorado.

173. DeSilver, Albert. "The Injunction." *The Nation*, 114 (January 25, 1922): 89–90.

Brief discussion of the use of injunctions to deny freedom of speech and assembly to labor union organizers. Written by the co-director of the ACLU.

174. Frankfurter, Felix and Nathan Greene. *The Labor Injunction*. New York: Macmillan, 1930.

Legal study of the injunction as a weapon against labor unions. Regarded as a classic in legal literature. Freedom of speech and assembly for union organizers was the ACLU's major issue in the 1920s. Frankfurter served on the ACLU National Committee; Greene later served on the ACLU Board of Directors. Frankfurter helped draft the 1932 Norris-LaGuardia Act which greatly restricted the use of injunctions in labor disputes.

175. Glaser, Martha. "Paterson, 1924: The ACLU and Labor." *New Jersey History*, 94 (1976, No. 4): 155–172.

A scholarly article on the ACLU's role in one of its most important cases during the 1920s. Good description of the suppression of First Amendment rights of labor union organizers.

176. Lane, Winthrop D. *Civil War in West Virginia*. New York: B. W. Huebsch, 1921. Reprinted: New York: Arno Press, 1969.

Account of industrial strife in the West Virginia coal fields, one of the ACLU's first major issues in 1920. Report partially sponsored by the ACLU. Publisher Ben W. Huebsch served on the ACLU Board of Directors for over forty years.

177. Lane, Winthrop. *The Denial of Civil Liberties in the Coal Fields*. New York: Doran, 1924.

Report on violations of First Amendment rights of coal miners, co-sponsored by the ACLU and the League for Industrial Democracy.

178. Murphy, Paul L. *The Passaic Textile Strike of 1926*. Belmont, CA: Wadsworth, 1974.

Collection of original materials on a major strike. ACLU was involved in the First Amendment aspects of the struggle. Good insights into the details of labor conflicts of the period.

179. Wood, Clement, McAlister Coleman and Arthur Garfield Hays. *Don't Tread on Me: A Study of Aggressive Legal Tactics For Labor*. New York: Vanguard Press, 1928.

Discussion of possible tactics to win First Amendment rights for labor unions and union organizers. Co-author Hays was one of the ACLU's most important figures from the 1920s through the early 1950s.

5. Sacco and Vanzetti Case

[See also #1151.]

180. Fraenkel, Osmond K. *The Sacco-Vanzetti Case*. New York: Knopf, 1931.

History of the Sacco and Vanzetti case by future ACLU general counsel.

181. Frankfurter, Felix. *The Case of Sacco and Vanzetti: A Critical Analysis for Lawyers and Laymen*. Boston: Little, Brown, 1927.

Extremely influential criticism of the prosecution of Sacco and Vanzetti by a prominent ACLU leader and future Supreme Court justice.

182. Joughin, G. Louis and Edmund M. Morgan. *The Legacy of Sacco and Vanzetti*. New York: Harcourt, Brace, 1948.

Detailed account of the Sacco and Vanzetti case. Sympathetic to their cause. Joughin was a long-time ACLU staff member.

6. Scopes Case

183. ACLU. *Anti-Evolution Laws.* New York: ACLU, 1925.

    Survey of state anti-evolution laws, as of 1925, with statements by prominent Americans opposing such laws.

184. Allen, Leslie H., ed. *Bryan and Darrow at Dayton.* New York: Arthur Lee, 1925.

    Abridged transcript of the 1925 *Scopes* trial.

185. Ginger, Ray. *Six Days or Forever?: Tennesse v. John Thomas Scopes.* Chicago: Quadrangle Books, 1969.

    A lively history of the 1925 Scopes "Monkey Trial" by a prominent historian. Still considered the standard work on the subject. Author is generally very sympathetic to the ACLU point of view.

186. Hays, Arthur Garfield. "The Strategy of the Scopes Defense." *The Nation,* 121 (August 5, 1925): 332.

    Vigorous reply to critics of the tactics used by Darrow in the *Scopes* trial. Hays served as co-counsel in the trial.

187. Hughes, Charles Evans. "Liberty and Law." *American Bar Association Journal,* 11 (September 1925): 563–569.

    ABA Presidential address. Reflects the impact of the *Scopes* case. Critical of the Tennessee anti-evolution law; a plea for tolerance. An important indicator of changing public attitudes as a result of the *Scopes* case.

188. Larson, Edward J. *Trial and Error.* New York: Oxford University Press, 1985.

    Scholarly account of the anti-evolution movement from the 1925 *Scopes* case to the "scientific creationism" cases of the 1980s. Extremely valuable perspective on the long-term impact of the *Scopes* case on American education.

189. Lawrence, Jerome and Robert E. Lee. *Inherit the Wind*. New York: Bantam Books, 1964.

    A successful Broadway play and later a motion picture, based on the *Scopes* trial. Embodies an exaggerated liberal stereotype of the case, with Darrow as a hero and Bryan as a comic buffoon.

190. Lippmann, Walter. *American Inquisitors: A Commentary on Dayton and Chicago*. New York: Macmillan, 1928.

    Commentary on the *Scopes* case by the leading American political columnist.

191. Scopes, John T. and James Presley. *Center of the Storm: Memoirs of John T. Scopes*. New York: Holt, Rinehart and Winston, 1967.

    Memoirs of the central figure in the famous *Scopes* case.

192. Weinberg, Arthur, ed. *Attorney for the Damned*. New York: Simon and Schuster, 1957.

    Contains excerpts from the transcript of the *Scopes* trial, along with excerpts from several of Darrow's other famous cases.

193. Wills, Garry. *Under God: Religion and American Politics*. New York: Simon and Schuster, 1990.

    A series of essays on the role of religion in American political life. Contains three chapters on the *Scopes* case and its aftermath with valuable insights.

194. *The World's Most Famous Court Trial: Tennessee Evolution Case*. Cincinnati: National Book Co., 1925.

    Abridged transcript of the *Scopes* trial.

7. Speech, Press, and Assembly, Freedom of

195. ACLU. *The Michigan Communist Trials*. New York: ACLU, 1923.

Pamphlet criticizing the prosecution of leading American Communists under Michigan criminal syndicalism law.

196. ACLU. *The Prosecution of Mary Ware Dennett for "Obscenity."* New York: ACLU, 1929.

    Pamphlet on a pivotal censorhip case in the late 1920s. Dennett was prosecuted under the Comstock Law for sending a sex education pamphlet through the mails. The case spurred the ACLU to develop a comprehensive attack on censorship in the arts.

197. ACLU. *State Laws Against Free Speech.* New York: ACLU, 1925.

    Brief survey of state criminal syndicalism and sedition laws.

198. ACLU. *"Unlawful Assembly" in Paterson.* New York: ACLU, 1925.

    Pamphlet on demonstration on behalf of strikers that resulted in arrest of Roger Baldwin, director of the ACLU. Arrest eventually led to important decision by New Jersey courts affirming First Amendment principles.

199. ACLU. *The Victory in New Jersey.* New York: ACLU, 1928.

    Pamphlet on the decision of the New Jersey Supreme Court overturning the conviction of Roger Baldwin for unlawful assembly (see #198). The first important First Amendment victory for the ACLU.

200. ACLU. *Who May Safely Advocate Force and Violence?* New York: ACLU, 1922.

    Pamphlet discussing the scope of First Amendment right to advocate force and violence.

201. Boyer, Paul S. *Purity in Print: The Vice-Society Movement and Book Censorship in America.* New York: Scribner's, 1968.

Detailed scholarly history of book censorship from the nineteenth century through the 1930s. Particularly good on the 1920s. Although no direct references to the ACLU, good material on cases handled by ACLU co-general counsel, Morris Ernst and Arthur Garfield Hays.

202. Chafee, Zechariah, Jr. *The Censorship in Boston.* Boston: Civil Liberties Union of Massachusetts, 1929.

    Account of a famous wave of censorship of books and plays in Boston in the mid-1920s and discussion of First Amendment issues. Pamphlet actually written by ACLU executive director Roger Baldwin but signed by Chafee.

203. Dennett, Mary Ware. *Who's Obscene?* New York: Vanguard Press, 1930.

    First-hand account of famous prosecution of Dennett for sending a sex education pamphlet through the mails.

204. DeSilver, Albert. "Repealing the War Laws." *The Nation,* 112 (April 20, 1921): 587–588.

    Article calling for the repeal of the Espionage and Sedition Laws.

205. Ernst, Morris L. "Radio Censorship and the Listening Millions." *The Nation,* 122 (April 28, 1926): 473–475.

    Article on censorship in the new radio industry.

206. Ernst, Morris L. "Who Shall Control the Air?" *The Nation,* 122 (April 21, 1926): 443–444.

    Article on threat to freedom of expression in radio industry posed by monopoly control of the industry.

207. Ernst, Morris L. and William Seagle. *To the Pure . . . A Study of Obscenity and the Censor.* New York: Viking, 1928.

    Discussion and critique of censorship by Ernst, ACLU general counsel and the leading attorney in censorship cases. One of Ernst's many writings on the subject of censorship, intended for a popular audience, which largely defined the issues for the next generation.

208. "Free Speech and the Schools." *The Independent*, 116 (June 5, 1926): 646–647.

    Article on the New York School Board's refusal to allow the ACLU to hold a meeting in a public school building.

209. Josephson, Harold. "Political Justice During the Red Scare: The Trial of Benjamin Gitlow." Michael Belknap, ed. *Political Trials*. Westport, CT: Greenwood, 1981. Pp. 153–176.

    Scholarly account of the trial of a leading American Communist that resulted in the landmark Supreme Court case of *Gitlow v. New York* (1925). The decision represented the ACLU's first important breakthrough in the Supreme Court.

210. Kirchwey, George W. *A Survey of the Workings of the Criminal Syndicalism Law of California*. Los Angeles: ACLU of Southern California, 1926.

    History and analysis of the California criminal syndicalism law, which was used more extensively in the 1920s than similar laws in other states.

211. Mencken, H. L. *The Editor, The Bluenose, and The Prostitute: H. L. Mencken's History of the "Hatrack" Censorship Case*. Carl Bode, ed. Boulder, CO: Roberts Rinehart, 1988.

    First-hand account of famous 1926 Boston censorhip case, involving Mencken and ACLU lawyer Arthur Garfield Hays. Includes commentary on the case by a historian and literary critic.

212. Nelles, Walter. "In the Wake of the Espionage Act." *The Nation*, 111 (December 15, 1920): 684–686.

    Article assessing the impact of wartime prosecutions under the Espionage Act.

213. Warren, Charles. "The New 'Liberty' Under the Fourteenth Amendment." *Harvard Law Review*, 39 (February 1926): 431–465.

Analysis of the significance of the Supreme Court's decision in *Gitlow v. New York* (1925), the ACLU's first significant victory in the Supreme Court.

D. THE 1930s

1. General

[See also #1130, #1131, #1132, #1134, #1135.]

214. ACLU. *Annual Reports, 1930–1939*. New York: ACLU, 1930–1939. New York: Arno Press, 1970.

Published annually by the ACLU. Detailed coverage of civil liberties issues and ACLU activities. Excellent resource for identifying various civil liberties issues.

215. ACLU. *Civil Liberty in American Cities—A Survey Based on 332 American Cities of Over 10,000 Population*. New York: ACLU, 1939.

Survey of the status of freedom of speech, press, and assembly in 332 cities.

216. ACLU. *Local Civil Liberties Committees Reports, 1938–1939*. New York: ACLU, 1939.

Supplement to 1939 ACLU *Annual Report*, covering activities of ACLU affiliates.

217. Auerbach, Jerold S. "The Depression Decade." Alan Reitman, ed. *The Pulse of Freedom*. New York: W. W. Norton, 1975. Pp. 40–76.

Excellent summary of the ACLU and civil liberties issues during the 1930s.

218. Chicago Civil Liberties Committee. *In Support of Freedom: How Civil Liberty is Guarded in Chicago and Illinois.* Chicago: Chicago Civil Liberties Committee, 1934.

   Pamphlet explaining the activities of the Chicago affiliate of the ACLU.

219. Clark, Grenville. "Civil Liberties: Court Help or Self Help?" *Annals of the American Academy of Political and Social Science,* 195 (January 1938): 1–11.

   Discussion of the role of the Supreme Court in protecting civil liberties by a prominent leader of the ABA who was sympathetic to the ACLU.

220. Clark, Grenville. "Conservatism and Civil Liberties." *ABA Journal,* 24 (August 1938): 640–644.

   Article by prominent ABA leader arguing that conservatives should be more active in supporting civil liberties. An important indicator of shift in public opinion toward greater support for civil liberties.

221. Dabney, Virginius. "Civil Liberties in the South." *Virginia Quarterly Review,* 16 (Winter 1940): 81–91.

   Survey of the state of civil liberties in the South.

222. Ernst, Morris L. *The Best is Yet . . .* New York: Harper Brothers, 1945.

   One of a series of memoirs of ACLU co-general counsel. Includes short chapters on several important ACLU cases. Author had a reputation for exaggerating his own role in these cases.

223. Fraenkel, Osmond K. "One Hundred and Fifty Years of the Bill of Rights." *Minnesota Law Review* (1939).

   Discussion of the role of the Supreme Court in protecting civil liberties up to the late 1930s. Author was then emerging as the ACLU's most important Supreme Court litigator.

224. Fraenkel, Osmond. "What Can Be Done About the Constitution and the Supreme Court?" *Columbia Law Review*, 37 (February 1937): 212–226.

Discussion of the hostility of the Supreme Court to New Deal economic measures and to civil liberties by the lawyer who would later become the ACLU's most important Supreme Court litigator. Article reflects the skepticism about the Supreme Court as a protector of indvidual rights prevalent among most ACLU leaders through the late 1930s.

225. Ickes, Harold L. *Nations in Nightshirts*. New York: ACLU, 1937.

Reprint of speech to the 1937 ACLU Annual Meeting by the then Secretary of the Interior of the United States.

226. Mitchell, Jonathan. "Civil Liberties Under Roosevelt." *The New Republic*, 81 (December 26, 1934): 186.

Civil libertarian critique of the Roosevelt Administration in the early years of the New Deal.

227. Ward, Paul. "The State of Civil Liberties." *The Nation*, 142 (June 10, 1936): 731–732.

Brief discussion of the state of civil liberties in 1936.

2. Academic Freedom

[See also #1137, #1149.]

228. ACLU. *The Case of Reed Harris*. New York: ACLU, 1932.

Pamphlet on the case of the editor of the Columbia University student newspaper who was expelled for his political views. In the 1950s Harris was attacked by Senator Joseph McCarthy for having sought the ACLU's help in this case.

229. ACLU. *The Gag on Teaching*. New York: ACLU, 1931. Second edition, 1936. Third edition, 1940.

Report on growing restrictions on rights of teachers, especially loyalty oaths.

230. ACLU. *The Principles of Academic Freedom.* New York: ACLU, 1934. Revised edition, 1937.

Early statement of ACLU policy on academic freedom.

231. ACLU. *School Buildings as Public Forums.* New York: ACLU, 1934.

Discussion of denial of right to hold meetings in public schools to radicals and ACLU representatives.

232. ACLU. *Special Oaths of Loyalty For School Teachers.* New York: ACLU, 1935.

Legal memorandum on growth of loyalty oaths for teachers.

233. ACLU. *What Freedom in New York Schools?* New York: ACLU, 1934.

Report on denial of freedom of speech and assembly to New York school teachers and students.

234. Meiklejohn, Alexander. "Teachers and Controversial Questions." *Harper's*, 177 (June 1938): 15–22.

Discussion of academic freedom issues related to the teaching of Communism, socialism, and other controversial issues. Author was a prominent member of the ACLU and one of the leading authorities on academic freedom and the First Amendment.

3. Aliens, Immigrants, Rights of

235. ACLU. *The Attempted Deportation of John Strachey.* New York: ACLU, 1935.

Pamphlet opposing the government's attempt to deport a noted author and radical.

236. ACLU. *Citizenship for Alien Pacifists.* New York: ACLU, 1938.

   Pamphlet on recent court cases involving the rights of alien pacifists.

237. ACLU. *The Right of Asylum.* New York: ACLU, 1935. Revised edition, 1937.

   Pamphlet on the legal rights of aliens.

238. ACLU. *Shall All Aliens Be Registered?* New York: ACLU, 1939.

   Pamphlet opposing federal legislation to require all resident aliens to register with the government.

4. Civil Rights

[See also #1146.]

239. ACLU. *A New Day for Indians.* New York: ACLU, 1938.

   Analysis of the 1934 Indian Reorganization Act which reflected many of the recommendations of the ACLU Committee on Indian Rights.

240. ACLU. *Black Justice.* New York: ACLU, 1931. Revised edition, 1938.

   Comprehensive survey of race discrimination in the United States. Report marked the beginning of a more active ACLU attack on race discrimination.

241. ACLU. *Civil Liberties for Indians!* New York: ACLU, 1932.

   Brief statement of ACLU policy on rights of Native Americans. Many of these recommendations were incorporated into the 1934 Indian Reorganization Act.

242. ACLU. *Indian Primer.* New York: ACLU, 1932.

   Pamphlet outlining the denial of rights to Native Americans.

243. ACLU. *The Oldest American Gets the Rawest Deal*. New York: ACLU, 1934.

   Brief report on the rights of Native Americans by ACLU Committee on Indian Rights.

244. Carter, Dan T. *Scottsboro: A Tragedy of the American South*. New York: Oxford University Press, 1971.

   Detailed scholarly history of the most famous civil rights case of the 1930s. Useful material on the ACLU's role in the important Supreme Court cases arising from the case.

245. Kluger, Richard. *Simple Justice*. New York: Vintage Books, 1977.

   Lengthy, detailed history of civil rights litigation leading up to *Brown v. Board of Education* (1954). Good material on initial proposal for legal attack on segregation by the Garland Fund (1929–1931) which was closely associated with the ACLU.

246. Martin, Charles H. *The Angelo Herndon Case and Southern Justice*. Baton Rouge, LA: LSU Press, 1976.

   Detailed scholarly history of one of the most important civil rights cases of the 1930s involving a black Communist organizer. The ACLU assisted in the Supreme Court appeal which resulted in an important decision on First Amendment rights.

247. Ransdell, Horace. *Report on the Scottsboro, Ala. Case*. New York: ACLU, 1931.

   ACLU-sponsored report on the famous Scottsboro case (see #243).

5. Communist-Related Issues

[See also #442, #1150, #1152.]

248. ACLU. *Alien and Sedition Bills Pending in Congress*. New York: ACLU, 1940.

Pamphlet criticizing various bills which eventually led to the 1940 Smith Act.

249. ACLU. *Minority Parties on the Ballot.* New York: ACLU, 1932. Revised editions, 1940, 1943.

Survey of state laws restricting access to the ballot for communists, socialists, and other radicals.

250. ACLU. *Oppose the Continuation of the Dies Committee!* New York: ACLU, 1939.

Pamphlet urging Congress not to renew the House Un-American Activities Committee.

251. ACLU. *Out of His Own Mouth!* New York: ACLU, 1939.

Pamphlet reprinting statement by Representative Martin Dies, Chair of the House Un-American Activities Committee to the effect that the ACLU was not a Communist organization.

252. ACLU. *Protest the Dies Commmittee Demand For Membership Lists!* New York: ACLU, 1940.

Pamphlet urging people to protest the attempt by the House Committee on Un-American Activities to obtain and publish the membership list of the Communist Party.

253. ACLU. *A Statement to Members and Friends of the American Civil Liberties Union.* New York: ACLU, 1940.

Official ACLU explanation of the trial and expulsion of Elizabeth Gurley Flynn from the Board of Directors for her membership in the Communist Party (see #264).

254. ACLU. *Still the Fish Committee Nonsense!* New York: ACLU, 1932.

Response to the 1931 Congressional investigation into alleged Communist activity (#270), which included testimony by Roger Baldwin.

255. ACLU. *Who's "Un-American?"* New York: ACLU, 1935.

ACLU reply to criticisms that it is "un-American." Primarily quotes conservatives and right-wing leaders who advocate lawless action.

256. Baldwin, Roger N. and Hamilton Fish, Jr. *Should Alien Communists Be Deported for Their Opinions?* New York: ACLU, 1934.

    Transcript of a debate between the director of the ACLU and the member of Congress who chaired the 1931 investigation into alleged Communist subversion in the United States. Debate held in Boston, March 14, 1931.

257. Britt, Stuart Henderson and Selden C. Menefee. "Did the Publicity of the Dies Committee in 1938 Influence Public Opinion?" *Public Opinion Quarterly*, 3 (July 1939): 449–457.

    Academic study of the impact of the first series of hearings by the House Un-American Activities Committee in 1938. Findings indicated a negative impact on the image of the ACLU.

258. Broun, Heywood. "Free Speech, With Reservations." *The New Republic*, 95 (July 13, 1938): 278. Reply: "Free Speech Again." *Ibid.*, 95 (August 3, 1938): 347–348.

    Article and response on controversy over possible libel suit by member of the ACLU Board of Directors against a right-wing critic of the ACLU for having called him a Communist. Possibility that the ACLU might represent the critic. Articles critical of the ACLU's position.

259. *Crisis in the Civil Liberties Union*. New York, 1940.

    Statement by dissident members of the ACLU criticizing the expulsion of Elizabeth Gurley Flynn from the Board of Directors (see #264). Includes documents related to the issue.

260. Dilling, Elizabeth. *The Roosevelt Red Record and its Background*. Chicago: The Author, 1936.

Right-wing attack on the New Deal. Accuses the ACLU of being communist-influenced and, in turn, of influencing the Roosevelt Administration.

261. Flynn, Elizabeth Gurley. "Why I Won't Resign From the ACLU." *New Masses* (March 19, 1940): 11–12.

    Defense of her own position and denial that the ACLU Board of Directors has the right to expel her from the Board (see #264).

262. Goodman, Walter. *The Committee: The Extraordinary Career of the House Committee on Un-American Activities*. New York: Farrar, Straus, and Giroux, 1968.

    A history of the House Un-American Activities Committee, with good material on the Committee's attacks on the ACLU during the first series of hearings in 1938.

263. Lamont, Corliss. *Freedom Is As Freedom Does*. New York: Horizon, 1956.

    General survey of assaults on civil liberties during the Cold War, by a prominent member of the ACLU Board of Directors during most of the period. One chapter is a highly critical account of the ACLU's performance during the Cold War, focusing on the 1940 expulsion of Elizabeth Gurley Flynn from the ACLU Board of Directors (see #264).

264. Lamont, Corliss, ed. *The Trial of Elizabeth Gurley Flynn by the American Civil Liberties Union*. New York: Horizon, 1968.

    Transcript of special ACLU Board of Directors meeting on May 7, 1940 where Board member Elizabeth Gurley Flynn was "tried" for being a member of the Communist Party and then removed by the ACLU Board. The incident is the source of criticism by leftists that the ACLU adopted an anti-Communist posture during the Cold War and failed to defend civil liberties vigorously.

265. McWilliams, Carey. "Sanity Restored." *The Nation*, 223 (July 3, 1976): 4–5.

　　Article on ACLU resolution disapproving the 1940 expulsion of Elizabeth Gurley Flynn from the Board of Directors.

266. Mencken, H. L. "The American Civil Liberties Union." *American Mercury*, 45 (October 1938): 182–190.

　　Article on the ACLU published as part of settlement of ACLU libel suit over an earlier article (#272) accusing the ACLU of having Communist ties.

267. Polenberg, Richard. "Franklin Roosevelt and Civil Liberties: The Case of the Dies Committee." *Historian*, 30 (February 1968): 165–178.

　　Detailed scholarly analysis of the response of the Roosevelt administration to attacks on it by the House Un-American Activities Committee between 1938 and 1940.

268. Simmons, Jerold. "The American Civil Liberties Union and the Dies Committee, 1938–1940." *Harvard Civil Rights—Civil Liberties Law Review*, 17 (Spring 1982): 183–207.

　　Detailed scholarly account of the relationship of the ACLU to the first round of hearings by the House Un-American Activities Committee, 1938–1940. Valuable insights into the internal controversies within the ACLU.

269. "Split in the American Civil Liberties Union." *The Nation*, 150 (May 18, 1940): 610.

　　Article on the removal of Elizabeth Gurley Flynn from the ACLU Board of Directors.

270. "Test of Consistency." *The Nation*, 207 (August 5, 1968): 69–70.

　　Article on ACLU repeal of 1940 policy barring Communists and members of other totalitarian groups from positions of leadership in the ACLU.

271. U.S. House of Representatives, Special Committee to Investigate Communist Activities in the United States. *Investigation of Communist Propaganda. Hearings.* 71st Cong., 2d and 3d Sess., 1930. *Report.* 71st Cong., 3d Sess., 1931.

    Congressional investigation into alleged Communist activity in the United States. Includes voluntary testimony by ACLU Executive Director Roger Baldwin on the meaning of free speech.

272. Varney, Harold Lord. "The Civil Liberties Union: Liberalism a la Moscow." *American Mercury,* 39 (December 1936): 385–399.

    Attack on the ACLU, accusing it of having Communist ties. Provoked protests by ACLU and libel suit. Led to publication of second article on the ACLU (See #266).

273. Varney, Harold Lord and Ernest Sutherland Bates. "The Civil Liberties Union: Political or Nonpartisan?" *Forum,* 99 (April 1938): 207–211.

    Right-wing attack on the ACLU, accusing it of left-wing sympathies.

274. Weybright, Victor. "Communists and Civil Liberties." *Survey Graphic,* 29 (May 1940): 290–293.

    Article on the expulsion of Elizabeth Gurley Flynn from the ACLU Board of Directors (#264). Sympathetic to the official ACLU position.

6. *Labor, Rights of*

[See also #1133.]

275. ACLU. *Call out the Militia.* New York: ACLU, 1938.

    Pamphlet discussing the use of state militias in strikes.

276. ACLU. *Civil Rights vs. Mayor Hague.* New York: ACLU, 1938.

Excerpts from federal court hearing on ACLU suit versus Mayor Hague of Jersey City, New Jersey. Suit eventually led to the landmark Supreme Court decision, *Hague v. CIO* (1939).

277. ACLU. *Justice—North Carolina Style.* New York: ACLU, 1930.

Pamphlet on the textile workers strike in Gastonia, North Carolina, one of the most celebrated strikes of the period.

278. ACLU. *The Kentucky Miners Struggle.* New York: ACLU, 1932.

Pamphlet on civil liberties issues related to the coal miners in Kentucky.

279. ACLU. *Legal Tactics For Labor's Rights.* New York: ACLU, 1937.

Discussion of tactics for labor union organizers.

280. ACLU. *Liberty Under the New Deal.* ACLU: New York, 1934.

Proceedings of an ACLU-sponsored conference on the New Deal in 1934. Presentations by Roger Baldwin, Mary Van Kleeck and other ACLU leaders express strong criticisms of the New Deal, particularly its policies toward labor unions.

281. ACLU. *More Candid Views of Mayor Hague.* New York: ACLU, 1938.

ACLU pamphlet on the fight for freedom of assembly in Jersey City, New Jersey. Features Mayor James Hague's blatant anti-civil liberties statements. The fight culminated in a landmark Supreme Court case, *Hague v. CIO* (1939).

282. ACLU. *Sedition in Illinois.* New York: ACLU, 1934.

Report on prosecution of unemployed workers under the Illinois sedition law.

283. ACLU. *A Strike is Criminal Syndicalism—in California*. New York: ACLU, 1930.

Brief account of labor struggles in Imperial Valley of California.

284. ACLU. *The Struggle for Civil Liberties in the Illinois Coal Fields*. New York: ACLU, 1933.

Report on the denial of civil liberties to coal miners in Illinois.

285. ACLU. *The Struggle For Civil Liberty on the Land*. New York: ACLU, 1936.

ACLU report on the denial of civil liberties to farm workers and tenant farmers.

286. Auerbach, Jerold S. *Labor and Liberty: The LaFollette Committee and The New Deal*. Indianapolis: Bobbs-Merrill, 1966.

Detailed scholarly history of the Senate investigation into violations of the rights of labor unions. Although not primarily a book on the ACLU, it contains an excellent treatment of the philosophical reorientation of the ACLU on the relationship of government and individual liberty during the 1930s. ACLU lobbied for the creation of the committee and supplied material to it from its files.

287. Daniel, Cletus. *The ACLU and the Wagner Act*. Ithaca, NY: Cornell University Press, 1980.

Critical account of the ACLU. Argues that the ACLU followed the position of the Communist Party on labor issues in the 1930s.

288. Greene, Nathan. *State Legislation Limiting Labor Injunctions*. New York: ACLU, 1939.

Author was then chair of the ACLU Committee on Labor's Rights. Includes model legislation on state law limiting the use of injunctions against strikes.

289. McKean, Dayton David. *The Boss: The Hague Machine in Action.* Boston: Houghton, Mifflin, 1940.

　　Contemporary account of the Jersey City struggle in which the ACLU played a major role that lead to the *Hague v. CIO* (1939) decision.

290. Riis, Roger W. "Free Speech for Whom?" *Forum*, 100 (December 1938): 312–316. Reprinted: *Reader's Digest*, 33 (December 1938): 32–37.

　　Member of the ACLU Board of Directors publicly criticizes the ACLU for initially refusing to support the free speech rights of automobile manufacturer Henry Ford. The National Labor Relations Board (NLRB) had issued an order restricting Ford's right to distribute anti-union material. This controversy was a pivotal event in the history of the ACLU which eventually changed its position and supported Ford's free speech rights.

291. Williams, Chester S. "Imperial Valley Mob." *The New Republic*, 78 (February 21, 1934): 39–41.

　　First-hand account of vigilante attacks on labor union organizers and ACLU leaders (particularly A. L. Wirin, attorney for ACLU of Southern California) in California agricultural region.

7. Nazi-Related Issues

[See also #1138.]

292. ACLU. *Shall We Defend Free Speech for Nazis in America?* New York: ACLU, 1934. Second edition, 1937.

　　Official ACLU statement explaining and defending its policy of defending the free speech rights of totalitarian groups. The initial version was written in response to the rise of domestic Fascist groups in 1934.

Revised version, with significant changes, issued in 1939 (#293). Later version published in 1977 (#673).

293. ACLU. *Why We Defend Free Speech for Nazis, Fascists—and Communists*. New York: ACLU, 1939.

Revised version of 1934 statement (#292) on the free speech rights of totalitarian groups. The decision to include Communists along with Nazis touched off a major controversy within the ACLU.

294. Hoke, Travis. *Shirts!* New York: ACLU, 1934.

ACLU-sponsored exposé of domestic Nazi groups. Commissioned in the wake of the Nazi triumph in Germany and the appearance of pro-Nazi groups in the United States.

295. Glaser, Martha. "The German-American Bund in New Jersey." *New Jersey History*, 92 (1974): 33–49.

Scholarly account of the controversies surrounding the major pro-Nazi group in the United States. Includes an account of an important decision by the New Jersey Supreme Court striking down a group libel law; decision was based on a brief by ACLU general counsel Arthur Garfield Hays.

296. Milner, Lucille. "Fighting Fascism by Law." *The Nation*, 146 (January 15, 1938): 65–67.

Discussion of anti-Nazi legislation in Europe by ACLU secretary. Argues against laws designed to restrict the activities of unpopular political groups.

8. Police Misconduct

297. ACLU. *Finger-Printing—For What?* New York: ACLU, 1936.

ACLU report opposing proposal for fingerprinting of all American citizens.

298. ACLU. *Methods of Combatting the Third Degree.* New York: ACLU, 1934.

   Proposal for methods to prevent police misconduct. Based largely on material in the government report on police abuse (#302).

299. ACLU. *Police Lawlessness Against Communists in New York.* New York: ACLU, 1930.

   Criticism of police brutality against demonstrators led by the Communist Party in New York City.

300. ACLU. *Thumbs Down!* New York: ACLU, 1937.

   Pamphlet opposing proposal for fingerprinting all citizens.

301. Chafee, Zechariah. "Remedies for the Third Degree." *Atlantic Monthly,* 148 (November 1931): 621–630.

   Recommendations for eliminating police misconduct. Based on #302 and similar to recommendations in #298.

302. U.S. National Commission on Law Observance and Enforcement. *Lawlessness in Law Enforcement.* Washington, DC: Government Printing Office, 1931. Reprinted: New York: Arno Press, 1969.

   Sensational exposé of police misconduct by the so-called Wickersham Commission. Report co-authored by Zechariah Chafee, Walter Pollak, and Carl Stern, lawyers associated with the ACLU, with material drawn, in part, from ACLU files.

9. Religious Liberty

303. ACLU. *Religious Liberty in the United States.* New York: ACLU, 1939.

   Pamphlet on religious freedom, concentrating on cases involving the Jehovah's Witnesses.

History of the ACLU

304. ACLU. *The Right of Atheists to Testify in Court.* New York: ACLU, 1932.

    Pamphlet on ACLU test case in New Jersey challenging denial of right of atheists to testify in court without swearing on the Bible.

10. Speech, Press, and Assembly, Freedom of

305. ACLU. *The California Red Flag Case.* New York: ACLU, 1930.

    Pamphlet on the case that resulted in the landmark Supreme Court decision, *Stromberg v. California* (1931).

306. ACLU. *Libels Against Race and Religion.* New York: ACLU, 1939.

    Pamphlet arguing against laws curbing "hate speech" directed at racial and religious minorities.

307. ACLU. *Ordinances Restricting Leaflet Distribution.* New York: ACLU, 1937. Originally in International Juridical Association. *Bulletin* (June 1937).

    Analysis of the current state of the law relating the leaflet distribution.

308. ACLU. *Radio Censorship.* New York: ACLU, 1934.

    Pamphlet on the problem of censorship in radio broadcasting.

309. ACLU. *The Right to Advocate Violence.* New York: ACLU, 1931.

    Pamphlet explaining the ACLU position on freedom of speech. Published in response to 1931 Congressional investigation of Communist activity (the Fish Committee) in which Roger Baldwin testified (#270).

310. ACLU. *Scandal and Defamation!* New York: ACLU, 1931.

    Pamphlet on the landmark freedom of the press case, *Near v. Minnesota* (1931).

311. ACLU. *What Rights For the Unemployed?* New York: ACLU, 1935.

   Report on restrictions on freedom of assembly for the unemployed.

312. ACLU. *What Shocked the Censor.* New York: ACLU, 1933.

   Complete record of cuts ordered by New York state film censors in 1932 and early 1933.

313. Civil Liberties Union of Massachusetts. *Censorship in Boston.* New York: ACLU, 1938.

   Pamphlet on recent censorship cases in Boston. See earlier version (#202).

314. Ernst, Morris L. and Alexander Lindey. *The Censor Marches On.* New York: Doubleday, 1940.

   Discussion of censorship issues, focusing on developments in the 1930s, by ACLU co-general counsel who litigated most of the important cases.

315. Ernst, Morris L. and Alexander Lindey. *Hold Your Tongue!* New York: William Morrow, 1932.

   Analysis of the law of libel and slander, written for a general audience. Co-author Ernst was ACLU co-general counsel.

316. Fennell, William G. *The Right of Assembly: A Study of the Law With Suggested Remedies.* New York: ACLU, 1935.

   Legal analysis of freedom of assembly, as of 1935, by a member of the ACLU Board of Directors.

317. National Council on Freedom from Censorship. *Freedom from Censorship.* New York: ACLU, 1933. Revised edition, 1937.

   Pamphlet surveying restrictions on freedom of expression in motion pictures, magazines, radio, books, and the theater. The National Council was a special project of the ACLU, organized to coordinate a national anti-censorship campaign.

History of the ACLU

11. Other Issues

318. ACLU. *Civil Liberties in American Colonies.* New York: ACLU, 1932. Revised edition, 1939.

    Survey of restrictions on civil liberties in areas controlled by the United States government.

319. ACLU. *Stop Wire-Tapping!* New York: ACLU, 1932.

    Brief ACLU report advocating federal legislation to outlaw wiretapping.

E. WORLD WAR II, 1940–1945

1. General

[See also #1181.]

320. ACLU. *Annual Reports, 1940–1945.* New York: Arno Press, 1970.

    Each annual report contains detailed information on civil liberties issues and ACLU cases. Valuable resource for identifying particular issues for each year.

321. ACLU. *Local Civil Liberties Committee Reports, 1939–1940.* New York: ACLU, 1940. *Ibid.,* 1941–1942 (1942). *Ibid.,* 1942–1943 (1943).

    Supplement to 1940 ACLU *Annual Reports* reporting on activities of ACLU affiliates.

322. ACLU. *Military Power and Civil Rights.* New York: ACLU, 1942.

    ACLU pamphlet explaining the civil liberties issues raised by the war and the official ACLU policies on each one.

323. ACLU. *Minority Parties on the Ballot.* New York: ACLU, 1940. Revised edition, January 1943.

Revision of earlier pamphlet (#249) on state laws restricting access to the ballot for Communists, Socialists, and other minority political parties. Detailed information on the 1940 elections. The 1943 edition covers the 1942 elections.

324. ACLU. *National Conference on Civil Liberties in the Present Emergency.* New York: ACLU, 1939.

    Proceedings of ACLU conference, October 13–14, 1939, on civil liberties issues raised by outbreak of war in Europe.

325. American Bar Association. Committee on the Bill of Rights. *Bill of Rights Review* (1940–1941).

    Journal devoted to civil liberties issues published by the ABA Committee on the Bill of Rights. Valuable coverage of important cases and activities of local ABA Bill of Rights Committees. The Committee was modelled after the ACLU and cooperated with the ACLU on several important cases.

326. "Americans vs. Fifth Columnists: A Symposium." *Survey Graphic*, 29 (November 1940): 545–550.

    Symposium on whether there is a Nazi "Fifth Column" in the United States and, if so, how the country should respond. Contributions by leading ACLU figures: Roger Baldwin, John Haynes Holmes, Morris Ernst, Dorothy Dudley Bromley, Dorothy Kenyon, and others not associated with the ACLU.

327. "Civil Liberties and the Fifth Column." *University of Chicago Round Table.* Chicago: University of Chicago Press, 1941.

    Transcript of an NBC Radio program featuring a debate on the question of whether there is a threat of Nazi subversion in the United States. Debate includes John A. Lapp, chair, Chicago Civil Liberties Committee.

328. Cushman, Robert. "Civil Liberty After the War." *American Political Science Review*, 38 (February 1944): 1–20.

Discussion of the future of civil liberties after World War II by a leading political scientist and civil liberties advocate.

329. Cushman, Robert. "The Impact of War on the Constitution." Robert Cushman, ed. *The Impact of War on America*. Ithaca, NY: Cornell University Press, 1942.

Excellent general survey of the impact of World War II on civil liberties by a prominent political scientist. Written in the early phases of the war.

330. Fraenkel, Osmond K. *Our Civil Liberties*. New York: Viking, 1944.

Survey of Supreme Court rulings on civil liberties issues, written by ACLU's foremost Supreme Court litigator. Revised editions, with various titles, published through the 1970s (see #536, #537).

331. Holmes, John Haynes. *What is Happening to Our Bill of Rights?* Boston: American Unitarian Association, 1941.

Review of current threats to civil liberties by the new chair of the ACLU Board of Directors.

332. Irwin, Theodore. "Civil Liberties in the Crisis." *Public Opinion Quarterly*, 4 (September 1940): 523–526.

Discussion of civil liberties issues as the United States nears entering World War II. Auther was then ACLU staff member.

333. Milner, Lucille. "Freedom of Speech in Wartime." *The New Republic*, 103 (November 25, 1940): 715.

Article on the suppression of free speech during World War I. One of several articles prepared by the ACLU as the United States was about to enter World War II.

334. Milner, Lucille B. and Groff Conklin. "Wartime Censorship in the United States." *Harper's*, 180 (January 1940): 187–195.

   Article on the suppression of free speech during World War I. One of several articles prepared by the ACLU as the United States was about to enter World War II.

335. Preston, William, Jr. "Shadows of War and Fear." Alan Reitman, ed. *The Pulse of Freedom*. New York: W. W. Norton, 1975. Pp. 77–122.

   Good summary of the ACLU and civil liberties issues during World War II.

336. Reisman, David. "Democracy and Defamation: Control of Group Libel." *Columbia Law Review*, 42 (May 1942): 727–780; (September 1942): 1085–1123; (November 1942): 1282–1318.

   Extremely important series of articles arguing that society has a right to control group libel, or hate speech. Perhaps the most articulate critique of the ACLU's position on freedom of speech. Reflects the impact of Nazi Germany on the thinking of American liberals.

337. Thomas, Norman. "Dark Days For Liberty." *Christian Century*, 59 (July 29, 1942): 929–931.

   Important criticism of "totalitarian liberals" who Thomas felt were too willing to compromise on civil liberties during wartime.

2. Academic Freedom

338. ACLU. *The Gag on Teaching*. Third edition. New York: ACLU, 1940.

   Third edition of pamphlet first published in 1931 (#229).

339. ACLU. *The Story of the Bertrand Russell Case*. New York: ACLU, 1940.

   Pamphlet on the denial of a teaching position at City College of New York to Bertrand Russell because of his allegedly "immoral" ideas. ACLU filed briefs in Russell's unsuccessful suit to obtain the teaching position.

340. ACLU. *What Freedom for American Students?* New York: ACLU, 1940. Excerpts reprinted as *A Student "Bill of Rights"* (1945).

   Pamphlet on academic freedom issues related to the rights of students.

341. Edwards, Paul. "How Bertrand Russell Was Prevented From Teaching at the College of the City of New York." Bertrand Russell. *Why I Am Not A Christian*. New York: Simon and Schuster, 1957. Pp. 207–259.

   Historical account of the denial of a teaching position at City College of New York to Bertrand Russell because of his allegedly "immoral" ideas. ACLU filed briefs in Russell's unsuccessful suit to obtain the teaching position.

342. Kallen, Horace, ed. *The Bertrand Russell Case*. New York: Viking, 1941.

   Collection of articles on the the refusal of the City of New York to hire Bertrand Russell at City College. Book sponsored by the ACLU. Includes material on the ACLU's intervention on behalf of Russell.

3. Civil Rights

343. ACLU. *Race Practices of National Associations*. New York: ACLU, 1945.

   Brief survey of racial practices of national organizations, with particularly important material on race discrimination by labor unions.

344. Hays, Arthur Garfield. "Rejoinder." *Politics*, 1 (April 1944): 88.

   Reply to criticisms of Dwight McDonald (#345) on Hays's handling of the *Lynn* case challenging racial segregation in the military.

345. McDonald, Dwight. "The Novel Case of Winfred Lynn." *The Nation*, 156 (February 20, 1943): 268–270.

   Discussion of the case of black American Winfred Lynn who was challenging racial segregation in the selective service system. McDonald headed the Lynn defense committee. Arthur Garfield Hays represented Lynn on behalf of the ACLU.

346. McDonald, Dwight. "On the Conduct of the Lynn Case." *Politics*, 1 (April 1944): 85–88.

   Discussion of government response to Lynn's challenge to the segregated draft and criticism of legal issues raised by attorney Hays on behalf of the ACLU (see reply, #343).

347. McDonald, Dwight. "The Supreme Court's New Moot Suit." *The Nation*, 159 (July 1, 1944): 13–14.

   Discussion of Supreme Court's response to appeal by Lynn in challenge to racial segregation in the selective service system (see #344).

348. Northrup, Herbert. "Race Discrimination in Unions." *The American Mercury*, 61 (August 1945): 90–95.

   Pioneering survey of racial discrimination by labor unions, written by member of ACLU Board of Directors. Article reprinted and distributed by the ACLU.

349. Northrup, Herbert R. "Unions, Restricted Clientele." *The Nation*, 157 (August 14, 1943): 178–180.

   Criticizes labor unions for discriminating against African-Americans.

350. Rauschenbush, Winifred. *How to Prevent a Race Riot in Your Home Town*. New York: ACLU, 1944.

   Response to racial disorders of 1943. Recommendations on how to promote racial justice and ease racial tensions.

4. Conscientious Objectors

[See also #1160, #1161.]

351. ACLU. *Conscience and the War*. New York: ACLU, 1944.

   Discussion of the rights of conscientious objectors under the 1940 Selective Service Act.

352. Cornell, Julien. *The Conscientious Objector and the Law*. New York: John Day, 1943.

   Detailed book-length discussion of legal issues surrounding the right of conscientious objection by counsel for National Commmittee on Conscientious Objectors (NCCO). Co-sponsored by the ACLU.

353. Cornell, Julien. *Conscience and the State*. New York: John Day, 1944.

   Short discussion of legal and administrative problems facing conscientious objectors, by legal counsel for NCCO.

5. Japanese-Americans, Internment of

[See also #1168, #1169, #1170.]

354. "$1,000 Reward; Information on Persons Committing Acts of Terrorism Against Returning Japanese-Americans." *Collier's*, 116 (September 22, 1945): 90.

   The ACLU offers cash reward for information leading to conviction of people who commit violence against Japanese-Americans returning from internment camps.

355. Bosworth, Allan R. *America's Concentration Camps.* New York: W. W. Norton, 1967.

Account of the Japanese-American internment written for a general audience. Superceded by more recent scholarship, especially #359. Contains an introduction by Roger Baldwin.

356. Dembitz, Nanette. "Racial Discrimination and the Military Judgment: The Supreme Court's Korematsu and Endo Decisions." *Columbia Law Review,* 45 (March 1945): 175–239

Sharply critical analysis of the Supreme Court's opinions in *Korematsu* and *Endo.* The author served in the Justice Department at the time of the original cases and later was a lawyer for a member of the Board of Directors of the ACLU.

357. Drinnon, Richard. *Keeper of Concentration Camps: Dillon S. Myer and American Racism.* Berkeley: University of California Press, 1987.

Detailed scholarly account of the government relocation centers for the Japanese-Americans during World War II. Highly critical of the role of the ACLU and ACLU executive director Roger Baldwin.

358. Grodzins, Morton. *Americans Betrayed.* Chicago: University of Chicago Press, 1949.

Detailed account of the evacuation and internment of the Japanese-Americans. Sharply critical of California political leaders for their role in the program.

359. Irons, Peter. *Justice at War: The Story of the Japanese-American Internment.* New York: Oxford University Press, 1983.

Detailed scholarly account of the legal proceedings over the evacuation and internment of the Japanese-Americans during World War II. A special focus on the Supreme Court cases. The author alleges misconduct on the part of the U.S. Justice Department. The author is a scholar-activist who served as attorney for the plaintiff's efforts to have their convictions overturned in the 1980s.

360. Irons, Peter, ed. *Justice Delayed: The Record of the Japanese American Internment Cases.* Middletown, CT: Wesleyan University Press, 1989.

  Legal materials on the original internment cases and subsequent efforts to have the convictions reversed. Includes briefs, transcripts and court opinions, 1943 to 1987.

361. Rostow, Eugene V. "The Japanese-American Cases—A Disaster." *Yale Law Journal*, 54 (June 1945): 489–533.

  Sharply critical of the government's action and the Supreme Court decisions in the internment of the Japanese-Americans. Calls for new appeal and reconsideration.

362. Rostow, Eugene V. "Our Worst Wartime Mistake." *Harper's*, 191 (September 1945): 193–201.

  Strong criticism of the government's internment program. Similar to #360 but written for a popular audience.

363. tenBroek, Jacobus, Edward N. Barnhart, and Floyd Matson. *Prejudice, War and the Constitution: Causes and Consequences of the Evacuation of the Japanese Americans in World War II.* Berkeley: University of California Press, 1954.

  Detailed account of the different aspects of the evacuation and internment. Sections focus on the history of anti-Japanese prejudice on the west coast, the evacuation program, and the test cases in the Supreme Court.

364. Weglyn, Michi. *Years of Infamy: The Untold Story of America's Concentration Camps.* New York: Morrow, 1976.

  Account of Japanese-American internment by a victim of the internment. Account reflects the point of view of the Northern California ACLU (and is dedicated to the affiliate's lawyer) and is critical of the national office of the ACLU in the internment cases.

6. Religious Liberty

365. ACLU. *Jehovah's Witnesses and the War.* New York: ACLU, 1943.

    Pamphlet on persecution of the Jehovah's Witnesses, including problems related to flag saluting, vigilante violence, and conscientious objector claims.

366. ACLU. *The Persecution of the Jehovah's Witnesses.* New York: ACLU, 1941.

    ACLU report on vigilante violence against Jehovah's Witnesses, particularly folowing the 1939 Supreme Court decision in *Gobitis*.

367. ACLU. *Provisions of State Constitutions Regarding Religious Freedom.* New York: ACLU, 1940.

    Survey of state laws on religious liberty, with particular emphasis on issues affecting the Jehovah's Witnesses.

368. Fennell, William G. *Compulsory Flag Salute in the Schools.* New York: ACLU, 1941.

    Survey of laws relating to compulsory flag salute, with discussion of constitutional issues, written by member of ACLU Board of Directors.

369. Manwaring, David R. *Render Unto Caesar: The Flag Salute Controversy.* Chicago: University of Chicago Press, 1962.

    Detailed scholarly study of the cases involving the refusal of Jehovah's Witnesses to salute the flag.

370. Penton, M. James. *Apocalypse Delayed: The Story of the Jehovah's Witnesses.* Toronto: University of Toronto Press, 1985.

Detailed scholarly history of the Jehovah's Witnesses, including the many court cases arising from their activities.

7. Speech, Press, and Assembly, Freedom of

371. ACLU. *Are You Free to Read—See—Hear?* New York: ACLU, 1945.

    Pamphlet examining censorship of books, magazines, radio, and the movies.

372. ACLU. *No More Post Office Censorship!* New York: ACLU, 1944.

    Pamphlet on ACLU opposition to proposed federal law criminalizing racial and religious "hate" speech.

373. ACLU. *Sedition!* New York: ACLU, 1942.

    Pamphlet on prosecution of Minneapolis Socialist Workers Party members in first use of the 1940 Smith Act.

374. ACLU. *Wartime Prosecutions for Speech and Publications.* New York: ACLU, 1944. Revised edition, 1945.

    Review of federal prosecutions involving freedom of speech and press during World War II.

375. ACLU. *What's Obscene?* New York: ACLU, 1945.

    Pamphlet arguing that censorship powers of the U.S. Post Office should be restricted.

376. Hays, Arthur Garfield. "Indictments Pull the Triggers." *The Nation*, 154 (May 9, 1942): 543–545.

    ACLU co-general counsel replies to criticism of ACLU policy of defending the free speech rights of Fascists during World War II (#379).

377. Meiklejohn, Alexander. "Free Speech For Fascists." *New Masses* (December 7, 1943).

Defense of free speech for alleged American fascists. Reply to a previous article by Earl Browder, head of the American Communist Party, calling for prosecution of Fascists.

378. Ribuffo, Leo. "United States v. McWillliams: The Roosevelt Administration and the Far Right." Michael Belknap, ed. *American Political Trials*. Westport, CT: Greenwood, 1981. Pp. 201–232.

Scholarly article on the major sedition proseuction during World War II, involving a group of right-wing and crypto-fascist individuals. Some material on the ACLU's ambivalent response to the case.

379. Rosenberg, James N. "Words Are Triggers: An Open Letter to Arthur Garfield Hays." *The Nation*, 154 (May 2, 1942): 511–512.

Criticism of ACLU policy of defending free speech rights of American fascists during World War II. Addressed to ACLU co-general counsel. See #376 for reply.

380. Washburn, Patrick S. *A Question of Sedition: The Federal Government's Investigation of the Black Press During World War II*. New York: Oxford, 1986.

Scholarly analysis of investigation and threatened prosecution of the black press for sedition. Some reference to ACLU activities.

F. THE COLD WAR, 1945–1960

1. General

[See also #1177.]

381. ACLU. "How Free is *Your* Town?" Symposium. "How Free is Free?" *The Nation*, 174 (June 28, 1952).

ACLU contribution to special issue of *The Nation* on the state of civil liberties at the worst point in the Cold War period.

382. ACLU. *It's Not Only Communists' Rights!* New York: ACLU, 1948.

    Statement of ACLU position on the rights of the Communist Party, loyalty tests, HUAC, and other Cold War issues.

383. ACLU. *Violence in Peekskill.* New York: ACLU, 1950.

    ACLU report on anti-Communist violence surrounding concert by singer Paul Robeson in Peekskill, New York.

384. Angell, Ernest and H. William Fitelson. "ACLU Officials Deny Communist Infiltration." *The New Leader*, 35 (November 17, 1952): 27.

    Reply to charges that the ACLU is Communist-influenced by then chairman of the ACLU Board of Directors (Angell) and another member of the Board.

385. "Argument in Indianapolis." *See It Now.* CBS Television. November 24, 1953.

    Edward R. Murrow television program on the refusal of the Indianapolis War Memorial Auditorium and several hotels to permit an ACLU meeting. Copy of the program is available at the Museum of Broadcasting, New York City. (See also #401.)

386. Buckley, William F., Jr. and L. Brent Bozell. *McCarthy and His Enemies.* Chicago: Henry Regnery, 1954.

    Defense of Senator Joseph McCarthy and his anti-Communist tactics. Includes section (pp. 76–86) on Dorothy Kenyon, the first person "named" by McCarthy, and who was a prominent member of the ACLU at the time.

387. Casper, Jonathan. *Lawyers Before the Warren Court: Civil Liberties and Civil Rights, 1957–1966.* Urbana: University of Illinois Press, 1972.

Political science study of the role of lawyers handling unpopular cases before the Warren Court. Based on anonymous interviews. Lawyers are characterized in terms of abstract "types."

388. Caughey, John W. *In Clear and Present Danger: The Crucial State of Our Freedoms.* Chicago: University of Chicago Press, 1958.

Survey of the violations of civil liberties during the Cold War. Written by a prominent figure in the Southern California ACLU.

389. Caughey, John W. "McCarthyism Rampant." Alan Reitman, ed. *The Pulse of Freedom.* New York: W. W. Norton, 1975. Pp. 123–175.

Good overview of the state of civil liberties in the Cold War period.

390. Dwyer, William L. *The Goldmark Case: An American Libel Trial.* Seattle: University of Washington Press, 1984.

Account of a case in Washington state in which a state legislator who was called a Communist sued for libel. Accusations also included that he was a member of the ACLU and that the ACLU was a Communist organization. Gives a good sense of the atmosphere of the Cold War period and the attacks on the ACLU. Foreword by Norman Dorsen, former president of the ACLU. (See also #393.)

391. Gellhorn, Walter, ed. *The States and Subversion.* Ithaca, NY: Cornell University Press, 1952.

Chapters on anti-Communist legislation in six states. Chapters on California, Illinois, Maryland, Michigan, New York, and Washington written by individual authors. Rich detail. Considerable material on ACLU activity in each state.

392. Halliday, Terence C. "The Idiom of Legalism in Bar Politics: Lawyers, McCarthyism, and the Civil Rights Era." *American Bar Foundation Research Journal*, 1984 (Fall 1984): 911–988.

   Analysis of the role of the legal profession during the Cold War. Although it does not deal with the ACLU directly, contains good material on the legal profession generally.

393. Jacobs, Paul. "Birchers Lose." *The New Republic*, 150 (February 8, 1964): 5.

   Article on completion of successful libel suit against John Birch Society members who called a state legislator and ACLU member in Washington state a communist (see #390).

394. Kendrick, Alexander. *Prime Time: The Life of Edward R. Murrow.* New York: Avon Books, 1970.

   Includes a brief account of the *See It Now* program on the 1953 incident in Indianapolis where the ACLU was denied permission to hold a meeting. (See also #385.)

395. Lamont, Corliss. "Corliss Lamont's Inside Story After 21 Years." *I.F. Stone's Weekly* (March 1, 1954): 4–6.

   Criticism of the ACLU for failing to to defend civil liberties vigorously enough by long-time Board member, on the occasion of his resignation from the Board. More complete version of these criticisms appears in #263.

396. "Legion and Civil Liberties." *The Nation*, 175 (September 6, 1952): 181.

   Article on American Legion attack on the ACLU, including the Legion's call for a federal investigation of the ACLU.

397. "Legion and the ACLU." *The New Republic*, 127 (September 8, 1952): 7.

   Article on American Legion attack on the ACLU.

398. McAuliffe, Mary S. "The American Civil Liberties Union During The McCarthy Years." Robert Griffith and Athan Theoharis, eds. *The Specter*. New York: New Viewpoints, 1974.

> Critical analysis of the ACLU's role during the Cold War period. Shorter version of #399.

399. McAuliffe, Mary S. *Crisis on the Left: Cold War Politics and American Liberals, 1947–1954*. Amherst: University of Massachusetts Press, 1978.

> Scholarly study of the role of liberals during the Cold War. Considerable material on the ACLU. Critical of the ACLU for failing to adequately defend civil liberties.

400. Sarton, May. *Faithful Are the Wounds*. New York: Rinehart and Co., 1955.

> Novel about the anti-Communist witch hunt, with some reference to the ACLU. Reflects the criticisms of the performance of the ACLU held by many leftists during the period.

401. "Skirmish in Indianapolis." *Commonweal*, 59 (December 4, 1953): 215.

> Account of controversy in Indianapolis, Indiana, where the ACLU affiliate was denied permission to hold a meeting in the War Memorial Building and several hotels (see #385).

402. Stouffer, Samuel. *Communism, Conformity, and Civil Liberties*. New York: Doubleday, 1955. Reprinted, Gloucester, MA: Peter Smith, 1963.

> Detailed academic study of public attitudes toward civil liberties at the height of the Cold War. Data indicate weak support for the rights of Communists, Socialists, and other unpopular groups.

403. "Whose Civil Liberties?" *American Legion Magazine* (May 1954).

Criticism of the ACLU for defending the rights of Communists and persons accused of being Communists.

404. Wilkinson, Frank. "The Era of Libertarian Repression, 1948–1973." *Akron Law Review*, 7 (Winter 1974): 280–309.

History and analysis of the Cold War by a victim of the anti-Communist crusade and later a prominent figure in the ACLU.

2. Academic Freedom

405. ACLU. *Academic Due Process*. New York: ACLU, 1958.

ACLU statement on academic freedom, focusing on due process rights of teachers and students threatened with disciplinary action.

406. ACLU. *Academic Freedom and Academic Responsibility*. New York: ACLU, 1952.

Statement of ACLU policies on academic freedom as of 1952.

407. ACLU. *Academic Freedom, Academic Responsibility, Academic Due Process*. New York: ACLU, 1966.

ACLU statement on academic freedom issues as of the mid-1960s.

408. ACLU. *Academic Freedom and Civil Liberties of Students*. New York: ACLU, 1958.

One of periodic restatements of ACLU position on academic freedom.

409. ACLU. *Civil Liberties of Teachers and Students*. New York: ACLU, 1949.

Statement of ACLU policies on academic freedom as of 1949.

410. ACLU. *Crisis at the University of California: A Statement to the People of California*. New York: ACLU, 1949.

ACLU statement on the loyalty oath crisis at the University of California. Written by Alexander Meiklejohn. Originally published by the ACLU-Northern California.

411. ACLU. *Crisis at the University of California II: A Further Statement to the People of California.* New York: ACLU, 1950.

    Revised version of #410. Update on events at the University of California.

412. ACLU—Greater Philadelphia Branch. *Academic Freedom: Some Recent Philadelphia Episodes.* Philadelphia: ACLU-Greater Philadelphia, 1954.

    Report on violations of academic freedom in the Philadelphia area by the ACLU affiliate.

413. Meiklejohn, Alexander. "Should Communists Be Allowed To Teach?" *New York Times Magazine* (March 27, 1949): 10, 64–66.

    Discussion of academic freedom issues, particularly the right of persons who are Communist Party members to teach in public schools and universities.

3. Blacklisting

414. Ceplair, Larry and Steven Englund. *The Inquisition in Hollywood: Politics in the Film Community, 1930–1960.* Berkeley: University of California Press, 1983.

    Detailed scholarly history of left-wing politics in Hollywood, the Congressional hearings on alleged Communism in the film industry, and the blacklisting of alleged Communists. Material on ACLU involvement in various aspects of the blacklisting controversy.

415. Miller, Merle. *The Judges and the Judged.* Garden City, NY: Doubleday, 1952. Reprinted: New York: Arno Press, 1971.

ACLU-sponsored report on blacklisting in the broadcasting industry. First comprehensive survey of the blacklisting problem.

416. O'Neill, William. *A Better World*. New York: Simon and Schuster, 1982.

    Scholarly study of liberals and Communism. Discussion of the blacklisting controversy in the ACLU. Critical of the ACLU from a neo-conservative perspective.

417. Pitzele, Merlyn S. "Is There a Blacklist?" *The New Leader*, 35 (May 12, 1952): 21–23.

    Critical review of *The Judges and the Judged* (#415) by an anti-Communist member of the ACLU Board. Controversy over the book precipitated a major split on the ACLU Board.

418. Pitzele, Merlyn S. "This Book is a Bad Mistake." *The New Leader*, 35 (June 16, 1952): 15, 18.

    Criticism of *The Judges and the Judged* (#415) by a dissident member of the ACLU Board of Directors.

4. Federal Bureau of Investigation

419. ACLU. *Report of ACLU Special Commission on the FBI Files to ACLU Board of Directors*. New York: ACLU, 1979.

    Report of a special commission established by the ACLU Board of Directors to review the 25,000 pages of FBI files on the ACLU (see #1354) obtained under the Freedom of Information Act. The files revealed a massive program of FBI spying on the ACLU since its founding in 1920. The report concluded that during the 1940s and 1950s several ACLU officials had acted improperly by maintaining secret relationships with the FBI.

420. Criley, Richard. *The F.B.I. v. The First Amendment*. Los Angeles: First Amendment Foundation, 1990.

Book on the FBI's spying on Frank Wilkinson beginning in the 1940s. Wilkinson was leader of the National Committee to Abolish the House Un-American Activities Committee, later the National Committee Against Repressive Legislation, and a prominent member of the ACLU.

421. Ernst, Morris L. "Why I No Longer Fear the FBI." *Reader's Digest*, 57 (December 1950): 135–139.

    Defense of the FBI by an ACLU co-general counsel and prominent member of the Board of Directors. Ernst was later found to have had a close personal relationship with FBI Director Hoover (see #424).

422. Neier, Aryeh. "Adhering to Principle: Lessons From the 1950s." *Civil Liberties Review*, 4 (November-December 1977): 26–32.

    An article written in response to revelations contained in the FBI files on the ACLU that some ACLU officials had cooperated with the FBI during the 1950s (see #419, #1354). The author was executive director of the ACLU when the article was written.

423. O'Reilly, Kenneth. *Hoover and the Un-Americans: The FBI, HUAC, and the Red Menace.* Philadelphia: Temple University Press, 1983.

    Detailed scholarly analysis of the relations between the FBI and the House Un-American Activities Committee during the Cold War. Many references to the ACLU and ACLU leaders.

424. Salisbury, Harrison. "The Strange Correspondence of Morris Ernst and John Edgar Hoover, 1939–1964." *The Nation*, 239 (December 1, 1984): 575–589.

    Critical account of the relationship between Ernst, a major figure in the ACLU, and the director of the FBI Based on FBI documents released under the Freedom of Information Act. Suggests impropriety by Ernst.

425. Theoharis, Athan. *Spying on Americans: Political Surveillance From Hoover to the Huston Plan*. Philadelphia: Temple University Press, 1978.

   Detailed scholarly history of political spying by government agencies in the twentieth century, with particular emphasis on the FBI. Some material on the role of the ACLU.

5. Federal Loyalty Program

426. Bontecou, Elizabeth. *The Federal Loyalty-Security Program*. Ithaca, NY: Cornell University Press, 1953.

   Detailed scholarly analysis of the federal loyalty program. Critical of the procedures and impact of the program.

427. Brown, Ralph S., Jr. *Loyalty and Security: Employment Tests in the United States*. New Haven, CT: Yale University Press, 1958.

   Scholarly study of loyalty and security tests for employment by a Yale law professor and long-time member of the ACLU Board of Directors.

428. Brown, Ralph S. "6,000,000 Second-Class Citizens." *The Nation*, 174 (June 28, 1952): 644–647.

   Critique of the federal loyalty program, the Hatch Act, and other restrictions on government employees.

429. Ernst, Morris L. "Some Affirmative Suggestions for a Loyalty Program." *American Scholar*, 19 (October 1950): 452–460.

   Proposal for revising the Federal Loyalty Program by the co-general counsel of the ACLU and the leading anti-Communist on the ACLU Board of Directors.

6. Fifth Amendment

430. Brown, Ralph S., Jr. "Lawyers and the Fifth Amendment: A Dissent." *American Bar Association Journal*, 40 (May 1954): 404–407.

    Criticism of proposed ABA policy that would disbar lawyers who took the Fifth Amendment in legislative investigations. Author was professor of law at Yale University and long-time member (1955–1991) of the ACLU Board of Directors.

431. Williams, C. Dickerman. "Problems of the Fifth Amendment." *Fordham Law Review*, 24 (1955–1956): 19–52.

    Discussion of Fifth Amendment issues by a member of the ACLU Board of Directors. Author eventually left the ACLU because of disagreement over official ACLU policy. A good indicator of the division of opinion within the ACLU during the period.

7. House Un-American Activities Committee

[See also #262.]

432. ACLU. *Why Should Congress Abolish the House Un-American Activities Committee?* New York: ACLU, 1962.

    Call for the abolition of HUAC.

433. Barrett, Edward L. *The Tenney Committee*. Ithaca, NY: Cornell University Press, 1951.

    Scholarly history and analysis of the California Fact-Finding Committee on Un-American Activities which was the only legislative investigating committee to officially label the ACLU a Communist "front." Critical of the committee and its tactics.

434. Bentley, Eric, ed. *Thirty Years of Treason*. New York: Viking, 1971.

Excerpts of testimony before the House Un-American Activities Committee. Includes testimony by ACLU leaders Arthur Garfield Hays and G. Bromley Oxnam (see #441).

435. Ferman, Irving. "A Comment By a Civil Libertarian." William F. Buckley, Jr., ed. *The Committee and its Critics.* New York: G. P. Putnam's, 1962. Pp. 242–253.

Defense of the House Un-American Activities Committee by a former director of the ACLU Washington legislative office. Represents the conservative, anti-Communist position within the ACLU during the period.

436. Gardner, Virginia. "Roger Baldwin: What Are You Hiding?" *New Masses,* 63 (May 20, 1947): 3–4.

Left-wing criticism of Roger Baldwin's relationship with legislative investigating committees, suggesting that he was collaborating with them in the anti-Communist witch hunt.

437. Gellhorn, Walter. "Report on a Report of the House Committee on Un-American Activities." *Harvard Law Review,* 60 (October 1947): 1193–1234.

Critical analysis of a HUAC investigation by an important member of the ACLU Board of Directors.

438. Malin, Patrick M. "Security and Civil Liberties: The Committee on Un-American Activities." *New Republic,* 135 (August 20, 1956): 3.

Discussion of HUAC by then-executive director of the ACLU.

439. Malin, Patrick Murphy. "Un-American Committee." *The Nation,* 183 (September 1, 1956): 2.

Criticism of the procedures of the House Un-American Activities Committee by the ACLU executive director.

440. Navasky, Victor. *Naming Names.* New York: Viking, 1980.

An analysis of people who cooperated with the anti-Communist witch hunt of the Cold War years by providing the names of other alleged Communists to the House Un-American Activities Committee. A much-praised book. Includes a critical account of the ACLU's performance in response to legislative investigations.

441. Oxnam, G. Bromley. *I Protest: My Experience With the House Committee on Un-American Activities.* New York: Harper and Brothers, 1954.

First-hand account of experience of being subpoenaed by the House Un-American Acitivites Committee by a prominent Protestant clergyman and ACLU leader.

442. Simmons, Jerold. *Operation Abolition: The Campaign to Abolish The House Un-American Activities Committee, 1938–1975.* New York: Garland, 1986.

Detailed scholarly history of the campaign to abolish the House Un-American Activities Committee. Good treatment of the strategy and tactics of the abolition movement and the division of opinion within the ACLU on this issue.

443. Wilkinson, Frank. "Abolition Campaign Makes National Progress." *Rights*, 5 (January—February 1958): 2–5.

Assessment of the abolish HUAC campaign by its leader. Written as the campaign was just beginning. Wilkinson was himself a victim of the Cold War and later a prominent leader in the ACLU.

444. Williams, C. Dickerman. "The Committee's Procedures." William F. Buckley, Jr., ed. *The Committee and Its Critics.* New York: G. P. Putnam's, 1962. Pp. 219–242.

Defense of the House Un-American Activities Committee by a former member of the ACLU Board of Directors.

8. Loyalty Oaths

445. ACLU. *The States and Subversion.* New York: ACLU, 1953.

    Short pamphlet summarizing material treated at length in #391. Brief overview of anti-Communist measures in six states, with particular emphasis on loyalty oaths.

446. Askin, Frank. "Loyalty Oaths in Retrospect: Freedom and Reality." *Wisconsin Law Review,* 43 (1968, No. 2): 498–504.

    Analysis of loyalty oaths, following a series of court decisions ruling them unconstitutional. Author is a long-time member of the ACLU Board of Directors.

447. Byse, Clark. "A Report on the Pennsylvania Loyalty Act." *University of Pennsylvania Law Review,* 101 (January 1953): 480–503.

    Analysis of Pennsylvania loyalty oath by member of Board of Directors of the Philadelphia ACLU.

448. Horowitz, Harold W. "Report on the Los Angeles City and County Loyalty Programs." *Stanford Law Review,* 5 (February 1953): 233–246.

    Analysis of legal issues surrounding loyalty oaths in Los Angeles which were challenged unsuccessfully by the ACLU Southern California affiliate.

449. Hyman, Harold M. *To Try Men's Souls: Loyalty Tests in American History.* Berkeley: University of California Press, 1959.

    Scholarly history of loyalty oaths in America. Primarily covers the period through World War I. Relatively little material on the Cold War period, but places it in historical perspective.

9. The Smith Act

[See also #1158, #1172.]

450. ACLU. *Civil Liberties versus the Smith Act.* New York: ACLU, 1951.

    ACLU statement criticizing the Smith Act and the prosecution of the top leadership of the Communist Party.

451. ACLU. *The Smith Act and the Supreme Court.* New York: ACLU, 1952.

    ACLU statement criticizing the Supreme Court's decision in *Dennis v. United States* (1951). Discusses possible strategies for combatting the impact of the decision.

452. Ernst, Morris L. "The 'Clear and Present Danger' Concept." *The New Leader,* 34 (July 2, 1951): 13.

    Discussion of the "clear and present danger" standard following the Supreme Court's revision of it in the 1951 *Dennis* case upholding the conviction of the leaders of the Communist Party under the Smith Act.

453. Ernst, Morris L. "Liberals and the Communist Trial." *The New Republic,* 120 (January 31, 1949): 7–8.

    Comment on the prosecution of the top leaders of the American Communist Party under the Smith Act. Argues that the Communist Party is a secret conspiracy. See reply by ACLU Executive Director in same issue (#1172).

10. Wiretapping

454. ACLU. *The Wiretapping Problem Today.* New York: ACLU, 1962.

    Report on legal status of and current practices on wiretapping. Report directed by Professor Herman Schwartz.

455. Ferman, Irving. "Don't Tap the Bill of Rights." *Machinists' Monthly Journal* (1954).

   Discussion of wiretapping by the director of the ACLU Washington legislative office.

456. Fly, James L. "Wiretapping Outrage." *The New Republic*, 122 (February 6, 1950): 14–15.

   Criticism of FBI wiretapping following revelations that the FBI illegally tapped a State Department employee being prosecuted for giving secrets to the Soviet Union. Author was then a member of the ACLU Board of Directors.

457. Malin, Patrick Murphy. "Is Wiretapping Justified?" *The Annals of the American Academy of Political and Social Science*, 300 (July 1955): 29–35.

   Discussion of civil liberties aspects of wiretapping by then-executive director of the ACLU. Arues that wiretapping is justified only in cases of treason and sabotage and that specific wiretaps should be permissible only with judicial authorization.

11. Other Issues

458. Bruce, J. Campbell. "Must Liberty Bow Her Head in Shame?" *Reader's Digest*, 61 (August 1952): 4–9.

   Article on the arbitrary denial of visas to persons seeking to visit the United States. Cases handled by the ACLU.

459. Hays, Arthur Garfield. "Full Disclosure: Dangerous Precedent." *The Nation*, 168 (January 29, 1949): 121–123.

   Criticism of proposal for a law requiring political groups which use the mails to disclose the names of their officers and sources of funds.

460. Kutler, Stanley I. "Government by Discretion: The Queendom of Passports." Stanley Kutler. *The American*

Inquisition. New York: Hill and Wang, 1982. Ch. 4, pp. 89–117.

Scholarly analysis of civil liberties issues related to passports during the Cold War. Good material on a number of cases involving the ACLU.

461. "On the History of the N.E.C.L.C." *Bill of Rights Journal* (December 1976): 1–39.

History of the Emergency Civil Liberties Committee (ECLC), later the National Emergency Civil Liberties Committee, created in 1951 by people who felt the ACLU's defense of civil liberties during the Cold War was not vigorous enough.

G. POST-WORLD WAR II AMERICA, 1945–1960

1. General

[See also #1051.]

462. ACLU. *Annual Reports, 1945–1960.* New York: Arno Press, 1970.

Detailed report of civil liberties issues and ACLU cases. Excellent resource for identifying particular issues.

463. ACLU. *Post-War Program For the Bill of Rights.* New York: ACLU, 1946.

Brief statement of ACLU objectives as of 1945.

464. ACLU. *What Do You Mean, Free Speech?* New York: ACLU, 1949.

ACLU statement on the free speech rights of anti-democratic groups.

465. "ACLU's Directors Prepare to Jettison its Principles." *I.F. Stone's Weekly* (October 31, 1953): 2. "Convulsions at the

ACLU." *Ibid.* (December 14, 1953): 3. "ACLU's Directors Decide Dictatorship is Best." *Ibid.* (January 11, 1954): 3.

Series of articles on conflict within the ACLU over policies related to the Cold War. Author critical of position of ACLU leadership.

466. "Baldwin to Work for World Civil Rights." *Christian Century*, 66 (November 9, 1949): 1316.

    Article on the retirement of ACLU Executive Director Roger Baldwin and his plans to continue working on international human rights issues.

467. Chafee, Zechariah, Jr. *Thirty-Five Years With Freedom of Speech*. New York: Roger Baldwin Civil Liberies Foundation, 1952.

    Reflections on thirty-five years of First Amendment law by the then-leading authority on freedom of speech. Provides a brief update on #97.

468. "Civil Rights in America." *The Annals of the American Academy of Political and Social Science*, 275 (May 1951).

    Symposium on civil rights and civil liberties issues. Articles by prominent figures in the ACLU, NAACP, and other organizations, as well as prominent scholars. Valuable articles on the role of the Supreme Court, church-state, criminal justice, racial equality, and other issues.

469. Fraenkel, Osmond K. *The Supreme Court and Civil Liberties*. New York: ACLU, 1945. Revised editions: 1949, 1952, 1955, 1957. Revised edition: New York: Oceana, 1960; revised, 1963.

    Survey of Supreme Court rulings on various civil liberties issues. See #330 for original version. Steadily expanded as the body of civil liberties law grows. Early versions (1945–1957) published as a pamphlet by the ACLU. 1960 and 1963 editions published in book form. (See also #536, #537.)

470. "Malin to Direct Civil Liberties Union." *Christian Century*, 67 (January 11, 1950): 35.

   Article on the appointment of the new executive director of the ACLU.

471. Malin, Patrick Murphy. *How Goes the Bill of Rights?* New York: ACLU, 1953.

   Speech by then-director of the ACLU assessing status of civil liberties in the United States in 1953.

472. Reitman, Alan. "The American Civil Liberties Union." *Encyclopedia of Labor* (1952).

   General description of the ACLU and its program, by the associate director of the ACLU.

473. Robison, Joseph. "Organizations Promoting Civil Rights and Liberties." *The Annals of the American Academy of Political and Social Science*, 275 (May 1951): 18–26.

   Survey of the activities of the various civil rights and civil liberties organizations as of 1951. Covers the ACLU, the NAACP, the American Jewish Congress, and others. A valuable portrait of the "rights industry" at this point in history.

474. Thomas, Norman. "Civil Liberty: A Look Back and Ahead." *New York Times Magazine* (November 28, 1954): 12+.

   Reflections on the development of civil liberties over the previous thirty years by one of the ACLU's founders.

2. Civil Rights

[See also #1156, #1159.]

475. ACLU. *A National Program For Civil Rights*. New York: ACLU, 1947.

   Pamphlet summarizing the recommendations of the President's Committee on Civil Rights.

476. Fraenkel, Osmond K. "The Federal Civil Rights Laws." *Minnesota Law Review*, 31 (March 1947): 302–327.

General survey of civil rights enforcement by the federal government, by the ACLU's most important Supreme Court litigator.

477. Kalven, Harry, Jr. *The Negro and the First Amendment*. Chicago: University of Chicago Press, 1966.

Extremely valuable discussion of the impact of the civil rights movement on First Amendment law in the 1950s and early 1960s. Although no discussion of the ACLU directly, the ACLU was involved in almost all of the cases cited.

478. Vose, Clement E. *Caucasians Only: The Supreme Court, The NAACP, and the Restrictive Covenant Cases*. Berkeley: University of California Press, 1959.

Detailed scholarly study of the cases culminating in the Supreme Court decision in *Shelley v. Kraemer* (1948). Valuable material on the role of the ACLU and ACLU affiliates in the various cases. Also valuable insights into the civil rights coalition in the post-World War II era.

3. Due Process/Police Misconduct

479. ACLU-Ilinois Division. *Secret Detention by the Chicago Police*. Glencoe, IL: The Free Press, 1959.

Pioneering study of persons arrested and detained by the Chicago police. The first empirical study of this aspect of police practices. The report found that thousands of persons, primarily the poor, were detained for long periods of time without bail and without ever seeing an attorney.

480. New York Civil Liberties Union. *If You Are Arrested*. New York: New York Civil Liberties Union, 1955.

Short pamphlet informing citizens of their rights if arrested. First distributed in 1955 in New York City and later by other ACLU affiliates. Extremely successful ACLU public education item. Subsequently revised many times to reflect changing Supreme Court decisions.

4. International Civil Liberties

[See also #1157, #1166, #1173, #1188, #1190, #1192, #1193, #1194, #1196, #1205.]

481. ACLU. *Civil Liberties and the International Scene.* New York: ACLU, 1953.

    Discussion of international civil liberties issues facing the United Nations.

482. ACLU. *Presenting the International League for the Rights of Man.* New York: ACLU, 1954.

    Brief description of the International League for the Rights of Man which was affiliated with the ACLU and its work on international human rights issues.

483. Ernst, Morris L. "Why Not A First Freedom Treaty?" *Survey Graphic*, 35 (December 1946): 445+.

    Proposal for an international treaty guaranteeing freedom of speech and press by the co-general counsel of the ACLU.

484. Hays, Arthur Garfield. "Civil Liberties in Germany." *The Survey*, 85 (January 1949): 6–11.

    Report on the status of civil liberties in post-war occupied Germany, following a visit by Hays and other ACLU figures.

5. Labor, Rights of

[See also #1164, #1180.]

485. ACLU. *Democracy in Trade Unions*. New York: ACLU, 1941. Revised editions, 1943, 1949.

   Statement of new ACLU policy on the rights of labor union members. Extremely important departure for the ACLU. Represented a break with previous position of strong support for unions during 1920s and 1930s. Ideas in this report eventually led to 1959 Landrum-Griffin Act.

486. ACLU. *Labor's Civil Rights*. New York: ACLU, 1940.

   Discussion of ACLU policies related to labor unions, primarily responding to criticism from the labor movement and leftists that the ACLU had shifted to the right.

487. ACLU. *A Labor Union "Bill of Rights"*. New York: ACLU, 1958. Revised edition, 1963.

   Pamphlet on the rights of labor union members. 1958 edition argues for enactment of federal legislation. 1963 edition analyzes the 1959 Landrum-Griffin Act.

488. Benson, Herman. "The Fight For Union Democracy." Seymour Martin Lipset, ed. *Unions in Transition: Entering the Second Century*. San Francisco: Institute for Contemporary Studies, 1986. Pp. 323–370.

   Account of history of campaign for union democracy by one of its leading advocates and important member of the ACLU.

489. Harrington, Michael. "Blue Collar Democracy." Alan Reitman, ed. *The Price of Liberty*. New York: Norton, 1968.

   Discussion of union democracy following passage of the Landrum-Griffin Act.

490. Rothman, Stuart. "Legislative History of the 'Bill of Rights' For Union Members." *Minnesota Law Review*, 45 (1960–1961): 199–219.

　　Scholarly history of the development of the 1959 Landrum-Griffin Act; material on the role of the ACLU in originating idea of union democracy.

491. Taft, Philip. "Democracy in Trade Unions." *American Economic Review*, 36 (May 1946): 359–369.

　　Early discussion of the issue of labor union democracy.

492. Thomas, Norman. "How Democratic Are Labor Unions?" *Harper's*, 184 (May 1942): 655–662.

　　Early statement on union democracy by leading member of the ACLU.

6. Religious Liberty

[See also #1276.]

493. Blum, V. C. "Are Catholics Second-Class Citizens?" *Catholic World*, 186 (March 1958): 418–424.

　　Accuses the ACLU of being anti-Catholic because of ACLU criticisms of Catholic activity regarding censorship and birth control.

494. Drinan, Robert F. "Dilemma of the ACLU." *America*, 102 (November 28, 1959): 2.

　　Critical commentary on ACLU position on church-state issues from a Catholic perspective.

495. Drinan, Robert F. "Religion and the ACLU." *America*, 99 (September 27, 1958): 663–665.

　　Expression of Catholic criticism of the ACLU on church-state issues by then-dean of Boston College Law School. In the 1960s Drinan became a prominent leader of the ACLU, particularly on issues of civil rights, the Vietnam War, and Watergate.

496. Lally, Msgr. Francis J. "Catholics—Civil Liberties." *America*, 98 (February 1, 1958): 508–509.

Statement of Catholic criticisms of the ACLU over issues of censorship, birth control, etc.

497. McCollum, Vashti. *One Woman's Fight*. Garden City, NY: Doubleday, 1951. Revised edition, 1952.

First-hand account by the plaintiff in the *McCollum* (1948) case challenging the Illinois "released-time" law. ACLU involved in the case.

498. Malin, Patrick Murphy. "ACLU Rejoinder." *Christian Century*, 74 (December 11, 1957): 1484.

Reply to criticisms that the ACLU is anti-Catholic, by the ACLU executive director.

499. Milner, Lucille B. "Church, State, and Schools." *The New Republic*, 113 (August 13, 1945): 177–180.

Discussion of emerging church-state issues by secretary of ACLU.

500. O'Meara, Dean Joseph, Jr. *Catholics and Civil Liberties*. Omaha, NE: American Freedoms Council, 1958.

Defense of Catholic position on social issues, primarily censorship and birth control, in the face of ACLU criticism.

501. Oxnam, G. Bromley. "Church, State, and Schools." *The Nation*, 168 (January 1, 1949): 67–70.

Statement supporting separation of church and state in the public schools by a prominent member of the ACLU Board and one of the founders of Protestants and Other Americans United For Separation of Church and State, one of the other leading separationist groups.

502. Pfeffer, Leo. "Amici in Church-State Litigation." *Law and Contemporary Problems*, 44 (Winter 1981): 83–110.

   Extremely valuable analysis of the role of *amicus curiae* briefs in church-state litigation, from the 1940s through the 1970s. Valuable material on the ACLU, especially in relation to other separationist advocacy groups. Pfeffer was arguably the most important Supreme Court litigator of church-state cases during the period, working with the ACLU on many important cases.

503. Pfeffer, Leo. *Church, State, and Freedom.* Boston: Beacon Press, 1953. Revised edition, 1967.

   Comprehensive survey of church-state issues through the early 1950s by staff attorney for the American Jewish Congress and frequent cooperating attorney for the ACLU. Extremely rich historical detail on religion in America.

504. Souraf, Frank. *The Wall of Separation: The Constitutional Politics of Church and State.* Princeton: Princeton University Press, 1976.

   Scholarly analysis of church-state litigation in the Supreme Court from the 1950s through the early 1970s. Extremely valuable analysis of the ACLU's role and the shift from cases initiated by the ACLU national office to cases initiated by the ACLU affiliates. Good insights into the internal politics of the ACLU.

7. Speech, Press, and Assembly, Freedom of

[See also #477.]

505. ACLU. *The Case Against Legal Restraints on Racial Libels and Anonymous Publications.* New York: ACLU, 1946.

   Pamphlet opposing laws punishing speech or publications offensive to racial or religious groups and opposing laws restricting the publication of anonymous political works.

506. ACLU. *Censorship of Comic Books.* New York: ACLU, 1955.

    Pamphlet attacking censorship of comic books.

507. ACLU. *Freedom from Censorship.* New York: ACLU, 1948.

    Summary of ACLU anti-censorship activities.

508. ACLU. *Policy Statement on Pressure Group Censorship.* New York: ACLU, 1952.

    ACLU statement defining the difference between the constitutionally protected right to protest and tactics that violate freedom of expression. Primarily addressed toward the Catholic Church and the National Office for Decent Literature. See #509 for later version.

509. ACLU. *Private Group Censorship and the NODL.* New York: ACLU, 1958.

    ACLU statement criticizing the the activities of the National Office for Decent Literature (NODL). Revised version of #508. Explains ACLU position on the difference between censorship and the right to protest. An important document in the history of the conflict between the ACLU and the Catholic Church.

510. ACLU. *Report on the Communications Industry.* New York: ACLU, 1946.

    Report critical of monopoly control of publshing and broadcasting industries. Recommends ACLU policy supporting anti-trust action by the federal government on the grounds that diversity of ownership promotes free exchange of ideas.

511. Ernst, Morris L. *The First Freedom.* New York: Macmillan, 1946.

    Discussion of the threat to freedom of expression posed by monoply control of the communications industry by the co-general counsel of the ACLU.

512. Ernst, Morris L. "Freedom to Read, See and Hear." *Harper's,* 191 (July 1945): 51–53.

Criticism of prevailing censorship practices by co-general counsel of the ACLU.

513. Ernst, Morris L. and Alan U. Schwartz. *Censorship: The Search For the Obscene.* New York: Macmillan, 1964.

Discussion and critique of censorship, written for the general audience. One of a series of books on censorship written by Ernst, long-time ACLU co-general counsel.

514. Ferlinghetti, Lawrence. "Horn on *Howl.*" Barney Rossett, ed. *The Evergreen Review Reader.* New York: Grove Press, 1968.

Article on the 1957 obscenity trial of Ferlinghetti, publisher of Allen Ginsberg's poem *Howl* in San Francisco. Ferlinghetti represented by the ACLU of Northern California. Case attracted international attention. Ferlinghetti acquitted.

515. Fowler, Albert. "Can Literature Corrupt?" *Modern Age*, 3 (Spring 1959): 125–133.

Discussion of the conflict between the ACLU and the National Office For Decent Literature over censorship (see #508, #509). Criticizes the ACLU for failing to explore possible cooperation with NODL.

516. Gardiner, Harold C., S. J. *The Catholic Viewpoint on Censorship.* Garden City, NY: Doubleday, 1961.

Statement of the Catholic Church position on censorship. Includes extensive coverage of the conflict between the ACLU and the Church. Includes copies of original documents in the controversy.

517. Holmes, John Haynes. "Sensitivity as Censor." *The Saturday Review*, 32 (February 26, 1949): 9+.

Defense of freedom of expression by then-chairperson of the ACLU Board of Directors. Criticizes liberal groups, particularly blacks and Jews, for advocating censorship of offensive materials.

518. National Council on Freedom from Censorship. *Freedom from Censorship.* New York: NCFC, 1946.

   Pamphlet criticizing prevailing censorship practices, by the National Council on Freedom from Censorship which functioned as a special ACLU committee on freedom of expression.

519. National Council on Freedom from Censorship. *The "Miracle" Decision.* New York: NCFC, 1952.

   Pamphlet on the 1952 Supreme Court decision (*Burstyn v. Wilson*) involving the film *The Miracle* which held that movies were protected by the First Amendment.

520. Raymond, Allen. *The People's Right to Know.* New York: ACLU, 1955.

   Comprehensive survey of government secrecy. An early statement of movement that culminated in the 1966 Freedom of Information Act.

521. Rice, Elmer. "Censorship." Elmer Rice. *The Living Theater.* New York: Harper, 1959. Pp. 276–286.

   Chapter on censorship in the theater by a noted playwright and prominent member of the ACLU Board of Directors. Includes material on theater censorship from the 1920s to the present.

522. Rice, Elmer. "Entertainment in the Age of McCarthy." *The New Republic*, 128 (April 13, 1953): 14–17.

   Survey of censorship in the arts. Argues that the anti-Communist mood of the period has led to increased censorship. Author was a noted playwrite and prominent member of the ACLU Board of Directors.

523. Rice, Elmer. "New Fashions in Censorship." *The Survey*, 88 (March 1952): 112–115.

   Argues that as the courts have increasingly held censorship by public officials to be unconstitutional the greatest threats to freedom of expression come from private pressure groups.

524. Walker, Jerry. "Civil Liberties Union Considers Free Radio." *Editor and Publisher*, 78 (December 1945): 34.

Report on discussions at the ACLU's 25th anniversary meeting about possible changes in FCC regulation of the radio industry.

H. THE 1960s AND 1970s

1. *General*

[See also #70, #71.]

525. ACLU. *Annual Reports, 1960–1970*. New York: Arno Press, 1970.

The annual reports for the late 1960s are not as detailed or as useful as they are through 1965. By that point, the scope of ACLU activity, including the number of affiliates, was too large to permit adequate summary in a single report. The report issued in January, 1967 covers the previous year and a half. The next report was issued in 1969 and is much less detailed than all previous reports. The reports for the years beginning in 1970 are not collected and published in a bound edition. They were usually issued as a part of the ACLU newsletter, *Civil Liberties*. No annual report was issued for several years in the late 1970s and early 1980s.

526. "ACLU Dinner." *The New Yorker*, 46 (December 19, 1970): 34–35.

Informal account of the dinner marking the fiftieth anniversary of the ACLU.

527. ACLU. *The Carter Administration and Civil Liberties: A Report on the First Year*. New York: ACLU, 1978.

Report on the civil liberties record of the Carter administration.

528. Andrews, Peter. "ACLU—Let There Be Law." *Playboy* (October 1971).

　　Favorable article on the ACLU, focusing on some of the most important ACLU cases.

529. Bishop, Joseph W. "Politics and the ACLU." *Commentary*, 52 (December 1971): 50–58.

　　Critical of the ACLU for its opposition to the Vietnam War. Accuses the ACLU of becoming a partisan political organization. An early statement of the emerging neo-conservative critique of the ACLU. See responses in *Commentary* (March 1972): 34–35; (April 1972): 30+; (May 1972).

530. Bishop, Joseph W. *Obiter Dicta*. New York: Atheneum, 1971.

　　Contains #508, an article critical of the ACLU's position in opposition to the Vietnam War, along with other essays.

531. Buckley, William F., Jr. "Decline of the ACLU." *National Review*, 24 (February 4, 1972): 118.

　　Criticism of the ACLU by a leading conservative spokesperson.

532. Casper, Jonathan D. *The Politics of Civil Liberties*. New York: Harper and Row, 1972.

　　Political science perspective on the development of the law of civil liberties. Illuminating analysis of the role of various interest groups, including the ACLU.

533. di Suvero, Henry. "The Movement and the Legal System." Jonathan Black, ed. *Radical Lawyers*. New York: Avon, 1971.

　　Discussion of legal strategy in political trials by former staff counsel for New York Civil Liberties Union.

534. Dorsen, Norman. "Can Civil Liberties Survive Massive Concentrations of Power?" *Detroit College of Law Review*, 1983 (No. 3): 1171–1180.

Published version of speech to the 1983 ACLU Biennial Conference by the president of the ACLU. Discussion of the prospects for civil liberties in the modern state.

535. Dorsen, Norman. *Frontiers of Civil Liberties*. New York: Pantheon, 1968.

Collection of essays and legal materials by then-general counsel and future president of the ACLU. Includes material on many landmark Supreme Court cases in which the author was directly involved (e.g., *Gideon v. Wainwright* /1963/; *In Re Gault* /1967/).

536. Fraenkel, Osmond. *The Rights You Have: A Practical Handbook of Civil Liberties*. New York: Warner Paperback, 1972.

A summary of civil liberties law, written for the layperson rather than the lawyer. Essentially a continuation of the series of books published by Fraenkel since 1944 (#330, #469, #537).

537. Fraenkel, Osmond. *The Supreme Court and Civil Liberties*. Dobbs Ferry, NY: Oceana, 1966.

Revision of Fraenkel's survey of the state of civil liberties law (see #330, #469, #536).

538. Friedman, Leon. "Up Against the Burger Court." *Civil Liberties Review*, 1 (Fall 1973): 156–161.

Discussion of the prospects for civil liberties before the conservative Burger Supreme Court.

539. Glasser, Ira. "The Constitution and the Courts." Alan Gartner, et. al. *What Nixon is Doing To Us*. New York: Harper and Row, 1973. Pp. 155–183.

Summary of leading civil liberties issues by then-executive director of the New York Civil Liberties Union and future executive director of the ACLU.

540. Glasser, Ira. "Life Under the New Feudalism." *Civil Liberties Review*, 1 (Winter/Spring 1974): 27–40.

   Discussion of civil liberties aspects of bureaucratic institutions of the modern welfare state.

541. Glasser, Ira. "Prisoners of Benevolence: Power versus Liberty in the Welfare State." Willard Gaylin, et al. *Doing Good: The Limits of Benevolence*. New York: Pantheon, 1978. Pp. 99–168.

   Discussion of civil liberties issues in the modern bureaucratic state by then-director of the New York Civil Liberties Union and future director of the ACLU. Offers good insight into the philosophical orientation of one of the major leaders of the "new" ACLU in the late 1960s and 1970s and the emphasis on the rights of persons dealing with modern bureaucratic institutions.

542. Glasser, Ira. "Repressive Institutions." *Trial Magazine*, 6 (June/July 1970): 28–29.

   Discussion of civil liberties issues related to the military, the public schools, mental hospitals, and prisons. Important statement of new thinking about civil liberties at a critical turning point in the organization's history.

543. Gumaer, David Emerson. "The ACLU: Lawyers Playing the Red Game." *American Opinion* (September 1969): 57–90.

   John Birch Society attack on the ACLU. Accuses the ACLU of aiding Communism.

544. Haskell, Gordon K. "Problems in the ACLU." *Dissent*, 15 (1968, No. 3): 229–232.

   Discussion of conflicts within the ACLU at a critical turning point in the organization's history. Conflicts resulted primarily from issues related to the Vietnam War.

545. Isbell, Florence. "Carter's Civil Libertarians." *Civil Liberties Review*, 4 (July-August 1977): 57–58.

    Discussion of persons with civil liberties commitments appointed to positions in the Carter administration, a number of whom had prior involvement with the ACLU. Illuminating discussion of the tension between civil liberties principles and political pressures.

546. Kelley, Dean. "Where Are Civil Liberties Headed?" *Civil Liberties Review*, 3 (February/March 1977): 11–51.

    Symposium on the 1976 ACLU Biennial Conference and the prospects for civil liberties.

547. McIlhaney, William H., II. *The ACLU on Trial*. New Rochelle, NY: Arlington House, 1976.

    Attack on the ACLU by a member of the John Birch Society. Accuses the ACLU of having Communist ties.

548. Neier, Aryeh. "Is Government Repression Working? Views of the American Civil Liberties Union Director." *Current*, 136 (January 1972): 3–6.

    Interview with the director of the ACLU, emphasizing the suppression of dissent by the federal government.

549. Neier, Aryeh. *Only Judgment: The Limits of Litigation in Social Change*. Middletown, CT: Wesleyan University Press, 1982.

    Reflections on the achievements and failures of ACLU litigation in the new civil liberties issues of the 1960s and 1970s: prisoners' rights, poverty, the Vietnam War, others. As executive director of the New York Civil Liberties Union and the ACLU (1970–1978), Neier was instrumental in initiating litigation in these areas. Extremely valuable insights into the role of ACLU litigation as a means of social change.

550. Neier, Aryeh. "Protest Movements Among the Disenfranchised." *Civil Liberties Review*, 1 (Fall 1973): 49–74.

Reflections on the achievements and failures of protest movements by powerless groups—racial minorities, women, the mentally retarded, the poor, etc, by the executive director of the ACLU.

551. Powledge, Fred. "Battle Over the Bill of Rights." *Life*, 62 (March 31, 1967): 22–25.

Sympathetic account of the ACLU and some of its major cases in the mid-1960s, with a special emphasis on Vietnam War-related issues.

552. Reitman, Alan. "Civil Rights and Liberties in the 1960s." *Encyclopedia of Social Work*. (1965).

Brief survey of civil rights and civil liberties issues in the mid-1960s by the ACLU associate director.

553. Samuels, Gertrude. "The Fight for Civil Liberties Never Stays Won." *The New York Times Magazine* (June 19, 1966): 14–15+.

Sympathetic account of the ACLU in the mid-1960s. Useful material on some of its major cases during the period.

554. Shattuck, John H. F. "You Can't Depend On It: The Carter Administration and Civil Liberties." *Civil Liberties Review*, 4 (January/February 1978): 10–27.

Analysis of the Carter administration's mixed record on civil liberties by the director of the ACLU Washington office.

555. Smoot, Dan. "The American Civil Liberties Union." *Dan Smoot Report* (July 27, 1964).

Extreme right-wing attack on the ACLU.

556. Tigar, Michael E. "Beyond Civil Liberties." Jonathan Black, ed. *Radical Lawyers*. New York: Avon, 1971. Pp. 43–51.

Book review of Norman Dorsen, *Frontiers of Civil Liberties* (#535). Good statement of radical left-wing critique of ACLU approach to civil liberties in the late 1960s.

557. "War Memorial Controversy Continues." *Christian Century*, 79 (June 1962): 739.

Controversy over denial of permission for Indiana ACLU to hold a meeting in the Indianapolis War Memorial building. See #385 for initial controversy in 1953.

2. Academic Freedom

[See also #61, #63.]

558. ACLU. *Academic Freedom in the Secondary Schools*. New York: ACLU, 1968. Revised edition, 1971.

Statement on the rights of students and teachers in secondary schools.

559. ACLU. *Combatting Undemocratic Pressures on Schools and Libraries*. New York: ACLU, 1964.

Pamphlet on strategies for public school and library officials to resist pressure to limit academic freedom.

560. "ACLU Guide Combats Pressures on Schools and Libraries." *Library Journal*, 89 (May 15, 1964): 2052.

Excerpts from new ACLU pamphlet on resisting public pressure to limit academic freedom in public schools and libraries.

561. "ACLU on Student Demonstrations." *School and Society*, 96 (October 26, 1968): 376–377.

Discussion of ACLU policy on the right of students to demonstrate.

562. ACLU. *ROTC and Educational Institutions*. New York: ACLU, 1970.

ACLU statement on threats to academic freedom posed by ROTC on college and university campuses.

563. "Committee Assesses Dangers That Accompany Government Support of University Research." *Science*, 131 (March 11, 1960): 716–717.

Article on recent ACLU committee report on threats to academic freedom accompanying increased support for research by the federal government.

564. Glasser, Ira. "Protecting Student Rights." *Current*, 115 (February 1970): 46–54.

Review of the issue of student rights and the activities of the New York Civil Liberties Union in protecting those rights. Glasser was then associate director of NYCLU concentrating on student rights issues.

565. Glasser, Ira. "Schools For Scandal—The Bill of Rights and Public Education." *Phi Delta Kappan* (December 1969): 190–194.

Important discussion of the rights of public school students. Valuable insight into the ACLU's new thinking about civil liberties issues at a critical turning point. Author was then associate director of the New York Civil Liberties Union and later executive director of the ACLU.

566. Lucas, Roy. "The Rights of Students." Norman Dorsen, ed. *The Rights of Americans*. New York: Random House, 1971. Pp. 572–590.

Analysis of the legal rights of students

567. New York Civil Liberties Union. *Student Rights Handbook For New York City*. New York: NYCLU, 1969.

Brief description of legal rights of students on First Amendment, due process, and equal protection issues. Written for students by NYCLU Student Rights Project.

568. Pemberton, John. "How Can Patriotism Be Taught?" *NEA Journal* (1967).

    Discussion of how patriotism can be taught in public schools without violating civil liberties principles, by then-executive director of the ACLU.

569. Reitman, Alan. *Corporal Punishment in the Public Schools*. New York: ACLU, 1972.

    Discussion of corporal punishment in public schools as a violation of civil liberties, by the ACLU associate director.

570. "Rights: NYCLU and Student Rights." *The New Yorker*, 43 (February 17, 1968): 24–25.

    Short article on ACLU role in defending the rights of public school students in New York City.

571. Timmons, Mary Sarazin. *The Constitutional Rights of Minnesota Public High School Students*. Minneapolis: Minnesota Civil Liberties Union Foundation, 1979.

    Analysis of legal rights of high school students in Minnesota, by the Minnesota Civil Liberties Union. Emphasis on First Amendment rights, equal protection, and due process rights.

572. Van Alstyne, William W. "The Rights of Teachers and Professors." Norman Dorsen, ed. *The Rights of Americans*. New York: Random House, 1971. Pp. 546–571.

    Discussion of the legal aspects of academic freedom.

573. "Whither Loyalty Oaths." *Senior Scholastic*, 90 (March 3, 1967): Supplement 4.

    Article on the future of loyalty oaths for teachers, following court decisions declaring such oaths unconstitutional.

3. Civil Rights

[See also #58, #549, #1260, #1270.]

574. Ackley, Sheldon. "To Overcome Discrimination Now." *Current*, 129 (May 1971): 35-38.

    Discussion of current civil rights issues by a prominent leader of the New York Civil Liberties Union.

575. ACLU. *How Americans Protest*. New York: ACLU, 1963.

    Extremely important statement of ACLU policy on civil rights demonstrations. Expresses strong support for sit-ins and other forms of militant protest. Indicative of shift in attitude of ACLU toward support for more militant forms of protest.

576. "The ACLU and the Urban Ghetto." *Civil Liberties* (September 1970).

    Brief description of ACLU activities in black ghettoes of Newark, New Jersey, Chicago, Illinois, and Los Angeles, California.

577. "ACLU Opens Southern Regional Office." *Christian Century*, 81 (November 1964): 1357.

    Article on the opening of the ACLU Southern Regional Office, with Charles Morgan as director. (See also #1269.)

578. Berube, Maurice R. and Marilyn Gittel, eds. *Confrontation at Ocean Hill-Brownsville*. New York: Praeger, 1969.

    Documents related to the crisis over the proposed decentralization of the New York City public schools and the resulting teachers' strike. Contains important New York Civil Liberties Union report (see #587) and related materials.

579. Cary, Eve. *Women and the Law*. Skokie, IL: National Textbook Co., 1977.

General survey of the law of women's rights as of the mid-1970s. Book published as part of a series in cooperation with the ACLU.

580. Castner, Lynn S. *Report on Administration of Justice and the Minnesota Indian.* Minneapolis: Minnesota Civil Liberties Union Foundation, 1967.

   Discussion of criminal justice issues related to Native Americans in Minnesota, by the executive director of the Minnesota Civil Liberties Union. Includes discussion of administration of justice on tribal reservation and in major urban settings.

581. Caughey, John. *To Kill a Child's Spirit: The Tragedy of School Segregation in Los Angeles.* Itasca, IL: F. E. Peacock, 1973.

   History of school desegregation litigation in Los Angeles in which the ACLU of Southern California played a major role. Author was a leader in the ACLU affiliate.

582. Dorsen, Norman. "Racial Discrimination in 'Private' Schools." *William and Mary Law Review,* 9 (Fall 1967): 39–58.

   Analysis of the application of existing civil rights laws to private educational institutions.

583. Ennis, Edward J. "The Rights of Aliens." Norman Dorsen, ed. *The Rights of Americans.* New York: Random House, 1971. Pp. 647–646.

   Article on the legal rights of aliens by then-chairperson of the ACLU Board of Directors.

584. Friedman, Leon, ed. *Southern Justice.* Cleveland, OH: Meridian Books, 1967.

   Articles on the southern civil rights movement in the mid-1960s, with contributions by several ACLU activists. Includes both analyses of legal issues and first-hand accounts of civil rights activity.

585. McDonald, Laughlin. *Racial Equality*. Skokie, IL: National Textbook Co., 1977.

General survey of the law of racial equality by the director of the ACLU Southern Regional Office. Book published as part of a series in cooperation with the ACLU.

586. Neier, Aryeh. "Civil Rights and Symbolic Language." *Current*, 104 (February 1969): 29–34.

Article on the importance of First Amendment protection for symbolic speech in civil rights protests.

587. New York Civil Liberties Union. *The Burden of Blame*. New York: NYCLU, 1968.

Extremely important New York Civil Liberties Union report on the crisis in New York City over the decentralization of the public schools and the 1968 New York teachers' strike. Report placed much of the blame on city school administrators and on the teachers' union. The report itself was highly controversial and had a significant impact on the school crisis.

588. Olds, William. *The White Man's Navy: Keeping Blacks Out*. New York: ACLU, 1979.

Report on race discrimination in the U.S. Navy.

589. Pollitt, Daniel H. "Timid Lawyers and Neglected Clients." *Harper's*, 229 (August 1964): 81–86.

Discussion of the problem of persons who are unable to obtain legal representation. Special focus on the problem of civil rights activists in the South. Some reference also to the problem of alleged Communists.

590. Whelton, Clark. "NYCLU's Trial From Within." *The Village Voice* (March 27, 1969).

Account of controversy within the New York Civil Liberties Union arising from the organization's role in the New York City school decentralization plan and the resulting teachers' strike. Describes unsuccessful attempt by moderate NYCLU faction to gain control of the organization.

4. Death Penalty

[See also #549.]

591. "ACLU Attacks Capital Punishment." *Christian Century*, 82 (September 22, 1965): 1150.

    Article on new ACLU policy opposing the death penalty on constitutional grounds.

592. ACLU of Georgia. *The Death Penalty in Georgia*. Atlanta: ACLU of Georgia, 1965.

    Pamphlet on race discrimination in the use of the death penalty in Georgia.

593. Bedau, Hugo Adam. *The Case Against the Death Penalty*. New York: ACLU, 1973. Revised editions, nd.

    Pamphlet explaining arguments against capital punishment. Written by a member of the ACLU who is also one of the leading experts on the death penalty. Pamphlet revised and reissued periodically.

594. Clark, Ramsey. "Spenkelink's Last Appeal." *The Nation*, 229 (October 27, 1979): 385.

    First-hand account of last-minute efforts to block the second execution in the United States since the mid-1960s. Attorneys involved with the ACLU Capital Punishment Project involved in the efforts.

595. Gottlieb, Gerald H. "Testing the Death Penalty." *Southern California Law Review*, 34 (Spring 1961): 268–281.

    Early discussion of the constitutional aspects of the death penalty.

596. Schwarzschild, Henry. "In Opposition to Death Penalty Legislation." Hugo Adam Bedau, ed. *The Death Penalty in*

America. Third Edition. New York: Oxford University Press, 1982. Pp. 364–370.

Excerpts from testimony before Congress in opposition to capital punishment by the director of the ACLU Capital Punishment Project.

5. Due Process/Police Misconduct

[See also #51, #62.]

597. ACLU. *If You Are Arrested*. New York: ACLU, nd.

    Revised version of pamphlet first issued in 1955 (#480) advising citizens of their rights if arrested. Revised versions issued to keep pace with new Supreme Court decisions.

598. ACLU. *Law and Disorder—The Chicago Convention and its Aftermath*. New York: ACLU, 1968.

    Report on the violations of civil liberties by the Chicago police during the demonstrations surrounding the Democratic Party convention.

599. ACLU. *Police Powers and Citizens' Rights: The Case For an Independent Police Review Board*. New York: ACLU, 1966.

    Pamphlet arguing in favor of a civilian review board for the New York City police department.

600. ACLU. *Preventive Detention*. New York: ACLU, 1972.

    Report opposing the concept of preventive detention, or allowing judges to deny bail to criminal suspects because of alleged dangerousness.

601. ACLU. *Your Rights Before the Grand Jury*. New York: ACLU, 1972.

    Pamphlet describing grand jury procedures and the rights of persons called to testify before grand juries.

602. ACLU of Georgia. *Police Procedures in Atlanta*. Atlanta: ACLU of Georgia, 1966.

ACLU affiliate report on police misconduct in the Atlanta police department.

603. ACLU-Greater Cleveland. *A Showing of Probable Cause.* Cleveland, OH: ACLU-Greater Cleveland, 1969.

ACLU report on police misconduct in a violent encounter between the police and residents of the Glenville neighborhood of the Cleveland black community.

604. ACLU-Southern California. *Law Enforcement—A Matter of Redress.* Los Angeles: ACLU-Southern California, 1969.

ACLU affiliate report on the problem of police misconduct in Los Angeles and the failure of the police department to discipline officers guilty of misconduct.

605. ACLU-Southern California. *Police Malpractice and the Watts Riot.* Los Angeles: ACLU-Southern California, 1965.

ACLU affiliate report on police misconduct in the 1965 riot in the black community of Watts.

606. Amsterdam, Anthony G. "The Rights of Suspects." Norman Dorsen, ed. *The Rights of Americans.* New York: Random House, 1971. Pp. 401–432.

Article summarizes the legal rights of criminal suspects as of 1970–71.

607. Askin, Frank. "Police Dossiers and Emerging Principles of First Amendment Adjudication." *Stanford Law Review*, 22 (1969–1970): 196–220.

Early discussion of police spying and the possibilities of challenging spying on First Amendment grounds.

608. Askin, Frank. "Surveillance: The Social Science Perspective." *Columbia Human Rights Law Review*, 4 (Winter 1972): 59+.

Discussion of surveillance of political activity by government agencies. Originally the Appendix to the brief in the Supreme Court case of *Laird v. Tatum*, unsuccessfully challenging surveillance by military intelligence. Author directed Constitutional Law Clinic at Rutgers Law School and served as co-general counsel of the ACLU.

609. Baker, Liva. *Miranda: Crime, Law, and Politics.* New York: Atheneum, 1983.

    Book-length study of the famous *Miranda* (1966) case. Good material on the important role of the ACLU amicus brief in influencing the Court's decision.

610. Buckley, William F., Jr. "Frisking: The Social Dividend; Searching Airline Passengers." *National Review*, 24 (December 22, 1972): 1422.

    Criticism of ACLU policy opposing unreasonable searches of airline passengers.

611. Chevigny, Paul. *Cops and Rebels: A Study of Provocation.* New York: Curtis Books, 1972.

    Discussion of police misconduct, particularly with respect to political dissidents, by former director of New York Civil Liberties Union police misconduct project. Book is a follow-up to #613.

612. Chevigny, Paul. *Police Complaints: A Handbook.* New York: ACLU, 1969.

    Pamphlet describing alternative courses of action for persons with complaints against the police.

613. Chevigny, Paul. *Police Power: Police Abuses in New York City.* New York: Vintage Books, 1969.

    Detailed report on police misconduct in New York City. Author was then director of special police misconduct project with the New York Civil Liberties Union. Contains useful data on misconduct and outcomes of citizen complaints.

614. Donner, Frank J. *The Age of Surveillance: The Aims and Methods of America's Political Intelligence System.* New York: Alfred A. Knopf, 1980.

　　Detailed analysis of illegal activities by the FBI, the military intelligence agencies, the Internal Revenue Service, and other agencies. Author was director of the ACLU Project on Political Surveillance in the 1970s. Book is based on material gathered by the project.

615. Ennis, Edward J. and Osmond K. Fraenkel. "Police Power and Citizens' Rights." Alan Reitman, ed. *The Price of Liberty.* New York: W. W. Norton, 1968. Pp. 165–186.

　　Discussion of police, police misconduct, and individual rights by two prominent ACLU leaders. Ennis was general counsel and later president of the ACLU. Fraenkel was long-time ACLU general counsel.

616. Gora, Joel M. *Due Process of Law.* Skokie, IL: National Textbook Co., 1977.

　　General survey of the law of due process as of the mid-1970s by former ACLU staff attorney. Book published as part of a series in cooperation with the ACLU.

617. Kamisar, Yale. *Police Interrogation and Confessions.* Ann Arbor: University of Michigan Press, 1980.

　　Valuable material on the role of the Illinois affiliate, and its legal director, Bernard Weisberg, in developing a novel argument for the *Escobedo* (1964) case. The same argument was later used successfully in *Miranda* (1966). One of the most detailed treatments of creative ACLU lawyering during the period of the Warren Court.

618. Neier, Aryeh. "Civilian Review Boards—Another View." *Criminal Law Bulletin,* 2 (October 1966): 10–18.

　　Discussion of civilian review boards by then executive director of the New York Civil Liberties Union.

619. Neier, Aryeh. *Crime and Punishment: A Radical Solution.* New York: Stein and Day, 1976.

   Discussion of crime policy by then-executive director of the ACLU. Recommendations emphasize decriminalization of use of drugs and alcohol.

620. Valentino, Linda and Greg Goldin. "The L.E.I.U.: McCarthyism By Computer." *The Nation*, 229 (August 25, 1979): 129.

   Critical analysis of the Law Enforcement Intelligence Unit (L.E.I.U), a cooperative arrangement between police departments to share intelligence files on criminal suspects.

621. Watters, Pat and Stephen Gillers, eds. *Investigating the FBI.* New York: Ballantine, 1973.

   Proceedings of a conference on the FBI and FBI misconduct. Sponsored by the Committee on Public Justice which was affiliated with the ACLU. The first serious attempt to examine the activities of the FBI.

6. Mentally Ill, Rights of the

[See also #44, #45, #549.]

622. ACLU-Metropolitan Detroit Branch. *Legal Rights of the Mentally Ill.* Detroit: ACLU-Metropolitan Detroit Branch, 1964.

   Early statement on the rights of the mentally ill.

623. Ennis, Bruce. *Prisoners of Psychiatry.* New York: Harcourt, Brace, Jovanovich, 1972.

   Detailed critique of civil liberties violations arising from prevailing psychiatric practices. Author was one of the leaders of the movement for the rights of the mentally ill and later ACLU legal director.

624. Ennis, Bruce J. "The Rights of Mental Patients." Norman Dorsen, ed. *The Rights of Americans*. New York: Random House, 1971. Pp. 484–498.

   Brief discussion of the legal rights of mental patients.

625. Rothman, David and Shelia M. Rothman. *The Willowbrook Wars: A Decade of Struggle for Social Justice*. New York: Harper and Row, 1984.

   Account of a famous case involving the rights of mentally retarded patients in a New York state hospital. Valuable material on the role of the ACLU and the development of the law of the rights of the mentally retarded.

626. Szasz, Thomas. "The ACLU's 'Mental Illness' Cop-Out." *Reason* (January 1974): 4–9. Response: *ibid.* (April 1974): 28.

   Criticism by a noted psychiatrist of ACLU policy on the issue of involuntary commitment of the mentally ill.

627. Szasz, Thomas. *Psychiatric Slavery*. New York: The Free Press, 1977.

   Discussion of the treatment of the mentally ill by a noted psychiatrist and critic of standard treatment practices. Includes discussion of an important ACLU case on the right to treatment, with a criticism of the ACLU's policy.

7. National Security

[See also #549, #721, #728, #731.]

628. ACLU. *The Case Against HUAC*. New York: ACLU, 1964.

   Call for the abolition of the House Un-American Activities Committee.

629. ACLU. *Controlling the FBI*. New York: ACLU, 1978.

Proposal for a legislative charter defining the powers of the FBI, particularly in terms of investigation of suspected subversive groups.

630. Dorsen, Norman, and Stephen Gillers, eds. *None of Your Business: Government Secrecy in America.* New York: Penguin Books, 1975.

    Collection of articles on government secrecy, national security, and related issues.

631. Dorsen, Norman, and John Shattuck. "Executive Privilege, Congress and the Courts." *Ohio State Law Journal*, 6 (1974, No. 1): 1–40.

    Discussion of civil liberties aspects of executive privilege by then co-general counsel of the ACLU (Dorsen) and staff member of the ACLU Washington office (Shattuck).

632. Halperin, Morton H. "Further Adventures of a Tappee." *Civil Liberties Review*, 1 (Winter/Spring 1974): 131–133.

    Personal account of the author's experience of being secretly wiretapped when working for the White House. Details on his subsequent lawsuit. Author later director of the ACLU Washington office.

633. Halperin, Morton, and Daniel Hoffman. *Freedom vs. National Security.* New York: Chelsea House, 1977.

    Comprehensive collection of materials on the subject of national security.

634. Halperin, Morton, and Jerry J. Berman, Robert L. Borosage, and Christine M. Marwick. *The Lawless State: The Crimes of the U.S. Intelligence Agencies.* New York: Penguin Books, 1976.

    Collection of articles on violations of civil liberties by the CIA, the FBI, and other government agencies.

635. Halperin, Morton. "National Security and Civil Liberties." *Foreign Policy*, (Winter 1975–1976): 125–160. Reprinted by Center for National Security Studies (1976).

    Short discussion of civil liberties aspects of national security.

636. Halperin, Morton and Daniel Hoffman. *Top Secret: National Security and the Right to Know*. Washington, DC: New Republic Books, 1977.

    Analysis of government secrecy under the national security rationale.

637. Shattuck, John H.F. "Tilting at the Surveillance Apparatus." *Civil Liberties Review*, 1 (Summer 1974): 74–78.

    Article on the difficulties of ending government spying, by the future director of the ACLU Washington office.

638. Wulf, Melvin W. "Introduction." Victor Marchetti and John D. Marks. *The CIA and the Cult of Intelligence*. New York: Dell, 1975.

    Discussion of the court case in which Wulf, legal director of the ACLU, defended the authors against the government's attempt to censor portions of the book.

8. Prisoners, Rights of

[See also #53, #549.]

639. ACLU. National Prison Project. *The Alabama Prison System*. New York: ACLU, 1978.

    Detailed report on conditions in the Alabama Prison system following a federal court decision declaring many of the conditions unconstitutional. One of the most important early prisoners' rights cases.

640. ACLU. National Prison Project. *Journal of the National Prison Project*, No. 13 (Fall 1987).

Special issue on the fifteenth anniversary of the National Prison Project. Valuable material on the origins of the project, important cases, and reflections by former project staff members.

641. Hirschkop, Philip J. "The Rights of Prisoners." Norman Dorsen, ed. *The Rights of Americans*. New York: Random House, 1971. Pp. 451–468.

    Seminal article by one of the founders of the prisoner's rights movement. Now dated in terms of prevailing legal doctrine, but extremely important as a historical document.

642. Hirschkop, Philip and M. A. Millemann. "The Unconstitutionality of Prison Life." *Virginia Law Review*, 55 (June 1969): 795–839.

    Pioneering article by ACLU cooperating attorney (Hirschkop) who brought some of the first constitutional challenges to prison conditions and was instrumental in creating the ACLU National Prison Project.

9. Privacy

[See also #23, #24, #54, #55, #549.]

643. ACLU. *The Case Against a Constitutional Convention on Abortion*. New York: ACLU, 1978

    Argument against a convention to amend the U.S. Constitution, particularly for an amendment outlawing abortion.

644. ACLU. *The Privacy Act: How It Affects You, How to Use It*. New York: ACLU, 1976.

    Brief guide to using the 1976 Privacy Act. Written for the layperson.

645. ACLU. *Privacy Report*. New York: ACLU, 1973–1975.

Periodical on privacy issues published by ACLU special project on privacy. See #660 for book by director of the project.

646. ACLU. "Protecting Civil Liberties: Right to Have an Abortion." *Current*, 95 (May 1968): 26–28.

    Excerpts from new ALCU policy affirming the right to have an abortion. The ACLU was perhaps the first national organization to call for legalizing abortion.

647. Buckley, William F., Jr. "Auction Time at the ACLU." *National Review*, 29 (July 22, 1977): 845.

    Criticizes ACLU affiliate for auctioning free abortion at a fund-raising event.

648. Faux, Marian. *Roe v. Wade: The Untold Story of the Landmark Supreme Court Decision That Made Abortion Legal*. New York: New American Library, 1989.

    Account of the landmark *Roe v. Wade* (1973) decision on the right to an abortion. Includes some detail on the role of the ACLU in the case and the companion case, *Doe v. Bolton*.

649. Glasser, Ira and Herman Schwartz. "Your Phone is a Party Line." *Harper's*, 245 (October 1972): 106–108.

    Article on the violations of privacy by wiretapping. Co-author Glasser was then executive director of the New York Civil Liberties Union and future executive director of the ACLU.

650. Greenawalt, Kent. "The Right of Privacy." Norman Dorsen, ed. *The Rights of Americans*. New York: Random House, 1971. Pp. 299–325.

    Discussion of right of privacy by ACLU leader, written in the period between *Griswold* (1965) and *Roe v. Wade* (1973).

651. Lister, Charles. "The Right to Control the Use of One's Own Body." Norman Dorsen, ed. *The Rights of Americans*. New York: Random House, 1971. Pp. 348–364.

　　Discussion of emerging civil liberties issues involving control over one's own body. Includes pre-*Roe v. Wade* discussion of right to abortion.

652. Mnookin, Robert H. "*Bellotti v. Baird*: A Hard Case." Robert H. Mnookin, ed. *In the Best Interest of Children*. New York: W. H. Freeman, 1985.

　　Detailed scholarly analysis of the case of *Belloti v. Baird* (1979) which held that minors had a right to obtain contraceptives. Illuminating detail on the often-bitter conflict between the ACLU and other activist individuals and organizations on the pro-choice side.

653. Neier, Aryeh. *Dossier: The Secret Files They Keep on You*. New York: Stein and Day, 1975.

　　Discussion of the threats to civil liberties in the growth of data files on individuals maintained by various government agencies. Author was ACLU executive director at the time.

654. Neier, Aryeh. "Marked For Life: Dissemination of Arrest Records." *New York Times Magazine* (April 15, 1973): 16–17; responses, *ibid.*, (May 13, 1973): 9.

　　Discussion of the violations of individual rights through public dissemination of arrest records.

655. "Open Criticism of a Secrecy Law." *Business Week* (June 17, 1972): 33.

　　Article on ACLU suit challenging the 1970 Bank Secrecy Act.

656. Pilpel, Harriet. "Birth Control and a New Birth of Freedom." *Ohio State Law Journal*, 27 (Fall 1966): 679–690.

　　Analysis of the 1965 *Griswold* decision affirming a right to privacy and its implications for broader constitutional law doctrine.

657. Pilpel, Harriet. "The Challenge of Privacy." Alan Reitman, ed. *The Price of Liberty*. New York: W. W. Norton, 1968. Pp. 19–44.

Early discussion of the right to privacy by important ACLU leader. Pilpel was primarily responsible for raising the issues of abortion rights and gay rights as civil liberties issues within the ACLU in the mid-1960s. She served as general counsel for both the ACLU and Planned Parenthood for many years.

658. Pilpel, Harriet. "Sex vs. the Law: A Study in Hypocrisy." *Harper's*, 230 (January 1965): 35–40.

Pioneering discussion of criminal abortion laws and laws prohibiting consensual adult sexual activity.

659. Shattuck, John. *Rights of Privacy*. Skokie, IL: National Textbook Co., 1977.

General survey of privacy rights by the director of the ACLU Washington legislative office. Book published as part of a series in cooperation with the ACLU.

660. Smith, Robert Ellis. *Privacy: How To Protect What's Left Of It*. Garden City, NY: Anchor Books, 1979.

Detailed comprehensive survey of privacy issues focusing on data files on individuals maintained by both government and private agencies. The author directed the ACLU privacy project in the early 1970s.

661. Westin, Alan. *Privacy and Freedom*. New York: Atheneum, 1967.

First comprehensive survey of the emerging issue of privacy rights. Particular emphasis on threats to privacy from data files maintained by public and private agencies. Author was associated with the ACLU for many years.

662. Wulf, Melvin L. "On the Origins of Privacy." *The Nation*, 252 (May 27, 1991): 700–704.

Extremely valuable memoir about the drafting of the ACLU amicus brief in the 1961 Supreme Court case of *Poe v. Ullman.* Justice John Marshall Harlan's dissent in *Poe* provided much of the basis for the Supreme Court's affirmation of a constitutional right of privacy in *Griswold* in 1965. Wulf was the associate legal director of the ACLU at the time. Very useful first-hand account of the drafting of an ACLU brief. Extremely important in terms of the origins of the constitutional right of privacy.

10. Religious Liberty

663. ACLU. *The Church/State Problem Has Been Handed to You: A Guide For Community Groups.* New York: ACLU, 1967.

    Pamphlet on current church/state issues with discussion of organizing strategies for opposing public funds for parochial schools.

664. Buckley, William F., Jr. "Preserve Us From Silent Night." *National Review,* 31 (January 5, 1979): 48–49.

    Article criticizing ACLU suit to ban singing of Christmas carols in a public school.

665. Drinan, Robert F., S.J. *Religion, The Courts, and Public Policy.* New York: McGraw-Hill, 1963.

    Discussion of Supreme Court decisions on the role of religion in American public life by a prominent Catholic theologian and lawyer. Represents a significant shift from the author's earlier criticisms of the ACLU (#494, #495). Anticipates his future role in the ACLU (#1227).

666. Muir, William K. *Prayer and the Public Schools.* Chicago: University of Chicago Press, 1967. Reissued as *Law and Attitude Change.* Chicago: University of Chicago Press, 1973.

    Scholarly analysis of the impact of the Supreme Court's 1962 decision outlawing prayer in the public schools. Good insights into the impact of ACLU litigation in the area of church and state.

667. "Nonsense From NYCLU." *America*, 115 (August 27, 1966): 201–202.

   Article critical of New York Civil Liberties Union position opposing public support for parochial schools.

668. Pfeffer, Leo. *Religious Freedom*. Skokie, IL: National Textbook Co., 1977.

   General survey of the law of religious liberty by a frequent ACLU cooperating attorney and the leading authority on separation of church and state. Book published as part of a series in cooperation with the ACLU.

669. Pfeffer, Leo. "The Right to Religious Liberty." Norman Dorsen, ed. *The Rights of Americans*. New York: Random House, 1971. Pp. 326–347.

   Brief survey of religious liberty issues as of 1971.

670. "Religious Liberty on Sunday: Real and Unreal." *America*, 104 (December 10, 1960): 361–362.

   Criticism of ACLU position opposing Sunday closing laws.

671. Smith, G.L. "Another Separation Trial." *Christian Century*, 96 (November 14, 1979): 1109–1110.

   Article on ACLU suit in Souix Falls, South Dakota opposing singing of Christmas carols in public schools.

672. "To Pick a Nit: Creche on Public Property." *America*, 104 (January 7, 1961): 434.

   Criticism of ACLU position opposing religious displays on public property.

11. Skokie

673. ACLU. *Why the American Civil Liberties Union Defends Free Speech for Racists and Totalitarians*. New York: ACLU, 1978.

Revised version of ACLU statement of the right of free speech for totalitarian groups. See #292 and #293 for earlier versions.

674. Arkes, H. "Marching Through Skokie." *National Review*, 30 (May 12, 1978): 588–593.

Conservative perspective on the Skokie crisis.

675. Bollinger, Lee. *The Tolerant Society: Freedom of Speech and Extremist Speech in America*. New York: Oxford University Press, 1986.

Discussion of the role of the First Amendment in American society by a legal scholar. The book was prompted by the Skokie case and the viewpoint is sympathetic to the ACLU's position.

676. Cohen, Carl. "Skokie—The Extreme Test." *The Nation*, 226 (April 15, 1978): 2–8.

Defense of the ACLU's position in the Skokie affair by an ACLU activist.

677. Dorsen, Norman. "Is There a Right to Stop Offensive Speech? The Case of the Nazis at Skokie." Larry Gostin, ed. *Civil Liberties in Conflict*. New York: Routledge, 1988. Pp. 122–135.

Reflections on the Skokie case by then-president of the ACLU.

678. Downs, Donald Alexander. *Nazis and Skokie: Freedom, Community, and The First Amendment*. Notre Dame, IN: Notre Dame University Press, 1985.

A history of the Skokie crisis and discussion of First Amendment theory. Thoughtful criticism of the ACLU's position on free speech.

679. Gibson, James L. and Richard D. Bingham. *Civil Liberties and Nazis: The Skokie Free-Speech Controversy*. New York: Praeger, 1985.

Scholarly study of the Skokie crisis. Includes valuable survey of the attitudes of ACLU members on various civil liberties issues, comparing their attitudes with the official policies of the organization and the attitudes of a comparison group of liberal political activists.

680. Goldberger, David. "Would You Defend an Unpopular Cause? On Defending Nazis." *Barrister*, 5 (Winter 1977).

    Article by the staff attorney for the Illinois ACLU during the Skokie crisis on the question of defending Nazis and other unpopular groups.

681. Haiman, Franklyn S. "Nazis in Skokie: Anatomy of the Heckler's Veto." *Free Speech Yearbook* (1978): 11–16.

    Discussion of the attempt to prevent Nazis from demonstrating in Skokie in terms of a "heckler's veto." Author was president of the Illinois ACLU during the Skokie crisis.

682. Hamlin, David. *The Nazi/Skokie Conflict: A Civil Liberties Battle*. Boston: Beacon Press, 1980.

    First-hand account of the Skokie crisis by the executive director of the ACLU Illinois affiliate during the crisis.

683. Hentoff, Nat. "Nazis March Toward the First Amendment." *The Village Voice* (August 1, 1977). "Hard Rains Falling at the ACLU." *Ibid.* (December 5, 1977). "Skokie: What the Mirror Shows." *Ibid.* (May 1, 1978).

    Series of articles on the Skokie crisis by a prominent ACLU member and journalist specializing in civil liberties issues.

684. Horowitz, Irving L. and V.C. Bramson. "Skokie, The ACLU, and the Endurance of Democratic Theory." *Law and Contemporary Problems*, 43 (Spring 1979): 328–349.

    Discussion of the issues raised by the Skokie case. Critical of the ACLU's position and its failure to defend the private rights of the Jewish community. Detailed and articulate critique of the ACLU's position.

685. LaMarche, Gara. "After Skokie: New Directions for Civil Liberties." *New York Affairs*, 6 (1980, No. 3).

    Discussion of the future of civil liberties in the aftermath of Skokie by prominent ACLU leader.

686. Lukas, J. Anthony. "The ACLU Against Itself." *The New York Times Magazine*, (July 9, 1978): 9–11+.

    Description of the ACLU's organizational problems following the Skokie crisis. Particularly valuable insights into the personalities of the ACLU's top leaders.

687. Lyles, J. C., "Skokie as Symbol." *Christian Century*, 95 (April 19, 1978): 411–412.

    Brief article on the Skokie crisis.

688. Mann, J. "Hard Times for the ACLU." *The New Republic*, 178 (April 15, 1978): 12–15.

    Account of the ACLU's organizational difficulties as a result of the Skokie incident.

689. Meiklejohn, Alexander. "Meiklejohn on Skokie." *Guild Practitioner*, 35 (Summer 1978): 84–96.

    Interview about the Skokie crisis with noted expert on the First Amendment in the official publication of the National Lawyers Guild. Eventually concludes that if he were the police chief in Skokie he would bar the Nazis from marching.

690. Neier, Aryeh. *Defending My Enemy*. New York: Dutton, 1979.

    First-hand account of the Skokie crisis by ACLU executive director during the crisis.

12. Speech, Press, and Assembly, Freedom of

[See also #727.]

691. ACLU. "Fair Trial and Free Press." *Law in Transition Quarterly*, 4 (March 1967): 44–51.

    Presentation of new (1966) ACLU policy on balancing the principles of the right to a fair trial and freedom of the press.

692. ACLU. *Obscenity and Censorhip—Two Statements of the American Civil Liberties Union.* New York: ACLU, 1963.

    Important statements of new policies by the ACLU, taking stronger stand on opposition to censorship of so-called obscenity.

693. ACLU. *Your Right to Government Information: How to Use the FOIA.* New York: ACLU, 1973.

    Pamphlet on how individuals can use the Freedom of Information Act. Written in layperson's terms.

694. ACLU, et al. "Coalition Statement on COP Report." *Newsletter on Intellectual Freedom*, 20 (May 1971): 57, 74

    Statement by a coalition of anti-censorship groups, including the ACLU, criticizing the 1970 report of the U.S. Commission on Pornography.

695. "ACLU Hits Customs' Seizure of Author's Manuscript." *Publishers Weekly*, 182 (November 19, 1962): 29.

    Article on ACLU challenge to censorship activities of the U.S. Customs Bureau.

696. "Constitutionality of Book Ban Challenged by NYCLU." *Library Journal*, 102 (March 1, 1977): 530.

    Article on New York Civil Liberties Union suit challenging removal of books from public school library by the school board.

697. Haiman, Franklyn S. *Freedom of Speech.* Skokie, IL: National Textbook Co., 1976.

   General survey of the law of freedom of speech by a long-time leader of the Illinois affiliate of the ACLU and member of the ACLU Board of Directors. Book published as part of a series in cooperation with the ACLU, and with Haiman as series editor.

698. Haiman, Franklyn S. "Speech v. Privacy: Is There a Right Not to be Spoken To?" *Northwestern University Law Review,* 67 (May-June 1972): 153–199.

   Discussion of the conflicting principles of free speech and the right to privacy by a long-time member of the ACLU Board of Directors.

699. National Ad Hoc Committee Against Censorship. Censorship Conference. *Proceedings.* New York: The Committee, 1976.

   Proceedings of a conference on censorship by an ad hoc coalition of groups on December 9, 1975. The group became the permanent National Coalition Against Censorship in 1976. (See also #18, the Coalition's newsletter #18.)

700. Pemberton, John de J., Jr. "Constitutional Problems in Restraints on the Media." *Notre Dame Lawyer,* 42 (1967): 881–887.

   Critical analysis of recent ABA report on fair trial and freedom of the press by then-executive director of the ACLU.

701. Pemberton, John de J., Jr. "The Right of Access to Mass Media." Norman Dorsen, ed. *The Rights of Americans.* New York: Random House, 1971. Pp. 276–296.

   Discussion of the legal issues surrounding the right of private citizens to have their views carried by private news media.

702. Pilpel, Harriet. Column. *Publishers Weekly* (1960s–1970s).

A weekly column on freedom of the press issues by prominent ACLU leader and general counsel.

703. "Policy Clarification Asked on Seizure of Book Imports." *Publishers Weekly*, 179 (March 6, 1961): 30.

    Article on ACLU challenge to censorship practices of the U.S. Customs Bureau.

704. Powledge, Fred. *An ACLU Guide to Cable Television*. New York: ACLU, 1972.

    ACLU-sponsored report on the emerging cable television industry. Analysis of First Amendment implications.

705. Powledge, Fred. *Public Television: A Question of Survival. A Report of the American Civil Liberties Union*. Washington, DC: Public Affairs Press, 1972.

    ACLU-sponsored report on public television. Argues that actions of the Nixon Administration threaten its survival.

706. Stevens, John D. "Proposal to ACLU: Newspapers Must Carry All Viewpoints." *Journalism Educator*, 23 (Fall 1968): 22–24.

    Article attacking "right of access" concept then under consideration by the ACLU.

707. Wagner, S. "ACLU to Take Marchetti Case to Supreme Court." *Publishers Weekly*, 202 (October 16, 1972): 25.

    Article on ACLU suit challenging the CIA's attempt to censor portions of the book *The CIA and the Cult of Intelligence*.

708. Wasby. Stephen L. "Public Law, Politics, and the Local Courts: Obscene Literature in Portland." *Journal of Public Law*, 14 (1965, No. 1): 105–130.

    Analysis of ACLU litigation and lobbying in response to anti-pornography efforts in Portland, Oregon.

709. Wulf, Melvin L. "Excess Access." *Civil Liberties Review*, 1 (Winter/Spring 1974): 128–130.

Argues against the concept of a "right of access" to the media. Author was then ACLU legal director.

13. Vietnam War

[See also #549.]

710. ACLU. *Choose Your War: Or, The Case of the Selective C.O.* New York: ACLU, 1969.

Pamphlet explaining the ACLU's support of the right of selective conscientious objection.

711. ACLU. *Dissent in Crisis.* New York: ACLU, 1969.

ACLU criticism of the so-called "anti-riot" act, making it a federal crime to cross state lines to engage in protest activities.

712. ACLU. *Why End the Draft?* New York: ACLU, 1971.

Proposal to abolish the draft on the grounds that selective service violates individual freedom.

713. ACLU-National Capital Area. *Mayday 1971—Order Without Law.* Washington, DC: ACLU-National Capital Area, 1972.

ACLU affiliate report on the violation of civil liberties in the mass arrests of demonstrators protesting the Vietnam War on May 1, 1971. ACLU suit eventually led to damage awards to many of those arrested.

714. "ACLU Reverses Itself." *Christian Century*, 85 (April 17, 1968): 476–477.

Article on the decision by the ACLU to provide legal assistance to Dr. Benjamin Spock, Reverend William Sloane Coffin, and others indicted by the federal government for opposing the Vietnam War.

715. ACLU-Southern California. *Day of Protest/Night of Violence.* Los Angeles: ACLU-Southern California, 1967.

    ACLU affiliate report on violent clash between anti-war demonstrators and the police at Century City, Los Angeles.

716. "An April Shower of Billy Clubs and a May Victory." *Christian Century,* 85 (May 15, 1968): 639.

    Article on the violent attack on anti-war demonstrators by the Chicago police in April and a subsequent protest march in May. The ACLU played a prominent role in the May march.

717. Bannan, John F. and Rosemary S. Bannan. *Law, Morality, and Vietnam: The Peace Militants and the Courts.* Bloomington: Indiana University Press, 1974.

    Scholarly treatment of major court cases involving anti-war activists. Valuable material on role of ACLU and/or ACLU affiliates in most of the cases.

718. Bishop, Joseph W., Jr. "The Reverend Mr. Coffin, Dr. Spock, and the ACLU." *Harper's,* 237 (July 1968): 6+.

    Criticism of ACLU's role in defending Coffin and Dr. Spock against federal prosecution for opposing the Vietnam War. Argues that the ACLU has adopted a "political" position.

719. Dershowitz, Alan M. "The First Amendment and the Vietnam War: The Cases of the Stanford Stalinist and the CIA Whistle-Blower." Alan Dershowitz. *The Best Defense.* New York: Vintage Books, 1983. Pp. 206–235.

    Discussion of the author's role as lawyer in two First Amendment cases. Includes material on the role of the ACLU in the case of a Stanford University professor fired because of his Marxist views.

720. Dorsen, Norman and David Rudovsky. "Some Thoughts on Dissent, Personal Liberty, and War." *American Bar Association Journal,* 54 (August 1968): 752–758.

Discussion of civil liberties issues arising from the Vietnam War by co-general counsel of the ACLU (Dorsen) and one of his law students (Rudovsky).

721. Friedman, Leon and Burt Neuborne. *Unquestioning Obedience to the President.* New York: Norton, 1972.

Discussion of legal issues surrounding the war powers of the president of the United States. Prompted by crisis over Vietnam War. Neuborne was staff attorney with New York Civil Liberties Union in the 1960s and early 1970s; later served as legal director of the ACLU, 1983–1986; litigated important cases challenging the constitutionality of the war.

722. Glasser, Ira. "Judgment at Fort Jackson: the Court Martial of Captain Howard B. Levy." *Law in Transition Quarterly*, 4 (September 1967): 123–156.

Discussion of the Howard Levy trial by the associate director of the New York Civil Liberties Union who assisted at the trial.

723. Harris, Richard. *Freedom Spent.* Boston: Little, Brown, 1976.

Collection of articles that originally appeared in *The New Yorker* on several civil liberties cases in the late 1960s and early 1970s. One deals with a protest case handled by New York Civil Liberties Union lawyers. Vivid account of a Vietnam War protest case.

724. Hentoff, Nat. "Commentary and Carbon Papers: Fantasizing the ACLU." *Civil Liberties* (March 1972): 1, 4.

Reply to criticisms of the ACLU for its position on the Vietnam War.

725. Mitford, Jessica. *The Trial of Doctor Spock.* New York: Knopf, 1969.

Account of Justice Department prosecution of Doctor Benjamin Spock and four others for conspiracy to obstruct the draft. Appendix 6, "The Role of the American Civil

Liberties Union in the Case of the Boston Five," provides detailed coverage of bitter internal ACLU split over the case.

726. Pemberton, John de J. "The War Protester." *Current History*, 55 (July 1968): 23–27, 48–49.

    Article on the rights of Vietnam War protesters by then-executive director of the ACLU.

727. Powledge, Fred. *The Engineering of Restraint: The Nixon Administration and the Press*. New York: ACLU, 1971.

    ACLU-sponsored report on efforts by President Richard Nixon to stifle criticisms of the administration's Vietnam War policy.

728. Schrag, Peter. *Test of Loyalty: Daniel Ellsberg and the Rituals of Secret Government*. New York: Simon and Schuster, 1974.

    Popular account of the government's prosecution of Daniel Ellsberg for releasing the Pentagon Papers. Particularly valuable for the material on Morton Halperin who served as a consultant to the defense in the trial and later became director of the ACLU Washington office. Particularly valuable insights into the development of national security as a civil liberties issue for the ACLU.

729. Sherrill, Robert. *Military Justice Is to Justice as Military Music is to Music*. New York: Harper and Row, 1970.

    Popular account of several cases involving protests by military personnel against the Vietnam War. Good material on the role of the ACLU in these cases. Includes a chapter on the Howard Levy case, an important event in the history of the ACLU.

730. Tigar, Michael E. "The Rights of Selective Service Registrants." Norman Dorsen, ed. *The Rights of Americans*. New York: Random House, 1971. Pp. 499–517.

Review of major court cases challenging selective service procedures, most of which were brought by the ACLU.

731. Ungar, Sanford J. *The Papers and the Papers: An Account of the Legal and Political Battle over the Pentagon Papers.* New York: E.P. Dutton, 1972.

Popular account of the Pentagon Papers cases. Some material on the ACLU's role.

14. Watergate

[See also #549, #1269.]

732. ACLU. *High Crimes and Misdemeanors.* New York: ACLU, 1973.

Discussion of grounds for impeachment of President Richard Nixon.

733. ACLU. *Watergate and Civil Liberties.* New York: ACLU, 1973.

ACLU interpretation of the civil liberties issues involved in the Watergate crisis.

734. ACLU. *Why President Richard Nixon Should Be Impeached.* Washington, DC: Public Affairs Press, 1973.

Pamphlet presenting the ACLU's case for the impeachment of President Nixon.

735. Friedman, Leon, ed. *United States v. Nixon.* New York: Chelsea House, 1974.

Collection of documents related to the Supreme Court case involving President Nixon's control of the White House tape recordings. Includes a copy of the ACLU brief in the case.

736. "Six Reasons: ACLU Calls on Congress to Initiate Impeachment Proceedings Against President Nixon." *The Nation,* 217 (October 22, 1973): 389.

Explains ACLU call for impeachment of President Richard Nixon.

15. Women, Rights of

[See also #26, #67, #549.]

737. ACLU. *The Case for Equality in State Jury Service*. New York: ACLU, 1966.

   Pamphlet urging support for federal legislation to prohibit discrimination against women in jury service in the states. Written by Dorothy Kenyon, long-time ACLU Board member.

738. ACLU. *The ERA: A Lifetime Guarantee*. New York: ACLU, 1978.

   ACLU pamphlet urging ratification of the Equal Rights Amendment to the U.S. Constitution.

739. Cary, Eve and Kathleen Willert Peratis. *Women and the Law*. Skokie, IL: National Textbook Co., 1977.

   Overview of women's rights issues as of the mid-1970s. Book published as part of a series on civil liberties issues in cooperation with the ACLU.

740. Cowan, Ruth. "Women's Rights Through Litigation: An Examination of the American Civil Liberties Union Women's Rights Project, 1971–1976." *Columbia Human Rights Law Review*, 8 (Spring 1976): 373–412.

   Detailed scholarly analysis of the cases brought by the ACLU Women's Rights Project during the first five years of its existence. Traces the major contribution of the Project to the development of the law of women's rights.

741. Dorsen, Norman. "Women, The Criminal Code, and the Correction System." New York City Commission on Human Rights. *Women's Role in Contemporary Society*. New York: Avon Books, 1972.

Discussion of the impact of the criminal justice system on women. Written by then-general counsel and future president of the ACLU.

742. Dorsen, Norman and Susan Deller Ross. "The Necessity of a Constitutional Amendment." *Harvard Civil Rights—Civil Liberties Law Review*, 6 (March 1971): 215–224.

    Argument in support of an Equal Rights Amendment to the Constitution.

743. Markowitz, Deborah L. "In Pursuit of Equality: One Woman's Work to Change the Law." *Women's Rights Law Reporter*, 11 (Summer 1989): 73–97.

    Scholarly analysis of the career of Ruth Bader Ginsburg who was primarily responsible for the initial ACLU women's rights cases in the early 1970s. The most important of these cases led to the first affirmation of women's rights by the U.S. Supreme Court.

744. Murray, Pauli. "The Negro Woman's Stake in the Equal Rights Amendment." *Harvard Civil Rights—Civil Liberties Law Review*, 6 (March 1971): 253–259.

    Discussion of the relevance of the ERA to black women by leading advocate of women's rights on the ACLU Board of Directors.

745. Murray, Pauli. "The Rights of Women." Norman Dorsen, ed. *The Rights of Americans*. New York: Random House, 1971. Pp. 521–545.

    Discussion of women's rights issues by early advocate of women's rights within the ACLU.

746. Murray, Pauli and Mary Eastwood. "Jane Crow and the Law." *George Washington Law Review*, 34 (December 1965): 232–241.

    Discussion of women's rights issues by two leading advocates of women's rights within the ACLU.

747. Norton, Eleanor Holmes. "A Strategy for Change." New York City Commission on Human Rights. *Women's Role in Contemporary Society.* New York: Avon Books, 1972.

    Norton was then chair of the New York City Commission on Human Rights. She had previously been staff attorney for the ACLU and would later become chair of the ACLU National Advisory Committee.

748. O'Connor, Karen. *Women's Organizations' Use of the Court.* Lexington, MA: Lexington Books, 1980.

    Political science analysis of women's rights litigation by the leading women's rights organizations in the 1970s. Concludes that ACLU's Women's Rights Project was more active and influential than any other organization.

749. O'Connor, Karen and Lee Epstein. "Beyond Legislative Lobbying: Women's Rights Groups and the Supreme Court." *Judicature*, 67 (September 1983): 134–143.

    Analysis of the role of the major women's rights groups in Supreme Court litigation. Argues that the ACLU Women's Rights Project handles more cases than any other women's rights group. For more extended analysis, see #748.

750. Seidenberg, Faith. "Family, Property, and Domicile Law in the State of New York." New York City Commission on Human Rights. *Women's Role in Contemporary Society.* New York: Avon Books, 1972.

    Discussion of certain aspects of the law affecting women in New York by leader of the New York Civil Liberties Union.

16. Other Issues

[See also #549.]

751. Hanks, Eva H. and John L Hanks. "The Right to a Habitable Environment." Norman Dorsen, ed. *The Rights*

of Americans. New York: Random House, 1971. Pp. 146–171.

Discussion of civil liberties aspects of the environmental movement.

752. "Inside the Great Campaign Finance Case of 1976: A Conversation With Ira Glasser." *Civil Liberties Review*, 4 (September-October 1977): 8–19.

Interview with Ira Glasser, then-executive director of the New York Civil Liberties Union, about the 1976 Supreme Court case, *Buckley v. Valeo*. NYCLU brought a suit successfully challenging major sections of the 1971 Federal Election Campaign Act because it violated the First Amendment. Good discussion of the origins of the case.

753. Rezneck, Daniel A. "The Rights of Juveniles." Norman Dorsen, ed. *The Rights of Americans*. New York: Random House, 1971. Pp. 469–483.

Discussion of the legal aspects of the rights of juveniles as of 1970–71.

754. Schrag, Philip G. "The Rights of Consumers." Norman Dorsen, ed. *The Rights of Americans*. New York: Random House, 1971. Pp. 128–145.

Discussion of the legal issues surrounding the rights of individuals as consumers.

755. Sparer, Edward V. "The Right to Welfare." Norman Dorsen, ed. *The Rights of Americans*. New York: Random House, 1971. Pp. 65–93.

Discussion of the rights of individual welfare recipients.

756. Summers, Clyde W, "The Rights of Unions and Union Members." Norman Dorsen, ed. *The Rights of Americans*. New York: Random House, 1971. Pp. 591–620.

Discussion of the civil liberties issues involving the rights of labor unions as organizations and union members as individuals.

III. Contemporary Civil Liberties Issues, 1980–1991

A. THE ACLU

1. General

[See #1, #2, #3, #7, #92.]

757. "ACLU Elects Calaway Treasurer." *Civil Liberties*, No. 369 (Spring 1990): 6.

   Article on the election of Jim Calaway as Treasurer of the ACLU. Emphasis on his role as fund-raiser.

758. ACLU. *National Attitudes Toward the ACLU.* New York: ACLU, 1989.

   Survey of public attitudes toward the ACLU. Commissioned by the ACLU and conducted by an independent survey research firm. Survey found generally favorable attitudes toward the organization.

759. "The ACLU on the Rebound." *National Law Journal* (September 5, 1983): 1+.

   Article on the ACLU's current program, emphasizing the organization's strength five years after the Skokie crisis. Written on the occasion of the 1983 ACLU Biennial conference in Washington, DC.

760. "Civil Liberties versus Political Agendas." Symposium. *Society*, 28 (January/February 1991): 5–22.

   Symposium on various aspects of ACLU policy, particularly economic rights. Includes two articles criticizing the ACLU and two responses by persons involved in the ACLU.

761. "Competing With the 'New Right' Where it Counts—at the Grassroots." *Civil Liberties*, No. 340 (December 1981): 4–5.

　　Interview with John Shattuck, director of the ACLU Washington Office, on the ACLU's new Bill of Rights Lobby, emphasizing grassroots support for legislative protection of civil liberties.

762. "The Danger of Civil Liberties." *The Guardian*, 34 (October 28, 1981): 19.

　　Criticism of ACLU policies, from a left-wing perspective. Emphasis on ACLU defense of free speech rights of racist groups.

763. Donohue, William A. "What the ACLU Means by 'Civil Liberties'." *The World and I* (June 1987): 621–631.

　　Conservative criticism of the ACLU for pursuing a partisan political agenda. For longer version, see #74 by the same author. See reply by historian and ACLU Board member, #793.

764. Dorsen, Norman. "The Need For a New Enlightenment: Lessons in Liberty From the Eighteenth Century." *Case Western Reserve Law Review*, 38 (1987–88, No. 4): 479–495.

　　Essay on the values underlying individual rights by then-president of the ACLU. Argues that the example of the eighteenth century Enlightenment provides inspiration for a renewed commitment to individual rights in contemporary society.

765. Dorsen, Norman. "The United States Supreme Court: Trends and Prospects." *Harvard Civil Rights—Civil Liberties Law Review*, 21 (Winter 1986): 1–26.

　　Analysis of trends in civil liberties decisions of the Supreme Court by then-president of the ACLU.

766. Etzioni, Amitai. "Too Many Rights, Too Few Responsibilities." *Society*, 28 (January/February 1991): 41–48.

A noted sociologist and social policy commentator argues that society has placed too much emphasis on individual rights at the expense of the needs of the community as a whole. Author cites several examples of ACLU policy. Author also founded and edits a journal, *The Responsive Community*, devoted to the same issue.

767. Glasser, Ira. "The American Civil Liberties Union and the Completion of the Bill of Rights." Adolph Grundman, ed. *The Embattled Constitution*. Malabar, FL: Krieger Publishing, 1986.

Discussion of the role of the ACLU in fulfilling the promises of the Bill of Rights by ACLU executive director.

768. Glasser, Ira, et. al. *An Imperial Judiciary: Fact or Myth?* Washington, DC: American Enterprise Institute, 1978.

Symposium on the role of the courts in American society. Participants include ACLU executive director Glasser and future Supreme Court justice Antonin Scalia.

769. Glasser, Ira. "Making Constitutional Rights Work." Norman Dorsen, ed. *Our Endangered Rights*. New York: Pantheon Books, 1984. Pp. 3–26.

Discussion of strategies for protecting civil liberties by the executive director of the ACLU.

770. Glasser, Ira. "The Reagan Administration is Moving America Away From Civil Liberties." *Civil Liberties*, No. 352 (Winter 1985): 3.

Interview with ACLU executive director on assaults on civil liberties by the Reagan administration

771. Glastris, Paul. ". . . One That Should be the Best, But Isn't." *The Washington Monthly*, 20 (March 1988): 27–23.

Criticism of ACLU policies, particularly ACLU opposition to drug testing for railroad employees, drunk driving road blocks, and searches of passengers at airports.

772. Harrington, James C. "The Texas Bill of Rights and Civil Liberties." *Texas Tech Law Review*, 17 (1986): 1487–1555.

Analysis of the opportunities for protecting civil liberties in Texas under the state constitution.

773. "Hart, Jackson and Mondale Answer ACLU's Questions." *Civil Liberties*, No. 349 (Spring 1984): 1+.

Three candidates for president in 1984 answer an ACLU questionnaire on civil liberties issues.

774. Hentoff, Nat. "What's Happening to the New York Civil Liberties Union?" *The Village Voice* (March 1, 1983). "NYCLU—The Change From Leadership to Timidity." *Ibid.* (March 8, 1983)."Who's Afraid of the NYCLU?" *Ibid.* (March 15, 1983). "Who Speaks for Civil Liberties in New York?" *Ibid.* (March 29, 1983).

Series of articles highly critical of the New York Civil Liberties Union and its executive director, Dorothy Samuels, in particular. Accuses the current leadership of the NYCLU of failing to take the kind of leadership that characterized the organization in the 1960s.

775. Hentoff, Nat. [Weekly Column]. *The Village Voice*.

A weekly column devoted to civil liberties issues. Individual columns frequently contain references to the ACLU, ACLU affiliates, including frequent criticisms of the ACLU from a civil libertarian perspective. See individual columns on specific topics (e.g., abortion rights, police misconduct, etc.).

776. LaMarche, Gara. "An Agenda For the 1990s." *The National Law Journal* (June 27, 1988).

Discussion of civil liberties strategies by then-director of the Texas Civil Liberties Union.

777. LaMarche, Gara. "ACLU: Vigilant in Texas." *Texas Lawyer* (July 31, 1985).

Description of the activities of the Texas ACLU affiliate by then-executive director.

778. Leo, John. "One Watchdog Missing in Action." *U. S. News and World Report*, 109 (November 5, 1990): 23.

Criticizes the ACLU for excessive support for abortion, including failing to defend anti-abortion protesters.

779. Loewenson, Carl H., Jr. "ACLU Turns to State Courts and Constitutions to Protect Rights." *Civil Liberties*, No. 352 (Winter 1985): 7

Discussion of recent ACLU cases in state supreme courts in response to increased hostility of U.S. Supreme Court to civil liberties.

780. Mayer, Milton. "The Trouble With the ACLU." *The Progressive*, 44 (February 1980): 48.

Published version of a speech to an ACLU chapter in California. Argues that the ACLU's interpretation of civil liberties fails to address the major problems in the world: racism, war, capitalism.

781. Neisser, Eric. "Civil Liberties Today." Monthly Column. *New Jersey Law Journal* (September 1986–   ).

Monthly column on civil liberties issues by legal director of the New Jersey Civil Liberties Union. Columns not necessarily restricted to New Jersey-related subjects.

782. Neisser, Eric. *Recapturing the Spirit: Essays on the Bill of Rights at 200*. Madison, WI: Madison House, 1991.

Collection of essays on the Bill of Rights by the legal director of the New Jersey Civil Liberties Union.

783. Neuborne, Burt. "The Supreme Court and the Judicial Process." Norman Dorsen, ed. *Our Endangered Rights*. New York: Pantheon Books, 1984. Pp. 27–45.

795. "Why the American Civil Liberties Union Does What it Does." *U.S. News and World Report*, 96 (March 26, 1984): 76.

    Brief article describing some of the more controversial ACLU policies.

2. 1988 Presidential Election, ACLU Role in

[See #92.]

796. Bennet, James. "ACLU Too, Buddy." *The New Republic*, 199 (October 17, 1988): 13–15.

    Discussion of the highly publicized controversy over Attorney General Richard Thornburgh's resignation from the ACLU in the 1970s.

797. Campisano, Mark S. "Card Games: The ACLU's Wrong Course." *The New Republic*, 199 (October 31, 1988): 10–12. Reply by Norman Dorsen and Ira Glasser. *Ibid.*, (December 12, 1988): 22–23.

    Critical account, arguing that the ACLU has moved out of the mainstream of American life. Reply by Dorsen, President of the ACLU, and Glasser, executive director.

798. Carlson, M. B. "Spotlight on the ACLU." *Time*, 132 (October 10, 1988): 36.

    Brief article on attacks on the ACLU during the 1988 presidential election campaign.

799. Crovitz, L. G. "A Primer on the ACLU." *The Saturday Evening Post*, 260 (December 1988): 2+.

    Description of the ACLU and its policies following the 1988 presidential election campaign.

800. Glasser, Ira. *Presidential Politics and the ACLU*. New York: ACLU, 1988.

    Reprint of an October, 1988 speech to the National Press Club by the executive director of the ACLU.

Responds to attacks on the ACLU during the 1988 presidential election campaign. Explains ACLU principles and discusses important cases from ACLU history.

801. Hackett, G. "The ACLU Battles Back." *Newsweek*, 112 (October 10, 1988): 44.

    Brief article on attacks on the ACLU during the 1988 presidential election campaign.

802. Judis, John. "How ACLU Left Itself Open to Right Wing Attacks." *In These Times*, 13 (November 9, 1988): 7.

    Critique of ACLU policies from a left-wing perspective. Article prompted by attacks on the ACLU during the 1988 presidential election campaign.

803. Ledbetter, Jim. "New Members, New Problems." *The Nation*, 248 (1989): 442–444.

    Discussion of the future of the ACLU following the 1988 presidential election campaign.

804. Lee, R. W. "What the ACLU Represents." *Conservative Digest*, 14 (December 1988): 60–63.

    Discussion of ACLU policies from a conservative perspective.

3. Bork, Robert, Nomination to the Supreme Court, ACLU Role in

[See #92.]

805. ACLU. "Why Robert Bork Is Not Qualified to Sit on the Supreme Court." *Civil Liberties*, No. 361 (Summer 1987): 4–5.

    Official ACLU statement explaining its reasons for opposing the nomination of Robert Bork to the Supreme Court.

806. ACLU. *Report on the Civil Liberties Record of Judge Robert Bork*. New York: ACLU, 1987.

817. Haiman, Franklyn S. "School Censors and the Law." *Communication Education*, 36 (October 1987): 327–338.

Article on the law of free speech with respect to school officials. Author is a long-time ACLU leader.

818. Hentoff, Nat. "When Nice People Burn Books." *Progressive*, 47 (February 1983): 42–44.

Criticism of censorship; cites recent efforts by liberals to censor forms of expression.

819. Hentoff, Nat. "Would You Fight For the Klan's First Amendment Rights?" *The Village Voice* (October 9, 1990).

Review of current and past cases involving attempts to deny the Ku Klux Klan the right to parade or speak. Includes material on ACLU defense of the Klan's First Amendment rights.

820. LaMarche, Gara. "Where are All the Censors?" *Columbia Magazine* (December 1987).

Discussion by a prominent member of the ACLU Board of Directors of current threats to freedom of expression. Notes that there are no longer any official government censors in the United States and that censorship is often a result of private group pressure.

821. LaMarche, Gara and William B. Rubenstein. "The Love That Dare Not Speak." *The Nation*, 251 (November 5, 1990): 524–526.

Survey of censorship of forms of expression relating to gays and lesbians. Authors are a member of the ACLU Board of Directors (LaMarche) and director of the ACLU Lesbian and Gay Rights Project (Rubenstein).

822. Marsh, Dave. *50 Ways to Fight Censorship*. New York: Thunder's Mouth Press, 1991.

Book on censorship by a leading rock music critic. Recommendation #19 is to "Join the American Civil Liberties Union."

823. Meires, G. "Klanwatch, ACLU Debate Stance Toward KKK." *The Guardian*, 40 (November 4, 1987): 4.

Discussion of differences of opinion on how to deal with the Ku Klux Klan between ACLU and Klanwatch.

824. Minnesota Civil Liberties Union. *A Report of a Survey on Censorship in Public Elementary and High School Libraries and Public Libraries in Minnesota*. Minneapolis: Minnesota Civil Liberties Union, 1983.

Survey of censorship in Minnesota libraries.

825. Modenbach, G. "ACLU Wrong About KKK's Rights." *The Guardian*, 35 (February 23, 1983): 16.

Criticism of ACLU's defense of First Amendment rights of Ku Klux Klan from left-wing perspective.

826. Morland, Howard. *The Secret That Exploded*. New York: Random House, 1981.

First-hand account of the publication of the "secret" of the hydrogen bomb and the attempt by the federal government to prohibit publication of the *Progressive* magazine. ACLU represented the magazine in the case.

827. Neier, Aryeh. "Surveillance as Censorship." *Unamerican Activities: The Campaign Against the Underground Press*. San Francisco: City Lights Press, 1981.

Article on government spying on independent or "underground" press by the former executive director of the ACLU. Argues that surveillance constitutes a form of censorship.

828. Norwick, Kenneth, "Censorship." Kenneth Norwick, ed. *Lobbying For Freedom in the 1980s*. New York: G. P. Putnam's, 1983.

Discussion of lobbying tactics to combat censorship.

829. Shattuck, John H. F. and Allan Adler. "The Freedom of Information Act: Vital to the Democratic Principles of Our Nation." *First Principles*, 6 (July/August 1981): 1–5.

839. Haiman, Franklyn S. "Pornography: Its Social and Legal Implications." *Women's Law Reporter*, 8 (Summer 1985): 3–10.

    Discussion of First Amendment aspects of pornography. Author is a long-time ACLU leader.

840. Lynn, Barry. "Civil Rights Ordinances and the Attorney General's Commission: New Developments in Pornography Regulation." *Harvard Civil Rights—Civil Liberties Law Review*, 21 (1986): 27–125.

    Discussion of threats to freedom of expression posed by feminist anti-pornography ordinances and the Attorney General's Commission on pornography by a staff member of the ACLU Washington office.

841. National Coalition Against Censorship. *The Meese Commission Exposed*. New York: ACLU, 1986.

    Proceedings of a January, 1986 conference criticizing the Attorney General's Commission on Pornography. The ACLU is a member of the Coalition and speakers at the conference include several ACLU leaders.

4. Racist/Sexist Speech/College Campus Speech Codes

842. Davis, A. "ACLU to Investigate Dartmouth College." *In These Times*, 12 (June 22, 1988): 28.

    Article on ACLU affiliate's plans to investigate possible due process violations in disciplinary actions against conservative students at Dartmouth College

843. Gale, Mary Ellen. "On Curbing Racial Speech." *The Responsive Community*, I (Winter 1990/91): 47–58.

    Discussion of the problem of racist speech by leading member of the ACLU Board of Directors and ACLU of Southern California. Argues in favor of a policy of restricting offensive speech that is targeted at protected classes of persons. A good statement of the minority position within the ACLU on the racist speech issue.

Article on ACLU suit challenging Arkansas law requiring the teaching of scientific creationism.

861. Dorsen, Norman. "The Religion Clauses and Nonbelievers." *William and Mary Law Review*, 27 (1986, No. 5): 863–873.

    Article on the legal rights of atheists and agnostics by then-president of the ACLU.

862. Gilkey, Langdon. *Creationism on Trial: Evolution and God at Little Rock*. Minneapolis: Winston Press, 1985.

    Account of the Arkansas creationism case, by a professor of theology who served as an expert witness for the ACLU in the case.

863. Gutman, Jeremiah and Ted Bohn. "The Civil Liberties of Religious Minorities." Marc Galanter, ed. *Cults and New Religious Movements*. Washington, DC: American Psychiatric Association, 1989.

    Article on the legal rights of unpopular religious groups, particularly so-called religious "cults." Co-author Gutman is a long-time member of the ACLU Board of Directors.

864. Hale, J. P. "Judicial Policy-Making." *America*, 145 (August 29–September 5, 1981): 89–92.

    Criticism of ACLU opposition to government funding of church-related child care agencies in New York, from a Catholic perspective.

865. LaFollette, Marcel Chotkowski, ed. *Creationism, Science, and the Law: The Arkansas Case*. Cambridge, MA: MIT Press, 1983.

    Collection of articles on the Arkansas creationism law trial.

866. LaMarche, Gara. "Rites and Rights." *Science Digest* (January 1982).

Defense of ACLU policy on defending the free speech rights of hate groups by member of ACLU Board of Directors.

855. Weiner, Jon. "Free Speech for Campus Bigots?" *The Nation*, 250 (February 26, 1990): 272–276.

Survey of current campus free speech controversies. Discussion of successful ACLU challenge to speech code at the University of Michigan.

5. Religious Liberty

856. "Away With a Manger." *The New Republic*, 189 (October 31, 1983): 4.

Criticism of ACLU suit against nativity scene on government property in Pawtucket, Rhode Island.

857. Bruno, Robert J. *Constitutional Analysis of a Voucher Plan in Minnesota*. Minneapolis: Minnesota Civil Liberties Union Foundation, 1988.

Analysis of voucher plan providing tuition reimbursement for parents who send their children to private or parochial schools. Argues that the idea violates the separation of church and state by providing state support for religious schools.

858. Cameron, S. C. "Does Your Church Meet in a School? It Won't If the ACLU Has its Way." *Christianity Today*, 28 (February 1984).

Article critical of ACLU position opposing meetings by religious groups in public school buildings.

859. Cook, H. "Monkey Trial Redivivus." *Christian Century*, 99 (January, 6–13, 1982): 6–7.

Article on ACLU suit challenging Arkansas law on the teaching of "creation science" in the public schools.

860. "'Creation'-Teaching Law Will Be Tested in Court." *Christianity Today*, 25 (September 4, 1981): 54–56.

850. Hentoff, Nat. "What's Happening to the ACLU?" *Village Voice* (May 15, 1990). "Putting the First Amendment on Trial." *Ibid.* (May 22, 1990). "A Dissonant First Amendment Fugue." *Ibid.*, (June 5, 1990). "An Endangered Species: A First Amendment Absolutist." *Ibid.*, (June 12, 1990). "Civil Liberties Shootout." *Ibid.*, (June 19, 1990).

Series of articles on the issue of college policies restricting racist speech. Good material on the debate within the ACLU over this issue. Author is critical of advocates of restrictive policies. Account of debate over racist speech in the Civil Liberties Union of Massachusetts.

851. LaMarche, Gara. "With Racism on the Rise, Do US Campuses Need to Limit Speech?" *Index on Censorship* (June 1990): 29–30.

International perspective on campus free speech issue by a prominent member of the ACLU.

852. Lawrence, Charles. "If He Hollers Let Him Go: Regulating Racist Speech on Campus." *Duke Law Journal*, 1990 (June, No. 3): 431–484.

Longer version of paper delivered at the 1989 ACLU Biennial Conference. Advocates restrictions on racist speech. Original paper was delivered at a panel session also featuring the original version of Strossen's contrary view (#853).

853. Strossen, Nadine. "Regulating Racist Speech on Campus: A Modest Proposal?" *Duke Law Journal*, 1990 (1990, No. 3): 484–573.

Discussion of racist speech issue by future president of the ACLU. Longer version of paper delivered at the 1989 ACLU Biennial Conference in response to Lawrence (#852).

854. Strum, Philippa. "The Right to Hear All Sides." *New Outlook*, 31 (June 1988): 26.

844. Gale, Mary Ellen. "Reimagining the First Amendment: Racist Speech and Equal Liberty." *St. John's Law Review*, 65 (Winter 1991): 119–185.

> Longer and more detailed version of #843.

845. Haiman, Franklyn S. "The Remedy is More Speech." *The American Prospect* (Summer 1991): 30–35.

> Article argues that the proper response to offensive speech is more speech rather than restriction. Author is long-time ACLU leader.

846. Haiman, Franklyn S. "Sexist Speech and the First Amendment." *Communication Education*, 40 (January 1991): 1–5.

> Article discusses First Amendment protection of offensive sexist speech. Author is a long-time ACLU leader.

847. Haiman, Franklyn S. "Words That May Injure: Contrasts in French and American Free Speech Law." *Free Speech Yearbook*, 28 (Carbondale: Southern Illinois University, 1990): 8–29.

> Article offers an international perspective on protection of offensive speech under the First Amendment. Author is a long-time ACLU leader.

848. Hentoff, Nat. "The ACLU Does the Right Thing." *The Village Voice* (November 13, 1990).

> Article on the October, 1990 ACLU Board of Directors meeting at which it adopted a policy opposing restrictions on racist speech.

849. Hentoff, Nat. "A Congressman Moves to Protect Free Speech at Colleges." *The Village Voice* (April 9, 1991).

> Article on federal legislation proposed by conservative congressman Henry Hyde to protect free speech on college campuses. ACLU endorses legislation.

Contemporary Civil Liberties Issues, 1980–1991 161

Discussion of First Amendment rights of so-called religious "cults" by prominent ACLU leader.

867. Lewin, R. "Creationism Goes on Trial in Arkansas." *Science*, 214 (December 4, 1981): 1101+.

    Article on ACLU suit challenging Arkansas law on the teaching of "creation science."

868. Lowther, W. "Darwin vs. the Creationists." *Maclean's*, 94 (December 21, 1981): 31.

    Article on ACLU suit challenging Arkansas scientific creationism law.

869. Lynn, Barry. "What is Equal Access?" *Civil Liberties*, No. 351 (Fall 1984): 5

    Discussion of ACLU opposition to new Equal Access law permitting student religious groups to hold meetings in public schools. Explains ACLU opposition to the law.

870. Nelkin, Dorothy. *The Creation Controversy: Science or Scripture in the Schools.* Boston: Beacon Press, 1982.

    Account of the Arkansas creationism case. Considerable background material on the history of science textbooks and the rise of scientific creationism.

871. Raloff, J. "Of God and Darwin." *Science News*, 121 (January 2, 1982): 12–13.

    Article on ACLU suit challenging Arkansas law requiring the teaching of scientific creationism.

872. Redlich, Norman. "Religious Liberty." Norman Dorsen, ed. *Our Endangered Rights.* New York: Pantheon Books, 1984. Pp. 259–280.

    Discussion of church and state issues, as of the mid-1980s.

873. Strossen, Nadine. "A Constitutional Analysis of the Equal Access Act's Standards Governing Public School Student

Religious Meetings." *Harvard Journal on Legislation*, 24 (Winter 1987): 117–190.

Detailed scholarly analysis of the federal Equal Access Act permitting religious groups to hold meetings in public school buildings under certain conditions. Author was then co-general counsel of the ACLU and future ACLU president.

874. Strossen, Nadine. "'Secular Humanism' and 'Scientific Creationism': Proposed Standards for Reviewing Curricular Decisions Affecting Students' Religious Freedom." *Ohio State Law Journal*, 47 (1986): 333–407.

Analysis of conflict between civil liberties principles of the free exercise of religion and separation of church and state by a prominent ACLU leader and future ACLU president.

875. Swomley, John. "The Decade Ahead in Church-State Issues." *Christian Century* (February 25, 1981).

Discussion of current church-state issues by a prominent member of the ACLU Board of Directors.

876. Swomley, John. "Public Schools Embattled Over Prayer." *Christian Century* (July 20, 1983).

Article on current controversies over prayer in public schools. Written by the chair of the ACLU Church-State Committee.

877. Swomley, John. "A Toe Hold for Religion in Public Education." *Christian Century* (February 15, 1984).

Article critical of the Equal Access Act permitting student religious groups to hold meetings in public schools under certain limited conditions. Written by the chair of the ACLU Church-State Committee. Argues that the Equal Access Act violates the separation of church and state.

878. Weatherly, J. "Creationists Concerned About Court Test of Arkansas Law." *Christianity Today*, 25 (September 18, 1981): 40–41.

Article on ACLU suit challenging Arkansas law on the teaching of "creation science."

C. DUE PROCESS OF LAW/CRIME/POLICE MISCONDUCT

[See #15, #31, #35, #51, #53 #62.]

1. General

879. ACLU. *Confronting Crime: New Directions*. New York: ACLU, 1990.

Report of an ACLU-sponsored conference on crime policy, September 14–16, 1989. Includes transcript of comments by leading police chiefs, criminologists, civil libertarians, and others. Suggests policies that would deal with crime without violating individual rights.

880. ACLU. *The Lessons of ABSCAM —A Public Policy Report by the American Civil Liberties Union*. New York: ACLU, 1982.

Discussion of civil liberties problems in the celebrated investigation of public corruption known as ABSCAM.

881. Berger, Vivian. "The Chiropractor as Brain Surgeon: Defense Lawyering in Capital Cases." *New York University Review of Law and Social Change*, 18 (1990–1991): 245–254.

Discussion of various aspects of representing persons facing capital punishment by law professor who is co-general counsel for the ACLU and who represents death row clients for the NAACP Legal Defense Fund.

882. Berger, Vivian. "Justice Delayed or Justice Denied?—A Comment on Recent Proposals to Reform Death Penalty

Habeas Corpus." *Columbia Law Review*, 90 (October 1990): 1665–1714.

Discussion of proposals to limit appeals by persons facing the death penalty. Written by law professor who is co-general counsel for the ACLU and who represents death row inmates for the NAACP Legal Defense Fund.

883. Berger, Vivian. "The Supreme Court and Defense Counsel: Old Roads, New Paths—A Dead End?" *Columbia Law Review*, 86 (January 1986): 9–116.

Discussion of recent developments in the law of the right to counsel by law professor who is co-general counsel for the ACLU.

884. Blumner, Robyn and Loren Siegel. "Where is U.S. Drug Policy Headed?" *Civil Liberties*, No. 373 (Spring/Summer 1991): 5.

Critical assessment of the "war on drugs" and its impact on civil liberties. Co-authored by the director of the Florida ACLU (Blumner) and a member of the ACLU national staff (Siegel).

885. Glasser, Ira. "Let's Get Real on Crime." *Civil Liberties*, No. 366 (Spring 1989): 12.

Criticism of popular "get tough" crime control proposals by the executive director of the ACLU. Argues in favor of policies that do not violate civil liberties and address the underlying causes of crime.

886. Glasser, Ira. "Taboo No More?" *Civil Liberties*, No. 368 (Fall/Winter, 1990): 12.

Discussion of the impact of the "war on drugs" on civil liberties by the executive director of the ACLU. Calls for open discussion of legalization of drugs as an alternative national policy.

887. Hentoff, Nat. "The Insatiable RICO Octopus." *The Village Voice* (October 3, 1989).

Article critical of federal Racketeer Influenced and Corrupt Organizations Act (RICO). Emphasizes potential threats to free speech. Article focuses on ACLU opposition to present law.

888. Hentoff, Nat. "RICO Stalks the Press." *The Village Voice* (October 17, 1989).

    Article on use of federal Racketeer Influenced and Corrupt Organizations Act (RICO) against anti-abortion newspaper. Cites ACLU opposition to current RICO law.

889. "Ollie's Allies." *The New Republic*, 199 (August 29, 1988): 4.

    Article on ACLU amicus brief on behalf of Oliver North, arguing that his conviction in the Iran-Contra affair was obtained in violation of his Fifth Amendment rights.

890. Jost, Kenneth. "The ACLU's Bad Bargain." *The National Law Journal* (May 8, 1989).

    Article critical of ACLU position opposing current Racketeer Influenced and Corrupt Organizations Act (RICO).

891. Rudovsky, David. "Criminal Justice: The Accused." Norman Dorsen, ed. *Our Endangered Rights*. New York: Pantheon Books, 1984. Pp. 203–220.

    Article summarizing developments in the law of due process related to criminal suspects as of the mid-1980s.

892. Schwartz, Louis B. "Civil Liberties vs. the ACLU." *The New Republic*, 183 (July 26, 1980): 20–23.

    Critical of ACLU opposition to proposed revision of federal criminal code. Argues that positive features of the proposed law outweigh the negative.

893. Shattuck, John H. F. and David Landau. "Civil Liberties and Criminal Code Reform." *Journal of Criminal Law and Criminology*, 72 (1981): 914–934.

Analysis of threats to civil liberties in proposed revision of federal criminal code.

894. Siegel, Loren. "Law Enforcement and Civil Liberties: We Can Have Both." *Civil Liberties*, 345 (February 1983): 5–8.

Discussion of civil liberties aspects of the "war on crime" by a member of the ACLU national staff. Argues that many crime control measures violate civil liberties and that other effective anti-crime measures are consistent with civil liberties principles.

895. Will, George F. "Is The ACLU Being Reasonable?" *Newsweek*, 101 (January 31, 1983): 80.

Conservative criticism of ACLU opposition to police sobriety check points.

2. Police Misconduct

896. ACLU. *On the Line: Police Brutality and Its Remedies*. New York: ACLU, 1991.

ACLU report on police misconduct. Issued in the wake of the highly-publicized beating of Rodney King by Los Angeles police officers in March, 1991.

897. Adler, Allan, and Jay Peterzell. "Courts Curtail Political Surveillance by Police Intelligence Units." *First Principles*, 6 (March/April 1981): 1–3.

Article summarizing recent law suits against spying on political groups by local police departments. Covers suits in New York City, Chicago, Detroit, along with other developments.

898. Balter, Michael. "Peering Cops." *Progressive*, 45 (September 1981): 18.

Discusses lawsuit by ACLU of Southern California challenging spying by Los Angeles police department.

899. Cassel, Doug. "Chicago FBI Settlement." *First Principles*, 6 (June 1981): 1–6.

Discussion of settlement of ACLU suit against FBI spying against political groups in Chicago. Argues that the settlement is the best one yet in any of the recent spying suits.

900. Donner, Frank. *Protectors of Privilege: Red Squads and Police Repression in Urban America.* Berkeley: University of California Press, 1990.

    History of police spying on political groups. Special emphasis in New York City, Philadelphia, Chicago, and Los Angeles. Other cities also covered. Extensive treatment of ACLU law suits designed to end police spying. Author was director of the ACLU Project on Political Surveillance in the 1970s. Material on the book based on the project's work.

901. Hentoff, Nat. "Chicago Shows Us Yokels How to Leash a Red Squad." *The Village Voice* (June 24, 1981).

    Article on settlement of ACLU suit against spying by the Chicago police. Critical of settlement in similar suit in New York City.

902. Hentoff, Nat. "The Dread 'Nunchakus'." *The Village Voice* (November 7, 1989).

    Article critical of police practices in arresting anti-abortion demonstrators in San Diego. Accuses the police of using unnecessary force. Critical of the local ACLU affiliate for failing to protest police tactics.

903. Hentoff, Nat. "How We All Got Screwed in the N.Y. Red Squad Case." *The Village Voice* (June 17, 1981).

    Article critical of settlement in New York Civil Liberties Union suit against spying by the New York City Police Department.

904. Hentoff, Nat. "NYPD Red Squad's Greatest Scam—Going Legit." *The Village Voice* (June 3, 1981).

    Article critical of settlement of New York Civil Liberties Union suit against spying by the New York City police department. Argues that the settlement legitimizes spying.

905. Hentoff, Nat. "Putting a Price Tag on the First Amendment." *The Village Voice* (October 10, 1989).

    Article on police tactics in arresting anti-abortion demonstrators. Praises staff of California ACLU affiliates for challenging practices that infringe on the rights of demonstrators. (See also #902.)

906. Jacobs, Jim and Richard Soble. "A Blow Against the Red Squads." *The Nation*, 232 (February 14, 1981): 168–170.

    Article on the settlement of ACLU law suits against police spying.

907. Peterzell, Jay. "Surveillance and Disruption of Anti-Nuclear Protest." *First Principles*, 6 (December 1980): 1+.

    Article on illegal surveillance of anti-nuclear energy protests by federal, state, and local police forces along with private security agencies.

908. "The Red Squad Settlements Controversy." *The Nation*, 233 (July 11, 1981): 43–46.

    Article on settlement of ACLU suits against police spying. Criticism of settlements on the grounds that they fail to elminate police spying completely. (See also #901, #903, #904.)

909. Stern, Gary M. *The FBI's Misguided Probe of CISPES*. Washington, DC: Center For National Security Studies, 1988.

    Article on FBI spying on the Committee in Solidarity with the People of El Salvador. Argues that the investigation violated the First Amendment rights of CISPES members.

910. Walker, Samuel. "The Politics of Police Accountability: The Police Spying Ordinance as a Case Study." Erika S. Fairchild and Vincent J. Webb, eds. *The Politics of Crime*

and Criminal Justice. Beverly Hills, CA: Sage Publications, 1985. Pp. 144–157.

History and analysis of a Seattle ordinance restricting police intelligence gathering. ACLU affiliate was a leading member of the coalition that advocated the ordinance. Ordinance was based on an ACLU proposal for controlling the FBI. Argues that the ordinance created an innovative procedure for independent monitoring of police activity.

D. EQUAL PROTECTION

1. Race Discrimination

[See #41, #58.]

911. ACLU. *In Contempt of Congress and the Courts*. New York: ACLU, 1984.

Criticism of the policies of the Reagan administration on civil rights. Argues that the administration failed to enforce existing civil rights laws, ignored the intent of Congress, and violated established case law on civil rights.

912. ACLU. *Ten Years of Struggling for Equal Justice for Mexican-Americans in South Texas*. New York: ACLU, 1982.

Report of activities of ACLU South Texas Project on behalf of Mexican-Americans. Published in both English and Spanish language editions.

913. Chepesiuk, Ron. "Advocate of the Disenfranchised." *The Progressive*, 54 (January 1990): 14.

Profile of Laughlin McDonald, director of ACLU Voting Rights Project.

914. Days, Drew S., III. "Racial Justice." Norman Dorsen, ed. *Our Endangered Rights*. New York: Pantheon Books, 1984, pp. 75–97.

Article on recent developments in the law of race discrimination, as of the mid-1960s.

915. Glasser, Ira. "Affirmative Action and the Legacy of Racial Injustice." Phyllis A. Katz and Dalmas A. Taylor, eds. *Eliminating Racism*. New York: Plenum, 1988. Pp. 341–357.

Discussion and defense of affirmative action as a strategy for eliminating racial discrimination, by the ACLU executive director.

916. Grossman, George S. *The Sovereignty of American Indian Tribes: A Matter of Legal History*. Minneapolis: Minnesota Civil Liberties Foundation, 1979.

Analysis of the legal status of Native American tribes by the Minnesota Civil Libertes Union.

917. Norton, Eleanor Holmes. "Affirmative Action: Race and Sex Conscious Remedies are Working—and Must Be Continued." *Civil Liberties*, No. 342 (May 1982): 5–6.

Argument in favor of affirmative action by former ACLU Associate legal director and future chair of ACLU National Advisory Committee.

918. Rocah, David. "One More Time: *Brown v. Board of Education*—Number 3—Reaches the Supreme Court." *Civil Liberties*, No. 373 (Spring/Summer 1991): 9.

Article on ACLU participation in current school desegregation suit in Topeka, Kansas, site of original 1954 *Brown v. Board of Education* suit.

2. Women's Rights

[See #26, #67, #748.]

919. ACLU. *Women's Rights Project—Information Sheet 1991*. New York: ACLU, 1991.

Summary of recent activities of the ACLU Women's Rights Project.

920. ACLU. *With Liberty and Justice For Women—The ACLU's Contributions to Ten Years of Struggle For Equal Rights.* New York: ACLU, 1982.

Ten-year progress report on the activities of ACLU Women's Rights Project.

921. ACLU and the NAACP Legal Defense Fund. *Justice Denied: The Loss of Civil Rights After the Grove City College Decision.* New York: ACLU, 1986.

Critical analysis of the decline in federal efforts to end sex discrimination in colleges and universities following the Supreme Court's decisiion in *Grove City College v. Bell* (1984).

922. Dworkin, Andrea. "The ACLU: Bait and Switch." *Yale Journal of Law and Feminism,* I (Spring 1989): 37–39.

Bitter attack on the ACLU. Accuses the ACLU of deceptive practices with respect to women's rights issues. See reply, #924.

923. Estrich, Susan R. and Virginia Kerr. "Sexual Justice." Norman Dorsen, ed. *Our Endangered Rights.* New York: Pantheon Books, 1984. Pp. 98–133.

Discussion of women's rights issues as of the mid-1980s.

924. Gale, Mary Ellen, and Nadine Strossen. "The Real ACLU." *Yale Journal of Law and Feminism,* 2 (Fall 1989): 161–187.

Reply to criticisms of ACLU regarding women's rights expressed by Andrea Dworkin (#922) by two prominent members of the ACLU Board of Directors, including the future president of the ACLU (Strossen).

925. Moss, Kary. "Substance Abuse During Pregnancy." *Harvard Women's Law Journal,* 13 (1990): 278–297.

Discussion of proposals to regulate and/or criminalize use of potentially dangerous substances by pregnant women. Written by staff attorney with the ACLU Women's Rights Project.

926. Shack, Barbara. "Women's Rights." Kenneth Norwick, ed. *Lobbying For Freedom in the 1980s.* New York: G.P. Putnam's, 1983.

    Discussion of tactics for lobbying for women's rights issues. Included in a collection of essays on lobbying on civil liberties issues.

E. NATIONAL SECURITY

[See #14, #38, #39, #57, #59.]

927. ACLU. *Ending the Cold War at Home: Public Policy Report.* Washington, DC: ACLU, 1991.

    Report issued for ACLU-sponsored conference on ending the Cold War at Home, February, 1991. Discusses Cold War-related violations of civil liberties, including government secrecy, restrictions on the rights of government employees, restrictions on the free flow of information and ideas, government spying, and other issues.

928. Adler, Allan. "Export Controls and Scientific Information." *First Principles,* 8 (January/February 1983): 1–4.

    Article on the use of export control laws to restrict the free flow of scientific information in and out of the United States.

929. Andres, Monica. "The Quality of Censorship: What the CIA Defines as Damaging to the National Security." *First Principles,* 5 (May 1980): 6–8.

    Critique of CIA standards in demanding censorship of publications on national security grounds.

930. Berman, Jerry J. "Political Surveillance in the Reagan Era." *First Principles*, 10 (May/June 1985): 1–3.

Article on recent FBI surveillance of political groups in the United States.

931. Center For National Security Studies. *Covert Operations and the Democratic Process: The Implications of the Iran/Contra Affair.* Washington, DC: CNSS, 1987.

Discussion of the civil liberties aspects of the Iran/Contra scandal.

932. Center For National Security Studies. *Former Secrets: Government Records Made Public Through the Freedom of Information Act.* Washington, DC: CNSS, 1982.

Summary of the most important revelations about government misconduct based on files obtained through the Freedom of Information Act. Includes list of books and articles based on material obtained through the FOIA.

933. Dorsen, Norman. "Foreign Affairs and Civil Liberties." *American Journal of International Law*, 83 (October 1989): 840–850.

Discussion of the civil liberties aspects of American foreign policy by then-president of the ACLU.

934. Glasser, Ira. "The ACLU and the F.O.I.A. Bill." *The Nation*, 238 (June 30, 1984): 786.

Further explanation of ACLU position on amendments to the Freedom of Information Act. See criticisms of ACLU, #954, #955, #956.

935. Glasser, Ira. "The Case for the New F.O.I.A. Bill." *The Nation*, 238 (June 2, 1984): 669–672.

Explains ACLU position in support of amendments to the Freedom of Information Act regarding certain CIA files. See criticisms, #954, #955, #956.

936. Glasser, Ira. "Nuclear Power, Rapid Technological Advancement, and Democratic Values." *New York*

University Review of Law and Social Change, 10 (1980–1981, No. 2): 347–355.

Discussion of threats to civil liberties posed by technology and nuclear power by the ACLU executive director.

937. Glasser, Ira. "The Power to Initiate War Must Be Returned to Congress." *Civil Liberties*, No. 348 (Winter 1984): 1.

Explanation of ACLU support for the 1971 War Powers Act requiring Congressional approval of commitment of American military forces to combat. Argues for the need to strengthen the law.

938. Godfrey, E. Drexel. "Our Wrong Rush to Unleash the C.I.A." *First Principles*, 5 (March/April 1980): 16+.

Argues against current proposals to ease restrictions on covert activity by the CIA. Author is a former CIA official.

939. Halperin, Morton H. "The Balancing Test." *First Principles*, 7 (May/June 1982): 12+.

Critique of recent Executive Order on the classification of government documents by the Reagan administration.

940. Halperin, Morton H. "The CIA on Campus." *First Principles*, 8 (November/December 1982): 1+.

Discussion of proposals to regulate clandestine CIA-sponsored research in American colleges and universities.

941. Halperin, Morton H. "Covert Operations: The Real Issue." *First Principles*, 5 (May 1980): 1–5.

General discussion of covert activity by the CIA and critique of current proposals for easing restrictions on those activities. Author is the director of the ACLU Washington office.

942. Halperin, Morton H. "Declaring War." *First Principles*, 9 (September/October 1983): 12+.

Discussion of the War Powers Act and the constitutional requirement that only Congress has the power to declare war.

943. Halperin, Morton H. "Evaluating Covert Operations." *First Principles*, 10 (November/December 1984): 8+.

Discussion of CIA covert operations by then-director of the Center for National Security Studies and future director of the ACLU Washington Office.

944. Halperin, Morton H. "National Security." Norman Dorsen, ed. *Our Endangered Rights*. New York: Pantheon Books, 1984. Pp. 281–295.

General survey of national security issues as of the mid-1980s by the director of the Center for National Security Studies and future director of the ACLU Washington Office.

945. Halperin, Morton H. "Reagan's National Security Censorship." *First Principles*, 8 (March/April 1983): 1–2.

Criticism of censorship under the national security rationale by the Reagan administration.

946. Halperin, Morton H. "The State of Reform." *First Principles*, 6 (October 1980): 1, 14.

Discusses current status of proposals in Congress to enact legislative charters governing the FBI and the CIA.

947. Halperin, Morton H. "What's Needed to Enact a CIA Charter." *First Principles*, 5 (July 1980): 1, 15.

Explains ACLU proposal for a legislative charter governing the activities of the CIA.

948. Halperin, Morton and Allan Adler. "There is No Deal." *The Nation*, 237 (September 24, 1983): 234.

Reply to criticisms of the ACLU's position on amendments to the Freedom of Information Act regarding the CIA (see #954, #955, #956).

949. Halperin, Morton H. and Gary M. Stern. "Lawful Wars: Restoring Congress' Role in the Overt and Covert Use of Force." *Foreign Policy*, 72 (Fall 1988): 5–27. Reprinted: Washington, DC: Center For National Security Studies, 1988.

   Article on the civil liberties aspects of the power to declare war. Argues in favor of restoring the authority of Congress to declare war.

950. "Hanging Together." *The Nation*, 233 (November 7, 1981): 459–461. "Discussion." *Ibid.*, 233 (November 21, 1981): 522.

   Article on ACLU opposition to proposed federal law creating criminal penalties for publishing the names of CIA agents.

951. "Hidden Issue: ACLU vs CIA." *The Nation*, 247 (October 31, 1988): 405.

   Article on the attacks on the ACLU during the 1988 presidential election. Argues that questions related to the CIA are the real issues behind the attacks.

952. "The Iran-Contra Affair." *Civil Liberties*, No 359 (Winter 1987): 1.

   Discussion of the civil liberties aspects of the illegal diversion of money from arms sales to Iran to support the Contras in Nicaragua.

953. Lynch, Mark H. "The FOIA and the CIA." *First Principles*, 9 (September/October 1983): 1–4.

   Published version of testimony on behalf of the ACLU before the Senate Intelligence Committee regarding the application of the Freedom of Information Act to the CIA.

954. MacKenzie, Angus. "The Operational Files Exemption." *The Nation*, 237 (September 24, 1983): 231–234. "Welcome Reversal." *The Nation*, 240 (April 27, 1985): 485.

Articles critical of ACLU position on proposed amendments to the Freedom of Information Act relating to the CIA.

955. McGehee, R. "ACLU and the F.O.I.A. Bill." *The Nation*, 38 (June 30, 1984): 786.

Article critical of ACLU position on proposed amendments to the Freedom of Information Act relating to the CIA.

956. Peck, Keenen. "Strange Bedfellows." *The Progressive*, 48 (November 1984): 28–31.

Criticism of ACLU position of proposed amendments to the Freedom of Information Act relating to the CIA.

957. Peterzell, Jay. "Reagan's Covert Action Policy (I)." *First Principles*, 7 (January 1982): 1–7. [Part Two], *ibid.*, 7 (February 1982): 1–10. [Part Three], *ibid.*, 7 (March 1982): 1–7. [Part Four], *ibid.*, 8 (September/October 1982): 1–9. [Part V], *ibid.*, 9 (January/February 1984): 1–5.

Multi-part series criticizing covert action policies by the Reagan administration.

958. Peterzell, Jay. *Reagan's Secret Wars*. Washington, DC: Center For National Security Studies, 1984.

Analysis of military actions conducted by the Reagan administration. Argues that they violate the law relating to congressional authority to make war.

959. Shattuck, John H. F. "National Security a Decade After Watergate." *democracy*, 3 (Winter 1983): 56–63.

Analysis of national security issues in the decade following the Watergate crisis by then-director of the ACLU Washington office. Argues that the courts and Congress have created a national security exception to the First Amendment.

960. "The Snepp Decision: Why the Court Made a Mistake." *First Principles*, 5 (June 1980): 1–4.

Analysis of 1980 Supreme Court decision upholding CIA censorship of book by former CIA agent Frank Snepp.

F. PRISONERS' RIGHTS

[See #15, #35, #53.]

961. ACLU. National Prison Project. *1990 AIDS in Prison Bibliography*. Washington, DC: National Prison Project, 1990.

Bibliography on the issue of AIDS in penal institutions.

962. ACLU. National Prison Project. *AIDS in Prisons: The Facts for Inmates and Officers*. Washington, DC: National Prison Project, nd.

Discussion of AIDS and policies related to AIDS in penal institutions.

963. ACLU. National Prison Project. *Bibliography of Women in Prison Issues*. Washington, DC: National Prison Project, nd.

Bibliography on issues related to women in penal institutions.

964. ACLU. National Prison Project. *The Prisoners Assistance Directory*. 8th edition. Washington, DC: National Prison Project, 1986.

Directory of services available to prisoners (e.g., legal assistance, family support, education, etc.). Revised regularly.

965. ACLU. National Prison Project. *Status Report*. Washington, DC: National Prison Project, periodically.

Report on current prisoners' rights cases handled by the National Prison Project.

966. ACLU. National Prison Project. *A Primer for Jail Litigators*. Washington, DC: National Prison Project, 1984.

    Litigation manual for lawyers challenging unconstitutional conditions in local jails.

967. Bronstein, Alvin J. "Criminal Justice: Prisons and Penology." Norman Dorsen, ed. *Our Endangered Rights*. New York: Pantheon Books, 1984. Pp. 221–234.

    Discussion of the state of prisoners' rights, as of the mid-1980s, by the director of the ACLU National Prison Project.

968. Bronstein, Alvin J. "Offender Rights Litigation: Historical and Future Developments." Ira P. Robbins, ed. *Prisoners' Rights Sourcebook*. Vol. 2. New York: Clark Boardman, 1980. Pp. 5–28.

    Overview of the history of prisoners' rights litigation, its impact, and its future, by the director of the ACLU National Prison Project.

969. Bronstein, Alvin J. "Reform Without Change: The Future of Prisoners' Rights." *Civil Liberties Review*, 4 (1977): 27–45.

    Pessimistic assessment of the impact of prisoners' rights litigation as of the mid-1970s by the director of the ACLU National Prison Project.

970. Jacobs, James B. *New Perspectives on Prisons and Imprisonment*. Ithaca, NY: Cornell University Press, 1983.

    Detailed and thoughtful analysis of the impact of prisoners' rights litigation by one of the leading authorities on the history of the prison. Includes specific reference to the ACLU National Prison Project. See especially the chapter on "The Prisoners' Rights Movement and Its Impacts."

G. PRIVACY

1. General

[See #54, #55.]

971. Bender, Paul. "Privacy." Norman Dorsen, ed. *Our Endangered Rights.* New York: Pantheon Books, 1984. Pp. 237–258.

    Overview of privacy rights issues as of the mid-1980s.

972. Gutman, Jeremiah. "Access." Herman Schuchman, et al., eds. *Confidentiality of Health Records: The Meeting of Law, Ethics, and Clinical Issues.* New York: Gerdner Press, 1982.

    Discussion of civil liberties aspects of access to and confidentiality of health records. Written by a long-time member of the ACLU Board of Directors.

2. Lesbian and Gay People, Rights of

[See #23, #37, #40.]

973. ACLU. Lesbian and Gay Rights Project. *AIDS: Basic Documents.* New York: ACLU, 1987.

    Collection of medical and legal materials related to AIDS. Excellent source of material.

974. ACLU. Lesbian and Gay Rights Project. *AIDS and Civil Liberties.* New York: ACLU, 1986.

    Short pamphlet on civil liberties issues related to AIDS.

975. ACLU. Lesbian and Gay Rights Project. *Epidemic of Fear: A Survey of AIDS Discrimination in the 1980s and Policy Recommendations for the 1990s.* New York: ACLU, 1990.

    Detailed analysis of AIDS and discrimination against persons with AIDS by the ACLU Lesbian and Gay Rights

Project. Includes recommendations for public policies related to AIDS that would not violate civil liberties.

976. Bullough, Vern L. "Lesbianism, Homosexuality, and the ACLU." *Journal of Homosexuality*, 13 (Fall 1986): 23– 33.

    History of ACLU policy on the rights of homosexuals from the 1950s through the 1980s.

977. Frieberg, P. "ACLU to Launch New Gay Rights Project." *The Advocate*, 414 (February 19, 1985): 16.

    Brief article on ACLU decision to create a special project on lesbian and gay rights.

978. Frieberg, P. "Nan Hunter to Head ACLU Lesbian/Gay Rights Project." *The Advocate*, 449 (June 24, 1986): 15.

    Brief article on Nan Hunter, director of new ACLU Lesbian and Gay Rights Project.

979. Gostin, Lawrence O., William J. Curran and Mary E. Clark. "The Case Against Compulsory Casefinding in Controlling AIDS—Testing, Screening and Reporting." *American Journal of Law and Medicine*, 12 (1986, No. 1): 7– 53.

    Detailed article arguing against compelled disclosure of sexual partners as a strategy for controlling AIDS. Co-author Gostin is a prominent member of the ACLU Board of Directors.

980. Hook, Ronald W. *The Constitutional Right of Privacy: Sodomy Laws*. Minneapolis: Minnesota Civil Liberties Union Foundation, 1981.

    Report on state sodomy laws by the Minnesota Civil Liberties Union.

981. Hunter, Nan. "AIDS Prevention and Civil Liberties: The False Security of Mandatory Testing." *AIDS and Public Policy Journal*, 2 (Summer/Fall 1987): 1–10.

Critique of mandatory testing for HIV infection by then-director of the ACLU Lesbian and Gay Rights Project.

982. Katz, Jonathan Ned. "Gay Couples Deserve the Rights and Benefits of Partnership." *Civil Liberties*, 363 (Winter 1988): 10.

   Article argues for granting gay couples the same legal rights enjoyed by heterosexual married couples.

983. Stoddard, Thomas B. "Gay Rights." Kenneth Norwick, ed. *Lobbying For Freedom in the 1980s*. New York: G. P. Putnam's, 1983.

   Discussion of tactics for lobbying on behalf of gay rights issues. Included in a collection of essays on lobbying on civil liberties issues.

984. Varady, M. "Dreaming Big/ACLU Attorney Susan McGreivy." *The Advocate*, 496 (April 12, 1988): 40.

   Sketch of staff attorney with ACLU of Southern California focusing on lesbian and gay rights issues.

3. Reproductive Freedom

[See #16, #24, #67.]

985. ACLU. *The Case Against a Constitutional Convention on Abortion*. New York: ACLU, nd.

   Pamphlet presenting ACLU arguments against anti-abortion proposal for a constitutional convention to draft an amendment outlawing abortion.

986. ACLU. Reproductive Freedom Project. *Docket*. New York: ACLU, annual.

   Summary of current cases being handled by the ACLU Reproductive Freedom Project. Published annually.

987. ACLU. Reproductive Freedom Project. *No Way Out: Young, Pregnant, and Trapped by the Law.* New York: ACLU, 1991.

    Pamphlet on problems facing pregnant minors as a consequence of recent laws restricting abortion rights.

988. ACLU. Reproductive Freedom Project. *Parental Notification Laws: Their Catastrophic Impact on Teenagers' Right to Abortion.* New York: ACLU, 1986.

    Report on the impact of so-called "parental notification" laws requiring minors to notify parents and/or obtain parental permission for abortions. For subsequent report, see #990.

989. ACLU. Reproductive Freedom Project. *Preserving the Right to Choose: How to Cope with Violence and Disruption at Abortion Clinics.* New York: ACLU, 1986.

    Pamphlet on legal issues surrounding anti-abortion tactics against abortion clinics. Includes discussion of strategies for responding to different kinds of disruptive tactics.

990. ACLU. Reproductive Freedom Project. *Shattering the Dreams of Young Women: The Tragic Consequences of Parental Involvement Laws.* New York: ACLU, 1991.

    Report on the impact of so-called "parental notification" laws requiring minors to notify and/or obtain parental permission for abortions. (See also #987, #988.)

991. ACLU. Reproductive Freedom Project. *The So-Called Human Life Amendment.* New York: ACLU, 1981.

    Pamphlet arguing against proposed amendment to the U. S. Constitution to prohibit abortions.

992. ACLU. Reproductive Freedom Project. *Women's Legal Guide to Reproductive Rights.* New York: ACLU, 1981.

    Summary of current reproductive rights issues.

993. Benshoof, Janet. "The Chastity Act: Government Manipulation of Abortion Information and the First Amendment." *Harvard Law Review*, 1010 (June 1985): 1916–1937.

Critical analysis of the federal "chastity act," involving federal government support of programs designed to prevent sexual activity outside of marriage. Written by the director of the ACLU Reproductive Freedom Project.

994. Benshoof, Janet. "The Establishment Clause and Government-Funded Natural Family Planning Programs: Is the Constitution Dancing to a New Rhythm?" *NYU Journal of International Law and Policy*, 20 (Fall 1987): 1–33.

Detailed discussion of federal government programs designed to promote natural family planning. Discusses possible violations of separation of church and state. Written by the director of the ACLU Reproductive Freedom Project.

995. Benshoof, Janet. "Reproductive Freedom." Kenneth Norwick, ed. *Lobbying For Freedom in the 1980s*. New York: G.P. Putnam's, 1983.

Discussion of tactics for lobbying on behalf of reproductive freedom issues. Included in a collection of essays on lobbying for civil liberties issues.

996. Bertin, Joan E. "Fetal Protection: Controlling Pregnancy." *BioLaw*, 2 (March 1991): S539–S547.

Detailed discussion of civil liberties aspects of proposed laws and policies designed to protect the health of the fetus. Written by the associate director of the ACLU Women's Rights Project.

997. LaMarche, Gara. "Civil Liberties Aspects of Childbirth Issues." *Consumers for Choices in Childbirth Newsletter* (Spring 1988).

Discussion of civil liberties aspects of childbirth, by a prominent ACLU leader. Includes, for example, discussion of the right of parents to choose nontraditional means of childbirth.

998. Staggenborg, Suzanne. *The Pro-Choice Movement: Organization and Activism in the Abortion Conflict.* New York: Oxford University Press, 1991.

Detailed analysis of the various pro-choice organizations. Good material on the role of the ACLU Reproductive Freedom Project. Places the activities of the project in the context of the broader pro-choice movement.

4. Right to Die

999. Hentoff, Nat. "Legalizing Death By Starvation." *The Village Voice* (January 10, 1989).

Article critical of ACLU position supporting the right to die in a case before the U.S. Supreme Court (*Cruzan v. Harmon*).

H. OTHER CIVIL LIBERTIES ISSUES

1. Children, Parents, Families, Rights of

[See #36, #48, #68.]

1000. ACLU. Children's Rights Project. *The ACLU Helped Put My Family Together Again.* New York: ACLU, 1988.

Pamphlet describes the activities of the ACLU Children's Rights Project, with an emphasis on children in foster care.

1001. Dershowitz, Alan M. "ACLU Takes a Wrong Turn." Alan Dershowitz. *Taking Liberties.* Chicago: Contemporary Books, 1988.

Criticism of ACLU position in highly publicized case involving parents who sought to return to the Soviet

Union and take their child with them. ACLU intervened on the basis of due process violations by Illinois officials in removing the child from the home. Author is a noted law professor and expert on civil liberties.

1002. Szasz, Thomas. "The ACLU vs Walter Polovchak." *Inquiry*, 3 (October 27, 1980): 6.

Criticism of ACLU role in highly-publicized case of Walter Polovchak whose parents sought to return to the Soviet Union. ACLU opposed removal of Polovchak from parents' custody without due process.

2. Economic Rights/The Poor/The Homeless

[See #52, 760.]

1003. ACLU. *Justice Evicted: An Inquiry into Housing Court Problems*. New York: ACLU, 1987.

Report on violations of the rights of tenants in New York City Housing Court. Prepared by the ACLU Access to Justice Project.

1004. ACLU. *No Justice For the Poor: How Cutbacks Are Destroying Legal Services*. New York: ACLU, 1983.

Analysis of impact of budget cuts on the Legal Services Corporation.

1005. ACLU and American Friends Service Committee. *The Hands That Feed Us: Undocumented Farmworkers in Florida*. New York: ACLU, 1986.

Report on civil liberties issues related to undocumented farmworkers in Florida.

1006. Blank, Susan. "The Homeless: ACLU Responds to the Emergency." *Civil Liberties*, 356 (Winter 1986): 1+.

Summary of ACLU activities on behalf of homeless people.

1007. Rocah, David. "Homelessness and Civil Liberties." *Civil Liberties*, No. 368 (Fall/Winter 1989): 5.

Discussion of civil liberties aspects of the problem of homeless people. Includes description of some ACLU cases on behalf of the homeless.

1008. Rocah, David. "Taking Liberty to the Streets." *Civil Liberties*, 369 (Spring 1990): 1+.

Article on the activities of the New York Civil Liberties Union on behalf of homeless people in New York City fighting city policy of rounding up people during extremely cold weather.

3. Employees, Rights of

[See #33, #34, #38, #42, #51, #57, #59, #63, #65.]

1009. ACLU. *Liberty At Work: Expanding the Rights of Employees in America*. New York: ACLU, 1988.

Collection of articles on various aspects of civil liberties in the workplace. Includes essays on drug testing of employees, free speech rights of employees, equal employment opportunity, and other issues.

1010. ACLU. *The Rights of Employees*. New York: ACLU, 1991.

ACLU Briefing Paper. Short pamphlet summarizing civil liberties of employees.

1011. Maltby, Lewis. "The Decline of Employment at Will—A Quantitative Analysis." *Labor Law Journal*, 41 (January 1990): 51–54.

Analysis of trends in the law relating to legal concept of employment at will, written by the director of the ACLU Task Force on Civil Liberties in the Workplace.

1012. Maltby, Lewis. *A State of Emergency in the American Workplace*. New York: ACLU, 1990.

Report on various civil liberties issues affecting employees by the director of the ACLU Task Force on Civil Liberties in the Workplace. Issues include: freedom of speech for employees, due process rights, control of off-duty behavior, etc.

1013. Slaff, George. "ACLU and Unions." *The Nation*, 235 (December 25, 1982): 690.

Criticism of ACLU policy with respect to labor unions, by prominent member of the ACLU.

4. Immigration

[See #27, #28.]

1014. ACLU. *Salvadorans in the United States: The Case for Extended Voluntary Departure.* New York: ACLU, 1984.

Pamphlet arguing in favor of granting refugees from El Salvador extended residency in the United States on the grounds that they are political refugees.

1015. Guttentag, Lucas. *Immigration Reform Act: Employer Sanctions and Discrimination Prohibitions—A Guide For Workers, Employers and Their Advocates.* New York: ACLU Immigration and Aliens' Rights Task Force, 1988.

Guide to legal aspects of a new federal law on immigration, written by the director of the ACLU task force on the rights of immigrants.

1016. Guttentag, Lucas. "Immigration-Related Employment Discrimination: IRCA's Prohibitions, Procedures and Remedies." *Federal Bar News and Journal*, 37 (January 1990): 23.

Guide to legal aspects of a new federal law on immigration, written by the director of the ACLU special project on the rights of immigrants.

1017. Harrington, James C., ed. *Los Derechos de Gene Indocumentada e Imigrante.* Austin: Texas Civil Liberties Union, 1985.

Pamphlet on the rights of immigrants and undocumented workers, in Spanish, edited by the then-legal director of the Texas Civil Liberties Union.

1018. Jussim, Daniel. "Terrorizing the Constitution: Government Moves to Deport Palestinians For Free Speech." *Civil Liberties,* 360 (Spring 1987): 1+.

Article on lawsuit by ACLU of Southern California and the national office of the ACLU opposing the federal government's attempt to deport seven Palestinians and one Kenyan on the grounds that they advocated terrorism.

1019. Schapiro, Steven R. and Wade Henderson. "Justice For Aliens." Norman Dorsen, ed. *Our Endangered Rights.* New York: Pantheon, 1984. Pp. 160–178.

Discussion of legal issues involving the rights of aliens, as of the mid-1980s, by two ALCU staff members.

5. International Civil Liberties

1020. Americas Watch Committee and the American Civil Liberties Union. *Report on Human Rights in El Salvador.* New York: Vintage Books, 1982.

Report on violations of human rights in El Salvador, with special reference to actions by the United States government in tolerating abuses.

1021. Strossen, Nadine. "Recent U.S. and International Judicial Protection of Individual Rights: A Comparative Legal Process Analysis and Proposed Synthesis." *Hastings Law Journal,* 41 (April 1990): 805–904.

Discussion of international civil liberties issues by the future president of the ACLU.

IV. General Civil Liberties Issues

A. CIVIL LIBERTIES, CONSTITUTIONAL LAW

[See also #79, #92, #97, #98, #109, #149, #675.]

1022. Abraham, Henry J. *Freedom and the Court.* Fifth edition. New York: Oxford University Press, 1988.

    Comprehensive survey of civil liberties issues, with emphasis on relevant Supreme Court decisions. Excellent introduction for the non-specialist.

1023. Brant, Irving. *The Bill of Rights.* Indianapolis: Bobbs-Merrill, 1965.

    History of the Bill of Rights, written for the general audience.

1024. Cortner, Richard C. *The Supreme Court and Civil Liberties Policy.* Palo Alto, CA: Mayfield Publishing, 1975.

    Scholarly analysis of the impact of Supreme Court decisions involving civil liberties on selected aspects of American social policy.

1025. Cortner, Richard C. *The Supreme Court and the Second Bill of Rights: The Fourteenth Amendment and the Nationalization of Civil Liberties.* Madison: University of Wisconsin Press, 1981.

    Detailed scholarly analysis of the impact of the Supreme Court's use of the Fourteenth Amendment to expand protection of individual rights at the state level. Good overview of the impact of the ACLU legal program.

1026. Dorsen, Norman, Paul Bender, Burt Neuborne, and Sylvia Law. *Political and Civil Rights in the United States.* Two volumes. Fourth edition. Boston: Little, Brown. 1979.

    Comprehensive law school case book on civil liberties. Revised edition of Thomas Emerson, David Haber, and Norman Dorsen, *Political and Civil Rights in the United States.* Co-author Dorsen served as president of the ACLU from 1976 to 1991. Extremely valuable as a sourcebook for materials on civil liberties issues.

1027. Emerson, Thomas I. *The System of Freedom of Expression.* New York: Random House, 1970.

    Comprehensive discussion of First Amendment rights by one of the leading legal scholars. Widely regarded as a classic work in the field of American law.

1028. Haiman, Franklyn S. *Speech and Law in a Free Society.* Chicago: University of Chicago Press, 1981.

    Comprehensive survey of First Amendment rights by a prominent scholar and long-time ACLU leader.

1029. Hall, Kermit L., ed. *Civil Liberties in American History.* Two Volumes. New York: Garland, 1987.

    Collection of previously published scholarly articles on civil liberties issues in American history. Excellent introduction to some of the most important scholarship in the field.

1030. Halpern, Stephen C., ed. *The Future of Our Liberties: Perspectives on the Bill of Rights.* Westport, CT: Greenwood Press, 1982.

    Collection of essays on selected civil liberties issues, as of the early 1980s.

1031. Hentoff, Nat. *The First Freedom: The Tumultuous History of Free Speech in America.* New York: Delacorte, 1980.

    History of several notable free speech cases and controversies in America. Written for a popular audience. Author is a prominent journalist specializing in civil liberties issues (see #775) and former member of the ACLU Board of Directors.

1032. Kairys, David. "Freedom of Speech." David Kairys, ed. *The Politics of Law: A Progressive Critique.* New York: Pantheon, 1982. Pp. 140–171.

Essay on the development of freedom of speech in the United States from a left-wing perspective. Critical of the ACLU's position on freedom of speech. Good material on the ACLU's early free speech cases.

1033. Kairys, David, ed. *The Politics of Law: A Progressive Critique.* New York: Pantheon, 1982.

Collection of essays on selected aspects of American law from a left-wing perspective. Includes several items related to civil liberties (see #1032).

1034. Kalven, Harry. *A Worthy Tradition: Freedom of Speech in America.* New York: Harper and Row, 1988.

Comprehensive scholarly discussion of the law of free speech by a noted legal scholar. Completed posthumously by the author's son.

1035. Kammen, Michael. *A Machine That Would Go of Itself: The Constitution in American Culture.* New York: Knopf, 1986.

Detailed scholarly discussion of the role of the Constitution in American history and culture by a prominent American historian. No material on the ACLU, but an excellent background to the development of civil liberties. (See also #1036.)

1036. Kammen, Michael. *Spheres of Liberty: Changing Perceptions of Liberty in American Culture.* Madison: University of Wisconsin Press, 1986.

Essays on the history of the Constitution in American life by a prominent American historian. Supplements #1036.

1037. Morgan, Richard E. *Disabling America: The 'Rights Industry' in Our Time.* New York: Basic Books, 1984.

   Neo-conservative critique of the impact of civil liberties litigation on American society. Argues that excessive emphasis on individual rights has undermined the effectiveness of important social institutions.

1038. Murphy, Paul M., ed. *The Bill of Rights in American Legal History.* Twenty volumes. New York: Garland, 1990.

   Collection of previously published scholarly articles on the history of the Bill of Rights. Contains over three hundred articles in twenty volumes. Excellent introduction to much of the best scholarship.

1039. Murphy, Paul L. *The Constitution in Crisis Times, 1918–1969.* New York: Harper and Row, 1972.

   Comprehensive scholarly history of constitutional law in the United States from 1918 to 1969 by a noted American historian and author of several books on the history of the ACLU (#85, #109, #149). Places the ACLU and the development of civil liberties in a broad historical context.

1040. Schwartz, Bernard, ed. *The Bill of Rights: A Documentary History.* Two volumes. New York: Chelsea House, 1971.

   Collection of documents on the history of the Bill of Rights. Excellent resource.

1041. Urofsky, Melvin I. *A March of Liberty: A Constitutional History of the United States.* New York: Knopf, 1988.

   Comprehensive scholarly history of constitutional law in the United States.

1042. Whipple, Leon. *The Story of Civil Liberty in the United States.* New York: Vanguard Press, 1927.

   The first book-length history of civil liberties in the United States. Carries the story through the 1920s. Extensive material on the pre-World War I period. Commissioned by the ACLU. The author was fired from his teaching job during World War I because of his political views.

B. LEGAL ROLE OF ACLU AND OTHER PUBLIC INTEREST GROUPS

[See also #75, #387, #392, #502, #504, #549, #740, #743, #748, #749.]

1043. Angell, Ernest. "The Amicus Curiae: American Development of an English Institution." *International and Comparative Law Quarterly*, 16 (1967): 1017–1044.

Analysis of the history of the amicus curiae brief by then-chairperson of the ACLU Board of Directors.

1044. Cortner, Richard C. "Strategies and Tactics of Litigants in Constitutional Cases." *Journal of Public Law*, 17 (1968): 287–307.

Scholarly analysis of the strategy and tactics used by advocacy groups in civil liberties cases.

1045. Epstein, Lee. *Conservatives in Court*. Knoxville: University of Tennessee Press, 1985,

Detailed scholarly analysis of conservative public interest law firms. Notes that conservative legal groups were consciously modelled after the ACLU. Valuable perspective on the impact of the ACLU on American society.

1046. Krislov, Samuel. "The Amicus Curiae Brief: From Friendship to Advocacy." *Yale Law Journal*, 72 (1963): 694–721.

Historical analysis of the transformation of the role of the amicus curiae brief between the 1930s and the 1960s.

1047. Graber, Mark A. *Transforming Free Speech: The Ambiguous Legacy of Civil Libertarianism.* Berkeley: University of California Press, 1991.

Scholarly analysis of the development of First Amendment law in the United States. Critical of the ACLU's position on the First Amendment.

1048. Halpern, Charles R. "The Public Interest Bar: An Audit" in Ralph Nader and Mark Green, eds. *Verdicts on Lawyers.* New York: Thomas Y. Crowell, 1976. Pp. 158–171.

Excellent analysis of the impact of public interest law groups, including the ACLU, on American society. Valuable insights into the positive contributions of the ACLU.

1049. Halpern, Stephen C. "Assessing the Litigative Role of ACLU Chapters." *Policy Studies Journal,* 4 (Winter 1975): 157–161.

Analysis of ACLU litigation effort by political scientist. Found that 95% of cases filed during six-month period were "enforcement" cases, involving violation of clearly established law. Reprinted in #1054.

1050. Rabin, Robert L. "Lawyers For Social Change: Perspectives on Public Interest Law." *Stanford Law Review,* 28 (1976): 207–261.

Scholarly analysis of the role of litigation as a strategy for social change. Includes some discussion of the ACLU.

1051. [Redlich, Norman]. "Private Attorneys-General: Group Action in the Fight For Civil Liberties." *Yale Law Journal,* 58 (1949): 574–598.

The first attempt to survey the work and impact of the public interest bar as of 1949. Examines the ACLU, the NAACP, and the Commission on Law and Social Action of the American Jewish Congress. Good discussion of the contributions of each organization. Perceptive and critical analysis of the ACLU as of 1949.

General Civil Liberties Issues

1052. Vose, Clement. "Litigation as a Form of Pressure Group Activity." *The Annals of the American Academy of Social and Political Science*, 319 (September 1958): 20–31.

    Early assessment of the role of public interest groups in using litigation to effect social change.

1053. Wasby, Stephen L. *Civil Liberties: Policy and Policy Making.* Lexington, MA Lexington Books, 1976.

    Collection of scholarly political science essays on civil liberties issues.

1054. Wasby, Stephen L. "Civil Rights Litigation by Organizations: Constraints and Choices." *Judicature*, 68 (April-May 1985): 337–352.

    Scholarly analysis of litigation strategies and tactics used by civil rights groups. Based primarily on the NAACP Legal Defense Fund, but with insights relevant to the ACLU.

1055. Wasby, Stephen. "How Planned is Planned Litigation?" *American Bar Foundation Research Journal*, 1984 (Winter, 1): 83–138.

    Scholarly analysis of strategies in civil rights litigation, focusing on the NAACP Legal Defense Fund. Valuable perspective on ACLU litigation strategies.

1056. Wasby, Stephen L. "Interest Group Litigation in an Age of Complexity." Allen Cigler and Burdett Loomis, eds. *Interest Group Politics*. Washington, DC: Congressional Quarterly, 1983.

    Scholarly analysis of litigation strategies adopted by civil rights groups.

1057. Weisbrod, Burton A., et al. *Public Interest Law: An Economic and Institutional Analysis.* Berkeley: University of California Press, 1978.

    Collection of scholarly articles on public interest law firms. First comprehensive attempt to assess the impact of public interest law advocacy on American law. No material directly on the ACLU, but provides useful perspective on the ACLU's role.

C. PUBLIC OPINION ABOUT CIVIL LIBERTIES

[See also #257; #402, #679, #758.]

1058. "Civil Liberties." [Special Issue]. *Journal of Social Issues*, 31 (1975, 2).

Special issue devoted to civil liberties. Several articles on public opinion and psychological aspects of attitudes toward civil liberties.

1059. Hyman, Herbert H. and Paul B. Sheatsley. "Trends in Public Opinion on Civil Liberties." *Journal of Social Issues*, 9 (1953, 3): 6–16.

Review of public opinion polls on various civil liberties issues from 1937 through 1953. Finds support for civil liberties in the abstract, but increasing support for limitations on rights related to Communists and other unpopular groups.

1060. Erskine, Hazel G. "The Polls: Freedom of Speech." *Public Opinion Quarterly*, 34 (Fall 1970): 483–496.

Review of public opinion polls regarding freedom of speech between 1936 and 1970.

1061. Erskine, Hazel G., and Richard L. Siegel. "Civil Liberties and the American Public." *Journal of Social Issues*, 31 (January 1975): 13–29.

Analysis of trends in public opinion about civil liberties between 1954 and 1974. Finds sharp rise in support on many issues.

1062. Mack, Raymond W. "Do We Really Believe in the Bill of Rights?" *Social Problems*, 3 (April 1956): 264–269.

Review of public attitudes about civil liberties in the mid-1950s. Finds weak support for civil liberties.

1063. McClosky, Herbert, and Alida Brill. *Dimensions of Tolerance: What Americans Believe About Civil Liberties*. New York: Russell Sage Foundation, 1983.

Comprehensive survey of public attitudes about civil liberties. Project undertaken in response to the 1977–1978 Skokie affair (see #673–#690). Serves as an update to #402 which surveyed public attitudes in the 1950s.

1064. Remmers, H.H., and R.D. Franklin. "Sweet Land of Liberty," *Phi Delta Kappan* (October 1962): 22–27.

Analysis of trends in public opinion about civil liberties between 1951 and 1960. Finds ambiguous trends, with support falling in some areas and rising slightly in others.

1065. Selvin, Hanan C., and Warren O. Hagstrom. "Determinants of Support for Civil Liberties." *British Journal of Sociology*, 11 (March 1960): 51–73. Reprinted in Seymour M. Lipset and Sheldon Wolin, eds. *The Berkeley Student Revolt*. Garden City, NY: Doubleday, 1965. Pp. 494–519.

Sociological study of public attitudes toward civil liberties.

1066. Triandis, Harry C. "Research Directions Suggested by the ACLU." *Journal of Social Issues*, 31 (1975, No. 2): 165–181.

Discussion of issues related to public opinion about civil liberties meriting future research. List of topics developed on the basis of suggestions from Alan Reitman, associate director of the ACLU, indicating issues that civil liberties activists would like to have answered.

1067. Simon, Rita J., and David Barnum, "Public Support for Civil Liberties—Israel and the U.S." *Research Annual*, 1 (1978).

Comparative study of public attitudes toward civil liberties in the United States and Israel.

D. INTERNATIONAL PERSPECTIVES

1068. "A Special First Amendment Issue." *Communications Lawyer*, 9 (Spring 1991).

Special issue on the occasion of the 200th anniversary of the Bill of Rights. Includes articles on freedom of speech and press in England, Israel, France, South Korea, and New Zealand. Article on the United States is written by Norman Dorsen, president of the ACLU (1976–1991).

1069. Benewick, Robert. "The Civil Lobby: A Comparative Analysis." *Government and Opposition*, 10 (1975, No. 4): 415–443.

Comparative study of the activities of the ACLU and the National Council for Civil Liberties.

1070. Dorsen, Norman. "A Transatlantic View of Civil Liberties in the United Kingdom." Peter Wallington, ed. *Civil Liberties 1984*. Oxford: Martin Robertson, 1984.

Essay comparing the missions and roles of the ACLU and the National Council for Civil Liberties. Written by the then-president of the ACLU, on the occasion of the fiftieth anniversary of the NCCL. Extremely valuable insights into unique role of the ACLU.

1071. Ewing, K.D., and C.A. Gearty. *Freedom Under Thatcher: Civil Liberties in Modern Britain*. Oxford: Clarendon Press, 1990.

Analysis of the development of civil liberties in England under Prime Minister Margaret Thatcher.

1072. Gostin, Larry, ed. *Civil Liberties in Conflict*. New York: Routledge, 1988.

Collection of essays on civil liberties issues in England and the United States. Edited by the former secretary of the National Council for Civil Liberties. Includes contributions by prominent members of the ACLU.

1073. Henkin, Louis A. *The Age of Rights*. New York: Columbia University Press, 1990.

Discussion of international human rights issues. Useful perspective on the development of rights in the United States.

1074. Hewitt, Patricia. *The Abuse of Power: Civil Liberties in the United Kingdom*. Oxford: Martin Robertson, 1982.

Critical analysis of the status of civil liberties in England, as of the early 1980s.

1075. Lilly, Mark. *The National Council for Civil Liberties: The First Fifty Years*. London: Macmillan, 1984.

Short history of the National Council for Civil Liberties in England. Written for a popular audience.

1076. Strossen, Nadine. "Recent U.S. and International Judicial Protection of Individual Rights: A Comparative Legal Process Analysis and Proposed Synthesis." *Hastings Law Journal*, 41 (1990): 805–904.

Comparative study of international human rights issues by then-general counsel and future president of the ACLU.

1077. Wallington, Peter, ed. *Civil Liberties 1984*. Oxford: Martin Robertson, 1984.

Collection of essays on civil liberties in England, as of the mid-1980s.

V. Individual ACLU Leaders

A. ROGER NASH BALDWIN

1. Books and Articles about

[See also #83, #127.]

1078. Donald, Peter. "Roger Baldwin at 96." *Libertarian Review* (January 1981): 27–31.

   Sympathetic portrait of Baldwin written shortly before his death.

1079. Duffus, Robert L. "The Legend of Roger Baldwin." *American Mercury*, 5 (August 1925): 408–414.

   Flattering portrait of Baldwin; helped to promote the "legend" of Baldwin as the personification of civil liberties.

1080. "Galahad of Freedom: The Story of Roger Baldwin." *The World Tomorrow*, 13 (January 1930): 33–36.

   Flattering portrait of Baldwin. Helped to promote the legend of Baldwin as the personification of civil liberties.

1081. Hoke, Travis. "Red Rainbow." *North American Review*, 234 (November 1932): 431–439.

   Sympathetic portrait of Baldwin in the early 1930s.

1082. Jensen, Oliver. "The Persuasive Roger Baldwin." *Harper's*, 203 (September 1951): 47–55.

   Sympathetic portrait of Baldwin written the year after his retirement as ACLU executive director.

1083. Lewis, Flora. "Looking Ahead at 87." *The Los Angeles Times* (September 10, 1971).

   Interview with Baldwin near the end of his life.

1084. MacDonald, Dwight. "The Defense of Everybody." *The New Yorker*, 29 (July 11, 1953): 31+; Part II, *ibid.*, 29 (July 18, 1953): 29+.

   Long, two-part article on Baldwin by a noted writer and social critic. Excellent insights into Baldwin's personality and style of leadership of the ACLU. Somewhat unbalanced in its treatment of ACLU history and civil liberties issues, however.

1085. "Roger N. Baldwin." *Current Biography 1940.* New York: H. W. Wilson, 1940. Pp. 43–44.

   Brief biographical sketch of the ACLU executive director in 1940.

1086. "Roger N. Baldwin." *Saturday Evening Post*, 210 (March 5, 1958): 8.

   Brief portrait of Baldwin.

1087. "Roger N. Baldwin." *Encyclopedia of the American Constitution.* Vol. 1. New York: Macmillan, 1986. P. 96.

   Brief biographical sketch.

1088. "Roger N. Baldwin." *Literary Digest*, 116 (October 28, 1933): 13.

   Brief biographical sketch.

1089. "Roger Baldwin Receives Medal of Freedom." *Civil Liberties*, 336 (February 1981): 1.

   Article on Baldwin receiving the Medal of Freedom from President Jimmy Carter.

1090. Sheehy, Gail. *Pathfinders.* New York: Bantam Books, 1981. Pp. 325–335.

Individual ACLU Leaders

Portrait of Baldwin, based on an interview, in book on notable figures who, in the author's opinion, have lived particularly creative lives.

2. Books and Articles by

[NOTE: Baldwin's voluminous writings are arranged first by time period and then alphabetically by title.]

a. 1910–1919

1091. "Conscience at the Bar." *The Survey*, 41 (November 9, 1918): 253. Also in "The Faith of a Heretic." *The Nation*, 107 (November 9, 1918): 54. *The World Tomorrow*, 1 (December, 1918): 305.

    Baldwin's statement to the Court during his trial for refusing to be inducted into the military. This speech was widely circulated and became an important statement of the principles of conscientious objection.

1092. "East St. Louis—Why." *The Survey*, 38 (August 18, 1917): 447–448.

    Letter to the editor offering an analysis of the 1917 race riot in East St. Louis, Illinois.

1093. "An Industrial Program for After the War." National Conference of Social Work. *Proceedings*, 45 (1918), 426–429.

    A proposed agenda for the social work profession regarding issues related to working people. Written largely by Baldwin. An important statement of his growing radicalism, circa 1916–1918.

1094. *Juvenile Courts and Probation*. With Bernard Flexner. New York: The Century Co., 1916.

    Textbook on juvenile court, co-authored by Baldwin. Probably the first detailed statement of professional principles for organizing and managing a juvenile court. Unofficially sponsored by the National Probation

Association. A good index of Baldwin's national stature in the field of social work at the time.

1095. "Missouri Legislature's Fruitless Session." *The Survey*, 34 (April 17, 1915): 71.

Brief article on the Missouri legislative session, emphasizing its failure to enact progressive legislation.

1096. "The National Conference at Seattle." *The Survey*, 30 (August 2, 1913): 590–594.

Brief report on the annual meeting of a national association of social workers

1097. "National Probation Officers Association." *The Survey*, 24 (June 11, 1910): 467–468.

A brief account of the formation of the National Probation Association. Baldwin was a founding member.

1098. "Negro Segregation By Initiative Election in St. Louis." *American City*, 14 (April 1916): 356.

Discussion of a racial segregation ordinance (forbidding white property owners from selling their property to blacks) enacted in St. Louis by popular referendum. Similar to many other local ordinances enacted at this time. An important event in Baldwin's political development, precipitating his first serious doubts about direct democracy.

1099. "New Tenants and Old Shacks." *The Survey*, 25 (February 18, 1911): 825–828.

A brief account of the campaign to improve housing for the poor in St. Louis in which Baldwin played a leading role.

1100. "Old Order—New Needs." *The Survey*, 34 (May 1, 1915): 114–115.

Brief discussion of social problems in urban society and the need for new programs to cope with poverty and related problems.

Individual ACLU Leaders

1101. "The Presentation of the Case." *The Child in the City.* New York: Arno Press, 1970. Pp. 341–348.

    Reprint of Proceedings of the Chicago Child Welfare Exhibition (1912). Discussion of one aspect of juvenile court proceedings. See #1095 for full statement of principles.

1102. "Prisons and Revolution." *The World Tomorrow*, 2 (August 1919): 221–224.

    One of the first expressions of Baldwin's radicalism upon leaving prison in 1919.

1103. "Social Work and Radical Economic Movements." National Conference of Social Work. *Proceedings*, 45 (1918): 396–398.

    A statement of the relationship of the social work profession to radical political and economic movements; written largely by Baldwin; an expression of his growing radicalism at this time.

1104. "St. Louis Pageant and Masque." *The Survey*, 32 (April 11, 1914): 52–53.

    Brief report on civic events in St. Louis.

1105. "St. Louis: Successful Fight for A Modern Charter." *National Municipal Review*, 3 (October 1914): 720–726.

    Brief account of the struggle for a new city charter in St. Louis, in which Baldwin was very active.

1106. "A State Children's Code and Its Enforcement." *The Survey*, 37 (December 30, 1916): 356–357.

    Discussion of issues surrounding child welfare legislation.

1107. "Statistics Relating to Juvenile Delinquents." National Conference of Charities and Corrections. *Proceedings*, 35 (1910), 523–532.

    Discussion of data related to juvenile delinquency. See #1095 for complete statement of principles.

1108. "Use of Municipal Ownership to Abolish Trans-Mississippi Freight and Passenger Pools at St. Louis." *National Municipal Review*, 4 (July 1915): 468–472.

> Discussion of municipal ownership of transportation facilities in St. Louis.

1109. "Wiping the Slate For Child 'Criminals'." *The Survey*, 33 (March 27, 1915): 691.

> Discussion of sealing juvenile court records. See #1095 for more general discussion.

b. 1920–1929

1110. "American Freedom Today." *The Socialist Review*, 9 (August 1920): 115.

> Brief discussion of the status of civil liberties shortly after the founding of the ACLU.

1111. "Civil Liberties." *Social Work Yearbook*. Vol. 1. New York: Russell Sage, 1929. Pp. 85–87.

> Summary of current civil liberties issues as of 1929.

1112. "The Conquest of Punishment." *The World Tomorrow*, 5 (August 1922): 241–242.

> Baldwin's views on the punishment of criminals. Argues against imprisonment and in favor of more humane response.

1113. "The Dutch War Resisters." *The Nation*, 124 (June 29, 1927): 723–724.

> Article on the fate of pacifists in the Netherlands. Written during Baldwin's trip to Europe.

1114. "He Who Gets Slapped at Geneva." *The Nation*, 124 (March 9, 1927): 259–260.

> Baldwin's observations of the League of Nations at work, based on his 1927 trip to Europe.

1115. "The Immorality of Social Work." *The World Tomorrow*, 5 (February 1922). 44–45.

   An expression of Baldwin's disillusionment with the social work profession in the early 1920s. A particularly revealing statement of his larger social outlook in this period.

1116. "Introduction." *Kropotkin's Revolutionary Pamphlets*. Roger N. Baldwin, ed. New York: Benjamin Blom, 1927.

   Introduction to a collection of pamphlets by a noted Russian anarchist. An expression of Baldwin's quasi-anarchistic outlook as of the 1920s.

1117. "Introduction." Alexander Berkman, ed. *Letters From Russian Prisons*. New York: Albert and Charles Boni, 1925. Reprinted: Westport, CT: Hyperion Press, 1977.

   Revealing statement of Baldwin's belief in philosophical anarchism.

1118. "A League of Nations Oppressed." *The Nation*, 124 (April 13, 1927): 397–398.

   Baldwin's observations of the League of Nations made during his 1927 trip to Europe.

1119. *Liberty Under the Soviets*. New York: Vanguard Press, 1927.

   An analysis of political and civil rights in the Soviet Union based on Baldwin's trip there in 1927. Particularly valuable material on the status of conscientious objectors, religious groups, and women. The book clearly reflects Baldwin's sympathy for the Soviet experiment as of 1927. The 1928 edition contains a brief additional note that reflects Baldwin's awareness of and hostility to the growing repression under Stalin.

1120. "Liberty Under the Soviets." *The Nation*, 125 (November 9, 1927): 505–507.

   A brief summary of some of the issues treated at length in #1120.

1121. "The Next War—in Mingo." *Labor Age*, 10 (November 1921): 1–2.

> A discussion of the suppression of civil liberties in the West Virginia coal mining fields, one of the ACLU's first major campaigns.

1122. "The Pacifist Attitude to Crime." *The World Tomorrow*, 11 (June 1928), 265–267. Reprinted in Devere Allen, ed. *Pacifism in the Modern World*. Garden City, NY: Doubleday, Doran & Co., 1929. pp. 79–90.

> Discussion of issues of crime and punishment from a pacifist perspective. Argues for more humane punishments than imprisonment.

1123. "A Strike Against the Government." *The Nation*, 119 (July 30, 1924): 120–121.

> Brief article on a major strike in Canada.

1124. "Voting Red in Austria." *The Nation*, 124 (June 15, 1927): 663–664.

> A first-hand account of the political strength of left-wing political movements in Vienna, Austria. Based on Baldwin's 1927 trip to Europe.

1125. *What Do You Mean 'Free Speech'?* New York: ACLU, 1923.

> Pamphlet setting forth ACLU position on the scope of free speech.

1126. "What the I.W.W Is Up Against." *The Socialist Review* (January 1921): 2–3

> Discussion of the continued suppression of the I. W. W. in the post-World War I years.

1127. "Where Are the Pre-War Radicals?" *The Survey*, 55 (February 1, 1926): 560

> Baldwin's contribution to a symposium on the apparent collapse of radicalism (and liberal reform) in the mid-1920s. The symposium provides extremely valuable

insights into the mood of the period among liberal reformers.

1128. "Working Outside." *The World Tomorrow*, 7 (July 1924): 202–203.

An extremely revealing expression of Baldwin's alienation from the mainstream of American life in the mid-1920s. Discusses the problem of finding work that does not force a person to compromise his or her principles.

c. 1930–1939

1129. "American Ideals (II): The Coming Struggle for Liberty." *Common Sense*, 4 (January 1935): 6–7.

Discussion of civil liberties issues as of the mid-1930s.

1130. "Civil Liberties." *Social Work Yearbook*. Vol. 2. New York: Russell Sage, 1933. Pp. 83–86

Summary of current civil liberties issues as of 1933.

1131. "Civil Liberties." *Social Work Yearbook*. Vol. 4. New York: Russell Sage, 1937.

A summary of civil liberties issues as of 1937.

1132. "Civil Liberties." *Social Work Yearbook*. Vol. 5. New York: Russell Sage, 1939. Pp. 76–79.

Summary of current civil liberties issues as of 1939.

1133. *Civil Liberties and Industrial Conflict*. With Clarence B. Randall. Cambridge, MA: Harvard University Press, 1938.

Discussion of issues related to labor and management. Written at a critical turning point in Baldwin's life, as he was turning away from his sympathy for Marxism.

1134. "Civil Liberties: Losses and Gains." *Social Work Today*, 4 (April 1937): 15–16.

> A brief summary of civil liberties issues as of 1937.

1135. "The Defense of the Bill of Rights by the American Civil Liberties Union." *Twice-a-Year*, 2 (Spring-Summer 1939): 205–210.

> A brief summary of the work of the ACLU as of 1939.

1136. "Fight the Gag Bills!" *New Masses*, 15 (April 2, 1935): 13–14.

> Statement opposing several bills in Congress that would punish radical political speech. These bills were defeated but similar bills resulted in the Smith Act in 1940.

1137. "Forces That Hamper the School From Without." *Social Frontier*, 2 (March 1936): 183–184.

> Discussion of assaults on academic freedom in the form of restrictions on the political beliefs and associations of teachers.

1138. "Free Speech for Nazis?" *The World Tomorrow*, 16 (November 1933): 613.

> An early explanation of the ACLU's defense of free speech for Nazis.

1139. "Freedom in the U.S.A. and the U.S.S.R." *Soviet Russia Today*, 3 (September 1934): 11.

> A statement of Baldwin's political views at the moment when he was most sympathetic to Communism.

1140. "Freedom in Teaching." *NEA Addresses and Proceedings* (1932). Pp. 244–245.

> Discussion of attacks on academic freedom.

1141. "Harvard Heretics and Rebels." With Corliss Lamont. *The Nation*, 142 (June 10, 1936): 733–735.

Individual ACLU Leaders

Discussion of the long history of famous religious heretics and political radicals who were graduates of Harvard College. Baldwin and Lamont were both Harvard graduates. Lamont was a wealthy radical and member of the ACLU Board of directors.

1142. "A Little Advice from the Left." *Hebrew Union College Monthly* (October 1931): 9–10.

General discussion of civil liberties in the early 1930s.

1143. "The Main Issues of Civil Liberty Under the New Deal." ACLU Conference on Civil Liberties Under the New Deal. December 8–9, 1934. *Proceedings* New York: ACLU, 1934.

Critique of early New Deal measures, especially of the administration's policies toward labor unions under the National Recovery Act. Reflects Baldwin's skepticism of the Roosevelt administration in its first years.

1144. "Modern Forms of Persecution." *Adult Bible Class Magazine* (July 1936): 293.

Brief discussion of general civil liberties issues.

1145. "The Myth of Law and Order." Samuel D. Schmalhausen, ed. *Behold America!* New York: Farrar and Rinehart, 1931.

Discussion of civil liberties focusing primarily on the denial of the First Amendment rights of working people and labor union organizers.

1146. "Negro Rights and the Class Struggle." *Opportunity*, 12 (September 1934): 264–269.

A statement of Baldwin's social and political philosophy at the moment when he was in his most left-wing phase. Places most of his hope on direct action by white and black workers and is particularly scornful of judicial protection of civil liberties.

1147. "Personal Liberty." *The Annals of the American Academy of Political and Social Science*, 185 (May 1936): 162–169.

General discussion of civil liberties issues in the mid-1930s.

1148. "A Puritan Revolutionist: The Story of Scott Nearing." *The World Tomorrow*, 13 (July 1930): 305–308.

A brief portrait of the famous radical Nearing, who was Baldwin's personal friend and colleague in the first years of the ACLU.

1149. "Radicals or Robots?: Are Our Schools and Colleges Going Red?" *Common Sense*, 2 (August 1933): 23–24.

Reply to charges that American education was dominated by Communists. Attacks growing restrictions on academic freedom in colleges and universities.

1150. "Red Scare." *Common Sense*, 4 (March 1935).

Discussion of the rising anti-Communist fever in the mid-1930s.

1151. "Sacco and Vanzetti—Undying Symbols." *Unity*, (August 16, 1937): 222.

Essay commemorating the tenth anniversary of the execution of Sacco and Vanzetti.

1152. "Should the Dies Committee Die?" *Twice-a-Year*, 2 (Spring-Summer 1939): 227–233.

A call for abolition of the House Un-American Actvities Committee after the first year of the Committee's operation.

1153. "Statement." *Twice-a-Year*, 1 (Fall-Winter 1938): 216.

Discussion of the principles of conscientious objection on the eve of World War II.

d. 1940–1949

1154. "The American Defense of Civil Liberties." *The New Leader*, 21 (July 3, 1948), 1, 15.

Individual ACLU Leaders

Discussion of civil liberties principles in the early years of the Cold War.

1155. "American Liberties, 1947–48." *Art and Action, 10th Anniversary Issue, Twice-a-Year, 1938–1948*. New York: Twice-a-Year Press, 1948. Pp. 529–536.

General discussion of civil liberties in post-World War II America.

1156. "Civil Rights." *Social Work Yearbook*. Vol. 10. New York: Russell Sage Foundation, 1949. Pp. 116–122.

General discussion of civil rights and civil liberties issues.

1157. "Civil Rights in Austria." *The New Leader*, 32 (February 26, 1949): 6.

Discussion of civil rights and civil liberties issues in post-World War II, based on Baldwin's recent visit.

1158. "Communist Conspirators and the Bill of Rights." *The Progressive*, 5 (April 1949), 14.

Discussion of the prosecution of the leaders of the American Communist Party under the Smith Act. Reflects Baldwin's opposition to the Smith Act and his uneasiness about having to defend Communists.

1159. "Congress Faces Civil Rights." *Christian Register* (November 1947): 425–426.

Discussion of civil rights issues in Congress following the report of President Harry Truman's Commission on Civil Rights.

1160. "Conscience Under the Draft." *The Nation*, 153 (August 9, 1941): 114–116.

Discussion of the status of conscientious objectors under the 1940 Selective Service Act.

1161. "Conscientious Objectors." *The Nation*, 151 (October 12, 1940): 326–328.

A discussion of the status of conscientious objectors under the 1940 Selective Service Act.

1162. "Freedom—More or Less." *Intercollegian*, 58 (April 1941): 135–136.

Discussion of threats to civil liberties on the eve of American entry to World War II.

1163. "Gilt-Edged Patriots: Presenting Merwin K. Hart." *Frontiers of Democracy*, 7 (November 15, 1940): 45–47.

Short article on prominent right-wing, anti-civil liberties spokesperson.

1164. "Have Public Employees the Right to Strike?—Yes." *National Municipal Review*, 30 (September 1941): 515–517.

Defense of the right of public employees to strike.

1165. "Hope For a World Bill of Rights." *The New Republic*, 119 (July 19, 1948): 9.

Discussion of international civil liberties issues.

1166. "International Agreements Can Protect Specific Rights." *The Annals of the American Academy of Political and Social Science*, 243 (January 1946): 134–138.

Discussion of international civil liberties issues following World War II. Argues in favor of ratification of international covenants on human rights.

1167. "Introduction." Walter Nelles. *A Liberal in Wartime: The Education of Albert DeSilver*. New York: W. W. Norton, 1940.

Introduction to biography of Albert DeSilver who served as the co-executive director of the ACLU with Baldwin from 1920 to 1924.

1168. "Japanese-Americans and the Law." *Asia*, 42 (September 1942): 518–519.

Discussion of the status of the Japanese-Americans in the early months of their evacuation from the west coast and internment.

1169. "Japanese-Americans in Wartime." *American Mercury*, 59 (December 1944): 665–670.

Discussion of the evacuation and internment of the Japanese-Americans.

1170. "Japan's American Revolution." *Current History*, (February 1948). Reprinted in *Reader's Digest*, 52 (March 1948): 75–78.

Discussion of the development of constitutional democracy in Japan under the American occupation, based on Baldwin's trip to Japan where he advised General Douglas MacArthur on civil liberties issues.

1171. "A Liberal Looks at Life." *Frontiers of Democracy*, 7 (May 15, 1941): 235–236.

General discussion of social and political questions prior to American entry into World War II.

1172. "Liberals and the Communist Trial." *The New Republic*, 120 (January 31, 1949): 7–8.

Discussion of the government prosecution of the top leaders of the American Communist Party under the Smith Act.

Response to Morris Ernst's contribution in the same issue (#453). Baldwin argues that the government has not proven its case against the Communist Party leaders.

1173. "Our Blunder in Korea." *The Nation*, 165 (August 2, 1947): 119–121.

Criticism of U.S. policy toward South Korea. Argues that the establishment of a puppet government is likely to enhance the popularity of Communism.

1174. "Our Counter-Espionage Statutes are Adequate." *Survey Graphic*, 29 (November 1940): 550.

Expression of opposition to the prosecution of political radicals under the new Smith Act.

1175. "The Prospects for Postwar Liberty." *The Progressive* (May 28, 1945): 4.

Brief assessment of the future of civil liberties on the occasion of the end of World War II.

1176. "The Question of Liberty." *The New Republic*, 105 (November 17, 1941): 649-651.

Discussion of civil liberties issues during wartime.

1177. "Reds and Rights." *The Progressive* (June 1948): 5-6.

Expression of the ACLU's opposition to anti-Communist measures in the first years of the Cold War.

1178. "Repression vs. Propaganda." *The Nation*, 154 (April 11, 1942): 444.

Discussion of freedom of speech during wartime.

1179. "The Truth Shall Make You Free." *Survey Graphic*, 35 (December 1946): 498-500.

Discussion of restrictions on the international flow of information.

1180. "Union Administration and Civil Liberties." *The Annals of the American Academy of Political and Social Science*, 248 (November 1946): 54-61.

A discussion of civil liberties aspects of the labor movement, including the rights of union members vis-a-vis union bureaucracies as well as the rights of unions.

1181. "What Liberties in Wartime?" *The New Leader*, 25 (December 5, 1942).

A review of civil liberties issues arising from World War II as of late 1942.

e. 1950–1981

1182. "Common Ground for Diversity." *Saturday Review*, 47 (May 16, 1964): 43–44.

    Discussion of issues related to tolerance of diverse opinions on controversial subjects.

1183. "Dayton's First Issue." Jerry R. Tompkins, ed. *D-Days at Dayton.* Baton Rouge: Louisiana State University Press, 1965.

    Baldwin's recollections of the 1925 *Scopes* trial.

1184. "Defenders of Civil Liberty." *America*, 14 (January 1962): 26–28.

    General discussion of civil liberties issues.

1185. "Defining Our Legal Liberties." *Saturday Review*, 49 (January 1, 1966): 28.

    General discussion of civil liberties issues.

1186. "Dissident Pioneer." *Rights*, 12 (February 1965): 31–33.

    Tribute to Alexander Meiklejohn, authority on the First Amendment, and an important figure in the ACLU.

1187. "Early Years of a Radical." *The Nation*, 182 (May 12, 1956): 414.

    Book review of autobiography of Elizabeth Gurley Flynn, *I Speak My Own Piece*. Discusses Flynn's relationship with the Communist Party and the ACLU (see #264).

1188. "Faint Outline of Global Law." *Saturday Review*, 41 (December 13, 1958): 31–32.

    Discussion of international human rights issues.

1189. "General Douglas MacArthur." *The Nation*, 198 (April 20, 1964): 385.

    Recollections of his experience with General MacArthur during the American occupation of Japan.

Notable for Baldwin's favorable view of the conservative military leader.

1190. "Hard Going For Human Rights." *The New Republic*, 125 (August 27, 1951): 10–11.

Assessment of the prospects for ratification of international covenants protecting human rights.

1191. "Haters Among Us." *Saturday Review*, 48 (June 19, 1965): 36.

Short article on racism in American society.

1192. "Hostility to the West." *The Nation*, 174 (June 7, 1952): 554.

Brief item on human rights issues in the Middle East.

1193. "Human Rights and Middle East Nationalism." *New Outlook*, 5 (July 1952): 7–11.

Discussion of human rights issues in the Middle East at a time when Baldwin was devoting his energies primarily toward international human rights issues.

1194. "Human Rights in the Middle East." *Hadassah Newsletter*, (July-August 1952): 4.

Discussion of human rights issues in the Middle East.

1195. "Ideals vs. Facts." *UN World*, 5 (August 1951): 19–21.

Discussion of issues related to international human rights.

1196. "The International Outlook for Civil Rights." *The Annals of the American Academy of Political and Social Science*, 275 (May 1951): 155–161.

Discussion of international human rights issues which became Baldwin's primary focus following his retirement as director of the ACLU in 1950.

1197. "Introduction." Allen R. Bosworth. *America's Concentration Camps*. New York: W.W. Norton, 1967.

Brief discussion of the evacuation and internment of the Japanese-Americans.

1198. "Jane Addams." *The Nation*, 190 (April 30, 1960): 375–376.

Recollections of the famous early social worker and feminist.

1199. "Jane Addams." *Jane Addams: A Centennial Reader* (New York: Macmillan, 1960).

An appreciation of feminist and social reformer Jane Addams who was one of the first members of the ACLU.

1200. "MacArthur: Man and Mission." *The Progressive* (May 1951), 31–32.

Review of biography of General Douglas MacArthur. A surprisingly favorable view of General Douglas MacArthur; reflects Baldwin's personal contact with MacArthur during his visit to Japan.

1201. "The Meaning of Civil Liberties." Introduction to *American Civil Liberties Union. Annual Reports.* New York: Arno Press, 1970), Vol. 1, pp. iii–xxxiii.

General discussion of ACLU history and the development of civil liberties.

1202. "Introduction." *A New Slavery. Forced Labor: The Communist Betrayal of Human Rights.* New York: Oceana, 1953.

Discussion of human rights violations in the Soviet Union. Reflects Baldwin's anti-Communist outlook of the period. For his earlier view of the Soviet Union, see #1120.

1203. "Norman Thomas: A Combative Life." *The New Republic*, 158 (January 13, 1968): 11–12.

An appreciation of Baldwin's closest friend and co-founder of the ACLU and long-time colleague in ACLU and other political movements. Written on the occasion of Thomas's death.

1204. "Norman Thomas: A Memoir." *Saturday Review*, 52 (April 12, 1969): 41–42.

> Recollections of Baldwin's closest friend and co-founder of the ACLU.

1205. "Palestine Refugees." *Current History*, 33 (November 1957): 295–298.

> Article on the question of Palestinian refugees in the Middle East.

1206. "Policemen of the Nation's Morality." *Saturday Review*, 43 (September 3, 1960): 43.

> Article criticizing advocates of censorship.

1207. *The Prospects for Freedom*. Felix Adler Lecture. New York: American Ethical Union, 1952.

> Pamphlet reprinting version of speech on general human rights issues.

3. Interviews with

1208. "The ACLU and the FBI: A Conversation Between Roger Baldwin and Alan F. Westin." *Civil Liberties Review*, 4 (November/December 1977): 17–25.

> Discussion of the relationship between the ACLU and the FBI following the release of the FBI's files on the ACLU and the revelation that some ACLU leaders had collaborated with the Bureau, in some cases in violation of ACLU policy.

1209. Baldwin, Roger. Interview. Columbia Oral History Collection. Columbia University, New York, NY.

> Extensive interview with Roger Baldwin conducted in the mid-1950s. Much material on his then-current work on international human rights issues following his retirement as director of the ACLU. Disappointing with respect to his activity as director of the ACLU.

1210. "Comment." *Civil Liberties Review*, 3 (June/July 1976): 5.

Response to interview published in earlier issue (#1212). Baldwin attempts to clarify the relationship between the ACLU and the Communist Party between 1920 and 1940.

1211. "Recollections of a Life in Civil Liberties—I." *Civil Liberties Review*, 2 (Spring 1975): 39–72. Part II. *Ibid.*, (Fall 1975): 10–40.

Excellent interview with Baldwin about the early years of the ACLU. The interviewer, Alan Westin, located many documents in the ACLU archives and used these to prompt Baldwin's memory.

4. Obituaries

1212. ACLU. *Roger Baldwin: A Remembrance.* New York: ACLU, 1982.

Collection of tributes to Baldwin published by the ACLU.

1213. "A Legacy of Freedom." *Inquiry*, 4 (October 19, 1981): 3.

1214. Donald, Peter G. "Last Words: Roger Nash Baldwin." *Rolling Stone*, (October 15, 1981): 24–25.

1215. Dorsen, Norman. "Roger N. Baldwin." *Harvard Magazine*, 84 (January/February 1982): 77.

1216. Haskell, Gordon. "Roger Baldwin." *Dissent*, 29 (Winter 1982): 102.

1217. Kairys, David. "Roger Baldwin." *In These Times*, 5 (September 9, 1981): 15.

1218. Morris, Willie. "Roger Baldwin." *The New Republic*, 150 (January 25, 1964): 8–10.

1219. Novack, George. "Roger Baldwin/Fighter For Liberties." *The Militant*, 45 (September 11, 1981): 22.

1220. Roche, John P. "Remembering Roger Baldwin." *The New Leader*, 64 (1981): 14–15.

1221. "Roger Baldwin: ACLU Founder Dead at 97." *Civil Liberties*, No. 339 (September 1981)

1222. Trinkl, J. "Baldwin of ACLU Dies." *The Guardian*, 33 (September 9, 1981): 7.

B. OTHER ACLU LEADERS

[See also #118, #144, #145, 154, #395, #441, 1186, #1187, #1204, #1205, #1199, #1200.]

1223. Budenz, Louis Francis. *This is My Story*. New York: McGraw-Hill, 1947.

Memoirs of a political radical who served as the ACLU's first publicity director in 1920, later joined the Communist Party, and eventually became a prominent anti-Communist during the Cold War.

1224. [Dennett, Mary Ware]. "Mary Ware Dennett." *Notable American Women*. Vol. 1. Cambridge, MA: Harvard University Press, 1980. Pp. 463–465.

Biographical sketch of a prominent birth control advocate who was active with the ACLU from its founding through the 1930s. Was the defendant in an important obscenity case involving a sex education pamphlet (see #196, #203).

1225. [Dorsen, Norman]. "Faculty Profile: Norman Dorsen." *NYU Law* (Spring, 1987): 5, 8.

Brief portrait of the president of the ACLU, 1976–1991.

1226. Drinan, Rev. Robert F. "I Gave Up Beating on the Justice Department For Lent." *Civil Liberties Review*, 1 (Fall 1973): 75–95.

Interview with prominent Catholic priest who became an ally of the ACLU on issues related to civil rights, the Vietnam War, Watergate, and national security. (See also #494, #495.)

1227. [Eastman, Crystal]. "Crystal Eastman." *Notable American Women.* Vol. 1. Cambridge, MA: Harvard University Press, 1980.

Biographical sketch of the co-founder of the Civil Liberties Bureau in 1917, forerunner of the ACLU.

1228. [Eastman, Crystal]. Cook, Blanche Wiesen. "Crystal Eastman." G.J. Barker-Benfield and Catherine Clinton. *Portraits of American Women.* New York: St. Martins, 1991. Pp. 423–446.

Biographical sketch of the co-founder of the Civil Liberties Bureau, forerunner of the ACLU.

1229. [Eastman, Crystal]. Cook, Blanche Wiesen, ed. *Crystal Eastman on Women and Revolution.* New York: Oxford University Press, 1978.

Collection of writings by the secretary of the American Union Against Militarism (AUAM) and the co-founder of the Civil Liberties Bureau, forerunner of the ACLU. Contains a good biographical essay by the editor.

1230. [Eastman, Crystal]. Kirchwey, Freda. "Crystal Eastman." *The Nation,* 127 (August 8, 1928): 123–124.

Obituary of the co-founder of the Civil Liberties Bureau, forerunner of the ACLU.

1231. Ernst, Morris L. *The Best is Yet . . .* New York: Harper and Brothers, 1945.

Memoirs of an important member of the ACLU Board of Directors and ACLU general counsel, 1929–1954. Contains valuable first-hand accounts of several ACLU cases.

1232. Ernst, Morris L. *A Love Affair With the Law.* New York: Macmillan, 1968.

   Memoirs of an important member of the ACLU Board of Directors and ACLU general counsel, 1929–1954. Relatively short and with less material on the ACLU than is found in #1233.

1233. [Ernst, Morris L.]. "Morris L. Ernst." *Current Biography 1961.* New York: H. W. Wilson, 1961.

   Short biographical sketch of prominent ACLU leader, then near the end of his career.

1234. [Ernst, Morris L.]. "Morris L. Ernst." *Current Biography 1976.* New York: H. W. Wilson, 1976. P. 466.

   Obituary.

1235. [Ernst, Morris L.]. "Morris L. Ernst." *Encyclopedia of the American Constitution,* Vol. 2. New York: Macmillan, 1986.

   Brief biographical sketch of ACLU co-general counsel, 1929–1954, and one of its most important leaders.

1236. [Ernst, Morris L.]. Rodell, Fred. "Morris Ernst: New York's Unlawyerlike Liberal Lawyer Is the Censor's Enemy, The President's Friend." *Life,* (February 21, 1941): 96–98.

   Portrait of ACLU co-general counsel and one of the leaders of the fight against censorship. Good insight into the non-ACLU activities of Ernst.

1237. Flynn, Elizabeth Gurley. *The Rebel Girl: An Autobiography: My First Life (1906–1926).* New York: International Publishers, 1973.

   Autobiography of a founding member of the ACLU. Does not cover the most controversial episode in her involvement with the ACLU (1940), however (see #264).

1238. [Flynn, Elizabeth Gurley]. Baxandall, Rosalyn Fraad. *Words on Fire: The Life and Writing of Elizabeth Gurley Flynn.* New Brunswick, NJ: Rutgers University Press, 1987.

Individual ACLU Leaders

Biographical essay on Flynn, together with a collection of her writings. Flynn was a founding member of the ACLU in 1920 but was expelled from the Board of Directors in 1940 because of her membership in the Communist Party (see #264).

1239. Flynn, Elizabeth Gurley. *The Alderson Story: My Life as a Political Prisoner.* New York: International Publishers, 1963.

    Flynn's account of her conviction and subsequent imprisonment for violating the Smith Act as a leader of the Communist Party. No material on the ACLU.

1240. [Flynn, Elizabeth Gurley]. "Elizabeth Gurley Flynn." *Notable American Women.* Vol. 4. Cambridge, MA: Harvard University Press, 1980. Pp. 242–246.

    Biographical sketch of a co-founder of the ACLU and prominent member of the Board of Directors in the 1920s and 1930s.

1241. [Flynn, Elizabeth Gurley]. Kizer, Benjamin H. "Elizabeth Gurley Flynn." *Pacific Northwest Quarterly*, 57 (July 1966): 110–112.

    Brief portrait of a co-founder of the ACLU and controversial member of the Board of Directors for many years.

1242. Fraenkel, Osmond K. Interview. Columbia Oral History Collection. Columbia University, New York, NY.

    Interview with long-time member of the ACLU Board of Directors, and the ACLU's most important Supreme Court litigator from the late 1930s through the early 1970s.

1243. [Fraenkel, Osmond K.] "Osmond K. Fraenkel." *Encyclopedia of the American Constitution.* Vol. 2. New York: Macmillan, 1986. P. 763.

    Brief sketch of the ACLU's most important Supreme Court litigator from the late 1930s through the 1970s.

1244. [Fraenkel, Osmond K.]. Dorsen, Norman. "An Appreciation of Osmond K. Fraenkel." *New York Law Journal* (June 14, 1983).

Brief sketch of the ACLU's most important Supreme Court litigator from the late 1930s through the 1970s. Fraenkel argued more civil liberties cases before the Supreme Court than any other person.

1245. [Fraenkel, Osmond K.]. "Nancy Wechsler Remembers Osmond and Jimmy." *Civil Liberties*, 348 (Winter 1984): 3.

Recollections by Nancy Wechsler of her father, Osmond Fraenkel, and her husband, newspaper editor James Wechsler.

1246. [Frankfurter, Felix]. Rauh, Joseph L. "Felix Frankfurter: Civil Libertarian." *Harvard Civil Rights—Civil Liberties Law Review*, 2 (1976): 496–530.

Article on the civil liberties aspects of the career of Supreme Court Justice Frankfurter. Frankfurter was an a member of the ACLU National Committee, 1920–1939, and an influential voice on many issues. Yet, he disappointed the ACLU once on the Supreme Court by taking a conservative position on many civil liberties issues.

1247. Garbus, Martin. *Ready for the Defense*. New York: Avon Books, 1972.

Memoirs of a prominent civil liberties attorney who served as the first director of the Roger Baldwin Civil Liberties Foundation (later the ACLU Foundation). The book covers five important cases handled by the author.

1248. [Glasser, Ira]. "Ira Glasser." *Current Biography Yearbook 1986*. New York: H. W. Wilson, 1986. Pp. 174–177.

Biographical sketch of ACLU executive director (1978–).

1249. Hays, Arthur Garfield. *City Lawyer*. New York: Simon and Schuster, 1942.

Autobiography of long-time member of the ACLU Board of Directors and co-general counsel, 1929–1954. One of the ACLU's most important lawyers from the 1920s through the 1940s. Valuable first-hand accounts of early civil liberties cases. Places ACLU activities in the context of other activities. (See also #144, #145.)

1250. [Hays, Arthur Garfield]. "Arthur Garfield Hays." *Encyclopedia of the American Constitution*. Vol. 2. New York: Macmillan, 1986. Pp. 909–910.

Brief biographical sketch of co-general counsel of the ACLU, 1929–1954, and one of its most important leaders.

1251. [Hays, Arthur Garfield]. "Arthur Garfield Hays." *Current Biography 1942*. New York: H. W. Wilson, 1942. Pp. 354–357.

Brief sketch of long-time ACLU co-general counsel, 1929–1954, and important member of the Board of Directors.

1252. Holmes, John Haynes. *I Speak for Myself: The Autobiography of John Haynes Holmes*. New York: Harper and Brothers, 1959.

Autobiography of a founding member of the ACLU and chairperson of the Board of Directors, 1940–1950. Holmes was also a prominent pacifist, civil rights activist, and one of the most prominent Protestant clergymen of his day. His memoirs are weak on his ACLU activities, but provide insight into his wide-ranging activities outside the ACLU.

1253. [Huebsch, Ben W.]. "Portrait." *Publishers Weekly*, 158 (December 9, 1950): 2426.

Short biographical sketch of a prominent American publisher (Viking Press) and long time member of the ACLU Board of Directors.

1254. Huebsch, Ben W. Interview. Columbia Oral History Collection. Columbia University. New York, NY.

Interview with noted publisher and long-time member of the ACLU Board of Directors. Co-founded Viking Press.

1255. Jackson, Gardner. Interview. Columbia Oral History Collection. Columbia University, New York, NY.

Interview with long-time political activist involved in civil liberties and liberal issues from the 1920s through the 1950s. Worked with the ACLU on the Sacco-Vanzetti case, opposition to the House Un-American Activities Committee, and other issues. Functioned as unofficial ACLU lobbyist in Washington, DC, for many years.

1256. [Kenyon, Dorothy]. "Dorothy Kenyon." *Notable American Women*. Vol. 4. Cambridge, MA: Harvard University Press, 1980. Pp. 395–397.

Biographical sketch of important member of the ACLU Board of Directors between the late 1930s and the 1960s. Kenyon was the first person named as a Communist by Senator Joseph McCarthy in 1950.

1257. [Kenyon, Dorothy]. "Judge Kenyon Meets the Press." *American Mercury*, 70 (June 1950): 700–708.

Article on the member of the ACLU Board of Directors who was the first person named by Senator Joseph McCarthy as a suspected Communist.

1258. [King, Carol Weiss]. "Carol Weiss King." *Notable American Women*. Vol. 4. Cambridge, MA: Harvard University Press, 1980. Pp. 397–398.

1259. Kunstler, William M. *Deep in My Heart*. New York: Morrow, 1966.

Memoirs of a prominent lawyer active in civil rights, civil liberties, and Vietnam War issues. Brief but vivid account of his work for the ACLU in Mississippi in the 1960s.

Individual ACLU Leaders

1260. Lamont, Corliss. *Basic Pamphlets.* New York: Basic Pamphlets, various dates.

    Series of short pamphlets on various topics, including civil liberties. Published occasionally between the early 1950s and the late 1980s.

1261. [Lamont, Corliss]. "Corliss Lamont." *Current Biography 1946.* New York: H. W. Wilson, 1947. Pp. 320-322.

    Brief sketch of one of the most important members of the ACLU Board of Directors (1934-1954).

1262. Lamont, Corliss. *Voice in the Wilderness: Collected Essays of Fifty Years.* Buffalo, NY: Prometheus Books, 1974.

    Collection of essays on humanism, civil liberties, socialism, and world peace. Not an autobiography, but provides valuable insight into the thinking of a prominent member of the ACLU Board of Directors, 1934-1954. Includes thirteen essays on civil liberties, many of them speeches or previously published articles.

1263. Lamont, Corliss. *Yes to Life.* New York: Horizon Press, 1981.

    Autobiography. Material on the ACLU repeats material found in more detail in #263 and #1263.

1264. [Malin, Patrick Murphy]. "Malin, Patrick Murphy." *Current Biography 1950.* New York: H. W. Wilson, 1950. Pp. 377-379.

    Biographical sketch of ACLU executive director, 1950-1962.

1265. [Malin, Patrick Murphy]. "Patrick Murphy Malin: The Lawyer You Didn't Know You Had." *True* (April 1961): 18.

    Sympathetic profile of the ACLU executive director.

1266. Morgan, Charles, Jr. *A Time to Speak.* New York: Holt, Rinehart and Winston, 1964.

Account of the author's civil rights activities in Birmingham, Alabama in the early 1960s. He and his family were forced to leave the city after he denounced the bombing of a black church which killed four black children in 1963. Morgan later became an important ACLU staff person (#1270).

1267. [Morgan, Charles, Jr.]. Branch, Taylor. "Can Chuck Morgan Keep Jimmy Carter Honest?" *Esquire*, 87 (February 1977): 14ff.

Article on the former director of the ACLU Washington Office. Concentrates on his political activities rathern than his ACLU activities.

1268. [Morgan, Charles, Jr.]. Powledge, Fred. "Profiles: Charles Morgan, Jr." *The New Yorker*, 45 (October 25, 1969): 63–64.

Article on the director of the ACLU Southern Regional Office, near the end of his tenure in that office. Sympathetic portrait.

1269. Morgan, Charles, Jr. *One Man, One Voice*. New York: Holt, Rinehart and Winston, 1979.

Memoirs of the director of the ACLU Southern Regional Office, and director of the ACLU Washington Office. Important first-hand account of his role in important civil rights and Vietnam War-related cases. Also valuable first-hand account of his role in the Watergate scandal and his efforts to get the ACLU to call for the impeachment of President Richard Nixon.

1270. Nearing, Scott. *The Making of a Radical: A Political Autobiography*. New York: Harper and Row, 1972.

Memoirs of a noted American political radical who was a victim of the repression of free speech during World War I. Contains several interesting episodes involving issues and people associated with the ACLU.

1271. [Neier, Aryeh]. "Aryeh Neier." *Current Biography 1978*. New York: H. W. Wilson, 1978. Pp. 322–326.

Biographical sketch of ACLU executive director, 1970–1978.

1272. [Norton, Eleanor Holmes]. "Defender of Unpopular Causes." *Ebony*, 24 (January 1969): 37–38.

Article on the career of Eleanor Holmes Norton, then a staff attorney with the ACLU. Good material on her role as an African-American defending the free speech rights of racists, notably Alabama Governor George Wallace, for the ACLU.

1273. [Norton, Eleanor Holmes]. "Eleanor Holmes Norton." *Who's Who of American Women, 1991–1992*. Wilmette, IL: Marquis Who's Who, 1991. P. 734.

Brief résumé of former ACLU staff counsel and chairperson of the ACLU National Advisory Council.

1274. [Norton, Eleanor Holmes]. "Some People Derive Their Energy From Struggle." *Civil Liberties Review*, 2 (Winter 1975): 90–110.

Interview with noted black attorney who served as assistant ACLU legal director, 1965–1970, and later as chair of the ACLU National Advisory Council in the 1980s.

1275. [Pemberton, John De J(arnette), Jr.] "John De J. Pemberton." *Current Biography 1969*. New York: H. W. Wilson, 1969. Pp. 327–329.

Biographical sketch of ACLU executive director (1962–1970).

1276. Pfeffer, Leo. "An Autobiographical Sketch." James E. Wood, ed. *Religion and the State: Essays in Honor of Leo Pfeffer*. Waco, TX: Baylor University Press, 1985. Pp. 487–534.

1277. [Pilpel, Harriet]. "Her Motto is 'Don't Tread on Me'." *Civil Liberties*, 333 (June 1980): 4.

Biographical sketch of long-time ACLU lawyer, general counsel, and expert on reproductive rights.

1278. [Pilpel, Harriet]. Law, Sylvia. "A Tribute: Harriet Fleischel Pilpel." *Family Planning Perspectives*, 23 (July/August 1991): 182–183.

   Obituary for Pilpel who served as general counsel for both the ACLU and Planned Parenthood and was a pioneer in the area of reproductive rights litigation.

1279. [Pollak, Walter]. "Walter H. Pollak." *Encyclopedia of the American Constitution*. Vol. 2. New York: Macmillan, 1986. P. 1423.

   Brief biographical sketch of one of the ACLU's most important lawyers in the 1920s and 1930s. (See also #154.)

1280. [Reitman, Alan]. Rosenthal, John. "Reitman Reminisces." *Civil Liberties*, No. 367 (Summer 1989): 6.

   Reflections of the long-time associate director of the ACLU (1949–1989) on the occasion of his retirement.

1281. Rice, Elmer. *Minority Report: An Autobiography*. New York: Simon and Schuster, 1963.

   Memoirs of a noted playwright who played an important role in the ACLU's anti-censorship activities from the late 1920s through the 1950s. Contains some useful material on the early years of the ACLU.

1282. [Seymour, Whitney North]. "Whitney North Seymour." *Current Biography 1961*. New York: H. W. Wilson, 1961. Pp. 417–419.

   Biographical sketch of important member of the ACLU Board of Directors, 1940–1954. Conservative influence on the ACLU during the period. The sketch does not mention his ACLU activities.

1283. Spivak, John L. *A Man in His Time*. New York: Horizon Press, 1967.

   Memoirs of a journalist who was hired by the ACLU to investigate and write reports on several civil liberties cases in the 1920s.

Individual ACLU Leaders

1284. Swomley, John M., Jr. *War, Peace and Justice: The Prophetic Record*. Kansas City: St. Paul School of Theology, 1985.

    Collection of essays by a leading pacifist who served on the ACLU Board of Directors in the 1970s and 1980s. Includes an extensive bibliography of the author's writings on pacifism, national security, civil rights, separation of church and state, abortion, and other issues.

1285. Thomas, Norman. Interview. Columbia Oral History Collection. Columbia University, New York, NY.

    Interview with co-founder of the ACLU and longtime member of the ACLU Board of Directors. Material concentrates on his poitical career, with little refence to his ACLU activities.

1286. [Thomas, Norman]. Bernard K. Johnpoll. *Pacifist's Progress: Norman Thomas and the Decline of American Socialism*. Chicago: Quadrangle Books, 1970.

    Biography of one of the founders of the ACLU and one of the most important members of the Board of Directors from 1920 through the 1950s. Very little material on his activities in the ACLU, however.

1287. [Thomas, Norman]. William A. Swanberg. *Norman Thomas: the Last Idealist*. New York: Scribner's, 1976.

    Biography of one of the founders of the ACLU and one of the most important members of the Board of Directors from 1920 thorugh the 1950s. Very little material on his activities in the ACLU, however.

1288. [Van Kleeck, Mary]. "Mary Van Kleeck." *Notable American Women*. Vol. 4. Cambridge, MA: Harvard University Press, 1980. Pp. 707–709.

    Biographical sketch of a noted feminist, expert on issues related to working women, and member of the ACLU Board of Directors in the 1930s. An important member of the left-wing faction of the Board during the period.

1289. Ward, Harry F. *The Labor Movement: From the Standpoint of Religious Values.* New York: Sturgis and Walton, 1917.

   Discussion of the labor movement and the problems of industrial society from the perspective of the Protestant social gospel. Ward served as chairperson of the ACLU Board of Directors, 1920–1940.

1290. Ward, Harry F. *The New Social Order.* New York: Macmillan, 1926.

   Discussion of social problems by the chairperson of the ACLU Board of Directors, 1920–1940.

1291. Ward, Harry F. *The Social Creed of the Churches.* New York: Abingdon Press, 1917.

   Discussion of social problems by the person who served as Chairperson of the ACLU Board of Directors, 1920–1940. Reflects the Protestant social gospel perspective before the emergence of civil liberties consciousness. Ward was a prominent Methodist minister and professor of theology.

1292. Weinberger, Harry. "A Rebel's Interrupted Autobiography." *American Journal of Economics and Sociology,* 2 (October 1942): 111–122.

   Short autobographical essay by an attorney who handled several of the most important civil liberties cases during World War I.

VI. Resources

A. ACLU OFFICES

1. National Offices

1293. ACLU National Office
   132 West 43rd St.
   New York, NY 10036
   212-944-9800

   [NOTE: The national office houses the executive director of the ACLU, the legal director, and the public education director. It also houses the following projects: AIDS and Civil Liberties Project, Children's Rights Project, Immigration and Aliens' Rights Task Force, Lesbian and Gay Rights Proejct. Reproductive Freedom Project, Women's Rights Project.]

1294. ACLU Washington Office.
   122 Maryland Avenue, NE
   Washington, DC 20002
   202-544-1681

   [NOTE: The ACLU Washington Office also houses the Center For National Security Studies, Project on Technology and Civil Liberties, and the National Security Litigation Project.

1295. National Prison Project
   1875 Connecticut Ave., NW
   Washington, DC 20009
   202-234-4830

1296. ACLU Mountain States Regional Office
6825 E. Tennessee Ave., Bldg. 2, #262
Denver, CO 80224
303-321-4828

1297. ACLU Southern Regional Office
44 Forsythe St., NW, #202
Atlanta, GA 30303
404-523-2721

2. ACLU Affiliate Offices

1298. Alabama Civil Liberties Union
P.O. 447
Montgomery, AL 36101
205-262-0304

1299. Alaska Civil Liberties Union
P.O. Box 201844
Anchorage, AK 99520-1844
907-276-2258

1300. Arizona Civil Liberties Union
Box 17148
Phoenix, AZ 85011-0148
602-650-1967

1301. ACLU of Arkansas
103 W. Capitol, #1120
Little Rock, AR 72201
501-374-2660

1302. ACLU of Northern California
1663 Mission St., #460
San Francisco, CA 94103
415-621-2488

Resources

1303. ACLU of Southern California
 1616 Beverly Blvd.
 Los Angeles, CA 90026
 213-977-9500

1304. ACLU of San Diego and Imperial Counties
 1202 Kettner Blvd., #6200
 San Diego, CA 92101
 619-232-2121

1305. ACLU of Colorado
 815 E. 22nd Ave.
 Denver, CO 80205
 303-861-2258

1306. Connecticut Civil Liberties Union
 32 Grand St.
 Hartford, CT 06106
 203-247-9823

1307. ACLU of Delaware
 First Federal Plaza
 702 King Street, #600A
 Wilmington, DE 19801
 302-654-3966

1308. ACLU of Florida
 225 NE 34th St., #102
 Miami, FL 33137
 305-576-2336

1309. ACLU of Georgia
 233 Mitchell St., SW, #200
 Atlanta, GA 30303
 404-523-5398

1310. ACLU of Hawaii
 P.O. Box 3410
 Honolulu, HI 96801
 808-545-1722

1311. Idaho National Chapter
Box 1897
Boise, ID 83701
208-344-5243

1312. ACLU of Illinois
203 N. LaSalle St., #1405
Chicago, IL 60601
312-201-9740

1313. Indiana Civil Liberties Union
445 N. Pennsylvania Street, #911
Indianapolis, IN 46204-1883
317-635-4056

1314. Iowa Civil Liberties Union
446 Insurance Exchange Building
Des Moines, IA 50309
515-243-3576

1315. ACLU of Kansas
201 Wyandotte St., #209
Kansas City, MO 64105
816-421-4449

1316. Kentucky Civil Liberties Union
425 W. Muhammad Ali Blvd., #230
Louisville, KY 40202
502-581-1181

1317. ACLU of Louisiana
921 Canal Street, #1237
New Orleans, LA 70112
504-522-0617

1318. Maine Civil Liberties Union
97A Exchange St.
Portland, ME 04101
207-774-8087

1319. ACLU of Maryland
2219 St. Paul Street
Baltimore, MD 21218
301-889-8555

1320. Civil Liberties Union of Massachusetts
19 Temple Place
Boston, MA 02111
617-482-3170

1321. ACLU of Michigan
1249 Washington Blvd., #2910
Detroit, MI 48226-1822
313-961-4662

1322. Minnesota Civil Liberties Union
1021 W. Broadway
Minneapolis, MN 55411
612-522-2423

1323. ACLU of Mississippi
921 N. Congress St.
Jackson, MS 39202
601-355-6464

1324. ACLU of Eastern Missouri
4557 Laclede AVe.
St. Louis, MO 63108
314-361-2111

1325. ACLU of Western Missouri
201 Wyandotte St., #209
Kansas City, MO 64105
816-421-4449

1326. ACLU of Montana
P.O. Box 3012
Billings, MT 59103
406-248-1086

1327. ACLU of the National Capital Area
1400 20th St., NW, #119
Washington, DC 20036
202-457-0800

1328. Nebraska Civil Liberties Union
P.O. Box 81455
Lincoln, NE 68501
402-476-8091

1329. ACLU of Nevada
325 S. Third St., #25
Las Vegas, NV 89101
702-366-1226

1330. New Hampshire Civil Liberties Union
11 South Main St.
Concord, NH 03301
603-225-3080

1331. ACLU of New Jersey
2 Washington Place
Newark, NJ 07102
201-642-2084

1332. ACLU of New Mexico
P.O. Box 80915
Albuquerque, NM 87108
505-266-5915

1333. New York Civil Liberties Union
132 West 43rd St., 2nd Floor
New York, NY 10036
212-382-0557

1334. North Carolina Civil Liberties Union
P.O. Box 28004
Raleigh, NC 27611
919-834-3390

Resources

1335. North Dakota National Chapter
[See Mountain States Regional Office, #1296].

1336. ACLU of Ohio
1223 West Sixth St., 2nd Floor
Cleveland, OH 44113
216-781-6276

1337. ACLU of Oklahoma
1411 Classen, #318
Oklahoma City, OK 73106
405-524-8511

1338. ACLU of Oregon
310 SW Fourth Avenue
Portland, OR 97204
503-227-3186

1339. ACLU of Pennsylvania
P. O. Box 1161
Philadelphia, PA 19105-1161
215-923-4357

1340. Rhode Island Civil Liberties Union
212 Union Street, #211
Providence RI 02903
401-831-7171

1341. ACLU of South Carolina
2712 Middleburg Dr.
Columbia, SC 29204
803-799-5151

1342. South Dakota National Chapter
[See Mountain States Regional Office, #1296].

1343. ACLU of Tennessee
P. O. Box 120160
Nashville, TN 37212
615-320-7142

1344. Texas Civil Liberties Union
3223 Smith St., #215
Houston, TX 77006
713-524-5925

1345. ACLU of Utah
#9 Exchange Place, #419
Salt Lake City, UT 84111-2709
801-521-9289

1346. ACLU of Vermont
100 State Street
Montpelier, VT 05601
802-223-6304

1347. ACLU of Virginia
6 N. 6th St., #400
Richmond, VA 23219-2419
804-644-8022

1348. ACLU of Washington
705 2nd Ave., #300
Seattle, WA 98104
206-624-2180

1349. West Virginia Civil Liberties Union
Box 3952
Charleston, WV 25339
304-345-9246

1350. ACLU of Wisconsin
207 E. Buffalo St., #325
Milwaukee, WI 53202
414-272-4032

1351. Wyoming National Chapter
[See Mountain States Regional Office, #1296.]

B. ARCHIVAL MATERIAL

1. Records of the National ACLU

1352. ACLU Archives. Seeley G. Mudd Library. Princeton University. Princeton, New Jersey.

The archives of the ACLU are enormous, covering events beginning with the ACLU's predecessor organization, the American Union Against Militarism (AUAM) in 1914. These records are extremely rich with considerable material about the ACLU itself, the ACLU affiliates, and civil liberties related issues and organizations on such subjects as civil rights, labor, immigration, and many others. The ACLU archives will be useful to scholars working on many of these other topics even though they have no direct interest in the ACLU. The ACLU archives are extremely well indexed and easy to use. For the years 1914 through 1945 there is a detailed card index which makes it possible to locate material quickly on specific individuals or subjects.

Although the archives of some ACLU affiliates are deposited in other libraries and museums (see below), the national office files do contain extensive although often incomplete material (minutes of meetings, correspondence, newsletters, etc.) on the various affiliates.

1353. *ACLU Records and Publications, 1917-1976*. Glen Rock, NJ: Microfilm Corporation of America, 1976.

Microfilm collection of the ACLU archives for the years, 1917-1975. Total of 96 reels of microfilm. Includes printed *Guide* to the collection.

1354. American Civil Liberties Union. Federal Bureau of Investigation files.

In the mid-1970s the ACLU obtained copies of the Federal Bureau of Investigation files on the organization (see #419, #422). Two copies of the original files currently exist. One is located at the ACLU national office and is available under certain restrictions. A second copy is available, without restrictions, in the reading room of the

Federal Bureau of Investigation library in Washington, DC.

1355. Bureau of Investigation Case Files, 1908–1922. National Archives, Record Group 65. Washington, DC.

Activities of the Bureau of Investigation, predecessor of the FBI, during World War I directed at critics of American war policy, pacifists, labor unions, and any person or organization deemed subversive by the Bureau of Investigation. Valuable material on people associated with the Civil Liberties Bureau, predecessor to the ACLU.

2. Records of ACLU Affiliates

[NOTE: The official files of the various ACLU affiliates have been handled in an inconsistent fashion. Some affiliates have deposited the records with a library or museum. Other affiliates still retain their old files in the office; some of these are available to outside researchers, some are not. There are also considerable variations regarding what materials are available to outside researchers. Because of privacy considerations, some material related to clients in ACLU cases is restricted. Because concern about privacy is a relatively recent phenomenon, these restrictions frequently do not exist for early material. [In any event, it is advisable to contact in advance either the ACLU affiliate office and/or the library holding the archival material to determine the size of the holdings, the years covered, and any restrictions.]

1356. Arizona Civil Liberties Union

Files are in the affiliate office.

1357. ACLU of Arkansas

University of Arkansas. Fayetteville, Arkansas.

1358. ACLU of Northern California

California Historical Society. San Francisco, California. See #77 for annotated guide to the archives.

1359. ACLU of Southern California.
University of California at Los Angeles (UCLA). Los Angeles, California

1360. ACLU of Colorado.
Metropolitan State College. Denver, Colorado.

1361. Connecticut Civil Liberties Union
University of Connecticut. Storrs, Connecticut.

1362. ACLU of Delaware
Files are in the affiliate office.

1363. ACLU of Florida
University of Florida. Gainesville, Florida.

1364. ACLU of Georgia
Files are in the affiliate office.

1365. ACLU of Hawaii
Files are in the affiliate office.

1366. ACLU of Illinois.
University of Chicago. Chicago, Illinois.

1367. Indiana Civil Liberties Union
Files are in the affiliate office.

1368. Iowa Civil Liberties Union.
Iowa State University. Ames, Iowa.

1369. ACLU of Kansas
Files are in the affiliate office.

1370. ACLU of Kentucky
University of Louisville. Louisville, Kentucky.

1371. Maine Civil Liberties Union

Files are in the affiliate office.

1372. ACLU of Maryland
University of Baltimore. Baltimore, Maryland.

1373. Civil Liberties Union of Massachusetts.
Massachusetts Historical Society. Boston, Massachusetts.

1374. ACLU of Michigan
Wayne State University. Detroit, Michigan.

1375. Minnesota Civil Liberties Union
Minnesota Historical Society. Minneapolis, Minnesota.

1376. ACLU of Mississippi
Files are scheduled to be deposited with the University of Mississippi, Oxford, Mississippi, in September, 1992.

1377. ACLU of Eastern Missouri.
Washington University. St. Louis, Missouri.

1378. ACLU of Western Missouri
Files are in the affiliate office.

1379. ACLU of Montana
Files are in the affiliate office.

1380. ACLU of the National Capital Area
Files are in the affiliate office.

1381. Nebraska Civil Liberties Union
Files are in the affiliate office.

1382. ACLU of Nevada
Files are in the affiliate office.

1383. New Hampshire Civil Liberties Union
Files are in the affiliate office.

Resources

1384. ACLU of New Jersey
Files are in the affiliate office.

1385. ACLU of New Mexico
Files are in the affiliate office.

1386. New York Civil Liberties Union.
Files currently in storage and not available.

1387. North Carolina Civil Liberties Union
Duke University. Durham, North Carolina.

1388. ACLU of Ohio
Ohio Historical Society. Columbus, Ohio.

1389. ACLU of Oklahoma
Files are in the affiliate office.

1390. ACLU of Oregon
Files are in the affiliate office.

1391. ACLU of Pennsylvania
Temple University. Philadelphia, Pennsylvania.

1392. Rhode Island Civil Liberties Union
Files are in the affiliate office.

1393. ACLU of South Carolina.
Winthrop College. Rock Hill, South Carolina.

1394. ACLU of Tennessee
Files are in the affiliate office.

1395. Texas Civil Liberties Union
University of Texas at Arlington. Arlington, Texas.

1396. ACLU of Utah
University of Utah. Salt Lake City, Utah.

1397. ACLU of Vermont
Files are in the affiliate office.

1398. ACLU of Virginia
University of Virginia Law School. Charlottesville, Virginia.

1399. ACLU of Wisconsin.
Wisconsin Historical Society. Madison, Wisconsin.

3. Personal Papers of ACLU Leaders

1400. Addams, Jane. Papers. Swarthmore College. Swarthmore, PA.

Important feminist, social worker, and pacifist. Co-founder of the ACLU. A small amount of material on the ACLU in the collection.

1401. Balch, Emily G. Papers. Swarthmore College. Swarthmore, PA.

Noted feminist and political activist. Associated with the ACLU in its early years. A small amount of material on the ACLU in the collection.

1402. Baldwin, Roger. Papers. Seeley G. Mudd Library. Princeton University. Princeton, NJ.

The collection of materials in the Roger Baldwin papers is relatively small and primarily covers Baldwin's early, pre-ACLU years. The material provides extremely valuable insights into his life and character. The most extensive and important material about Baldwin's career is found in the ACLU archives.

1403. Baldwin, Roger. FBI files.

Copy of Federal Bureau of Investigation files on Baldwin, obtained through the Freedom of Information Act. File not complete, as the FBI refused to release some pages of material. Available at Reading Room of the FBI

Library, Washington, DC. Original copy in the possession of Professor Samuel Walker, University of Nebraska at Omaha.

1404. Beale, Howard K. Papers. Wisconsin Historical Society. Madison, WI.

Small collection of material related to historian Beale's activities with the ACLU from the 1930s through the 1950s, primarily on academic freedom and conscientious objector issues.

1405. Bingham, Alfred M. Papers. Yale University. New Haven, CT.

Small collection of materials related to the ACLU in the late 1930s and early 1940s.

1406. Borchard, Edwin M. Papers. Yale University. New Haven, CT.

Small collection of materials related to the ACLU, primarily from the 1930s.

1407. Bronstein, Alvin J. Papers. c/o Bronstein, National Prison Project. Washington, DC.

Microfilm copy. Papers related to Bronstein's work on prisoners' rights and the ACLU National Prison Project.

1408. Chafee, Zechariah. Papers. Harvard University Law School. Cambridge, MA.

Noted legal scholar. Small collection of materials related to the ACLU.

1409. Clark, Grenville. Papers. Dartmouth College. Hanover, NH.

Important collection of material related to the American Bar Association's Committee on the Bill of Rights (1938–1942), which cooperated with the ACLU on a number of landmark Supreme Court cases during the period.

1410. Darrow, Clarence. Papers. Library of Congress. Washington, DC.

Famous trial attorney who handled the *Scopes* case (1925) for the ACLU. Relatively few items related to the ACLU.

1411. Doty, Madeline A. Papers. Smith College. Northampton, MA.

Noted feminist and pacifist. Leader of the Women's International League for Peace and Freedom in the 1920s and 1930s. Married Roger Baldwin in 1919; divorced in 1935. Materials in the collection shed interesting light on aspects of Baldwin's personal life.

1412. Dunn, Robert W. Papers. Tamiment Library. New York University. New York, NY.

Small collection of materials related to Dunn's ACLU activities, primarily on labor issues.

1413. Eastwood, Mary. Papers. Schlesinger Library. Radcliffe College. Cambridge, MA.

Small but valuable collection of materials primarily related to women's rights issues in the ACLU.

1414. Ernst, Morris L. Papers. Humanities Research Center. University of Texas. Austin, TX.

Large and valuable collection of materials on one of the most important figures in ACLU history. Ernst served as co-general counsel of the ACLU from 1929 to 1954, handled many important censorship and early reproductive rights cases.

1415. Evans, Elizabeth Glendower. Papers. Schlesinger Library. Radcliffe College. Cambridge, MA.

Noted feminist and pacifist. Small collection of materials related to the ACLU.

1416. Fly, James L. Papers. Columbia University. New York, NY.

Former Chairperson of the Federal Communications Commission and member of the ACLU Board of Directors. Small collection but some important material on Cold War issues in the 1950s.

1417. Flynn, Elizabeth Gurley. Papers. Tamiment Library. New York University. New York, NY.

Disappointingly small collection of papers on a co-founder of the ACLU and one of the most controversial figures in ACLU history (see #264).

1418. Flynn, Elizabeth Gurley. Papers. Wisconsin Historical Society. Madison, WI.

Small but valuable collection of papers on a co-founder of the ACLU and one of the most controversial figures in ACLU history (see #264).

1419. Fraenkel, Osmond K. Papers. Harvard University Law School. Cambridge, MA.

Disappointing collection of materials on the ACLU premier Supreme Court litigator from the late 1930s through the early 1970s. Contains the original copy of Fraenkel's diary but this item is closed to scholars until the year 2033 (but see item #1420). Also contains a copy of an "autobiography" which Fraenkel began, but this item is thin and unreliable.

1420. Fraenkel, Osmond K. Excerpts from Diary. Seeley G. Mudd Library. Princeton University. Princeton, NJ.

Contains a transcribed copy of the portions of Fraenkel's diary (see #1419) that relate to the ACLU. Extremely valuable source which has been widely used by historians. Must be handled with extreme caution, however. Original copy is closed to scholars and there is no way to verify the accuracy of the transcription or to put the material here in the context of material that was not transcribed.

1421. Frankfurter, Felix. Papers. Harvard University Law School. Cambridge, MA.

   Disappointing in terms of material on the ACLU, despite the fact that Frankfurter was an extremely important figure in the organization from 1920 through 1939.

1422. Frankfurter, Felix. Papers. Library of Congress. Washington, DC.

   Disappointing in terms of the material on the ACLU, despite the fact that Frankfurter was an extremely important figures in the organization from 1920 through 1939.

1423. Hays, Arthur Garfield. Papers. Seeley G. Mudd Library. Princeton University. Princeton, NJ.

   A relatively small and disappointing collection of material. Primarily legal briefs and suppporting papers. Little if any personal material. The most valuable material on Hays (correspondence, etc.) is contained in the ACLU papers.

1424. Holmes, John Haynes. Papers. Library of Congress. Washington, DC.

   Valuable collection of material on one of the founders of the ACLU and chairperson of the Board of Directors, 1940–1950.

1425. Huebsch, Ben W. Papers. Library of Congress. Washington, DC.

   Relatively small collection of material on Huebsch, who was one of the longest serving members of the ACLU Board of Directors.

1426. Kenyon, Dorothy. Papers. Smith College. Northampton, MA.

   Small but useful collection on one of the early advocates of women's rights in the ACLU.

Resources 255

1427. Lamont, Corliss. Papers. Columbia University. New York, NY.

Disappointingly small collection of material on one of the most important figures in ACLU history. Lamont served on the Board from 1934 to 1954 (see Item #263).

1428. Luscomb, Florence. Papers. Schlesinger Library. Radcliffe College. Cambridge, MA.

Noted feminist and political activist. Small collection of material related to the ACLU.

1429. MacDonald. Dwight. Papers. Yale University. New Haven, CT.

Prominent writer and political activist. Relatively little material on the ACLU. Important material relates to MacDonald's articles on Roger Baldwin (#1084) for the *The New Yorker*.

1430. Meiklejohn, Alexander. Papers. Wisconsin Historical Society. Madison, WI.

Noted scholar and authority on the First Amendment. Some valuable material on the ACLU.

1431. Murray, Pauli. Papers. Schlesinger Library. Radcliffe College. Cambridge, MA.

Noted feminist and civil rights activist. Small but valuable collection of material on women's rights issues in the ACLU in the 1960s.

1432. Neier, Aryeh. Papers. ACLU Office. New York, NY.

Papers related to Neier's career as executive director of the ACLU, 1970–1978. Contained in storage in the basement of the ACLU office.

1433. Oxnam, G. Bromley. Papers. Library of Congress. Washington, DC.

Prominent Methodist minister and political activist. Important member of the ACLU Board of Directors. Leader on Church-State issues.

1434. Rice, Elmer. Papers. Humanities Research Center. University of Texas. Austin, TX.

Noted American playwright. Leader of ACLU anti-censorship activities from the late 1920s through the 1950s (see #1281).

1435. Riis, Roger W. Papers. Library of Congress. Washington, DC.

Small collection of material on the ACLU.

1436. Roe, Gilbert. Papers. Contained in LaFollette Family Papers. Library of Congress. Washington, DC.

Small collection of material related to attorney who handled a number of important cases during World War I.

1437. Sanger, Margaret. Papers. Library of Congress. Washington, DC.

A few items on free speech issues by the most famous advocate of birth control in America.

1438. Schroeder, Theodore. Papers. Southern Illinois University. Carbondale, IL.

Important material on the first significant advocate of free speech and founder of the Free Speech League, which preceded the ACLU.

1439. Seymour, Whitney North. Papers. New York Public Library. New York, NY.

Closed to scholars until the year 2008. Potentially valuable material. Seymour was one of the most influential members of the ACLU Board of Directors from 1939 to 1954. He was a particularly conservative influence on major issues during World War II and the Cold War.

1440. Thomas, Norman. Papers. New York Public Library. New York, NY.

Large collection of material on one of the founders of the ACLU and one of its most important Board members for over thirty years. Relatively disappointing on the ACLU, however. The material does not begin until about 1940 and, consequently, there is little on the important first two decades. Other important ACLU-related material may be found in the ACLU papers.

1441. Van Kleeck, Mary. Papers. Smith College. Northampton, MA.

Valuable collection of material on an important ACLU Board member in the 1930s, an advocate of labor's rights, and member of the left-wing faction on the ACLU Board in the late 1930s.

1442. Wald, Lillian. Papers. Columbia University. New York, NY.

Valuable set of materials about one of the leaders of the AUAM whose resignation in the summer of 1917 led to the founding of the Civil Liberties Bureau. Especially good collection of materials on the AUAM, 1914–1917.

1443. Wald, Lillian. Papers. New York Public Library. New York, NY.

Little material on the ACLU. Important ACLU-related material is found in #1442.

1444. Weinberger, Harry. Papers. Yale University. New Haven, CT.

Small collection of material by attorney who handled some of the most important civil liberties cases during World War I.

1445. Wood, L. Hollingsworth. Papers. Columbia University. New York, NY.

Leader of the Civil Liberties Bureau (1917–1919) and co-founder of the ACLU (1920). Small collection of material on the ACLU.

4. Records of Other Organizations

[NOTE: The following items include the official archives of other organizations which contain material related to the ACLU].

1446. American Fund for Public Service Papers. Rare Books and Manuscript Division. New York Public Library. New York, NY.

Popularly known as the "Garland Fund." The Fund was organized and indirectly controlled by Roger Baldwin. During the 1920s it was the principal source of grants for ACLU-related causes (see #136).

1447. American Union Against Militarism Papers. Swarthmore Peace Collection. Swarthmore College. Swarthmore, PA.

The AUAM was the parent organization of the ACLU. Much of the material in the AUAM papers is also found in the ACLU archives but the material here is more complete and better organized.

1448. International Labor Defense Papers. Schomburg Library. New York Public Library. New York, NY.

The ILD was a left-wing organization providing legal assistance to radicals and labor unions. It worked with the ACLU on a number of important cases.

1449. National Association for the Advancement of Colored People (NAACP) Papers. Library of Congress. Washington, DC.

Contains some useful material on the ACLU, particularly for the years 1920–1945.

1450. National Committee Against Repressive Legislation (NCARL) Papers. Wisconsin Historical Society. Madison, WI.

Successor to the National Committee to Abolish the House Committee on Un-American Activities. Contains valuable material on the anti-HUAC campaign and on its director, Frank Wilkinson.

1451. National Commmittee to Abolish the House Un-American Activities Committee.

Same as #1450.

1452. National Committee on Conscientious Objectors (NCCO) Papers. Swarthmore College. Swarthmore, PA.

Organization created during World War II to assist conscientious objectors. Functioned as a de facto ACLU Committee during the war. Valuable material on ACLU activities during the period.

1453. New York Bureau of Legal First Aid Papers. Tamiment Library. New York University. New York, NY.

One of the early organizations combatting the denial of civil liberties during World War I. Activities were eventually absorbed into the Civil Liberties Bureau and then the ACLU.

1454. Swarthmore Peace Collection. Swarthmore College. Swarthmore, PA.

Large and extremely valuable collection, containing the papers of many organizations and individuals involved in pacifist and conscientious objector issues. Material from World War I, World War II, the Korean War, and the Vietnam War. Includes the papers of the AUAM (#1447), predecessor of the ACLU, and other organizations and individuals associated with the ACLU.

Name Index

Note: Entries are indexed by item number, not by page number.

ABA, *see* American Bar Association
Abraham, Henry J., 1022
Abrams, Jacob, *see Abrams v. United States*
Ackley, Sheldon, 574
ACLU Foundation (Roger Baldwin Foundation), 467, 1247
Addams, Jane, 1198, 1199, 1400
Addlestone, David, 66
Adler, Allan, 810, 829, 897, 817, 948
Adler, Felix, 1207
Adult Bible Class Magazine, 1144
Advocate, The, 977, 978, 984
AIDS and Public Policy Journal, 981
Akron Law Review, 404
Allen, Devere, 1122
Allen, Leslie H., 184
America, 494–496, 667, 670, 672, 864, 1184
American Academy of Political and Social Science, 219, 457, 468, 473, 1052, 1147, 1166, 1180, 1196
American Bar Association (ABA), 75, 187, 219, 220, 325, 430, 700, 1409

American Bar Association Journal, 75, 187, 220, 430, 720
Committee on the Bill of Rights, 325, 1409
American Bar Foundation, 392, 1055
American Bar Foundation Research Journal, 392, 1055
American City, 1098
American Defense Society, 134
American Economic Review, 491
American Enterprise Institute, 768
American Ethical Union, 1207
American Freedoms Council, 500
American Friends Service Committee, 1005
American Fund for Public Service ("Garland Fund"), 136, 245, 1446
American Jewish Congress, 473, 503, 1051
American Journal of Economics and Sociology, 1292
American Journal of International Law, 933
American Journal of Law and Medicine, 979
American Legion, 131, 396, 397, 403, 785

American Legion Magazine, 403, 785
American Mercury, 266, 272, 348, 1079, 1169, 1257
American Opinion, 543
American Political Science Review, 328
American Prospect, The, 845
American Protective League, 102
American Psychiatric Association, 863
American Scholar, 429
American Union Against Militarism, 93, 94, 100, 1227–1230, 1352, 1442, 1445, 1447, 1454
American Unitarian Association, 331
Americans United for Separation of Church and State, 501
Americas Watch Committee, 1020
Amsterdam, Anthony G., 606
Andres, Monica, 929
Andrews, Peter, 528
Angell, Ernest, 384, 1043
Annals of the American Academy of Political and Social Science, 219, 457, 468, 473, 1052, 1147, 1166, 1180, 1196
Annas, George, 33, 49
Arkes, H., 674
Arsenault, Ray, 128
Asbury, Herbert, 211
Asia, 1168
Askin, Frank, 446, 607, 608
Atlantic Monthly, 301
Attorney General's Commission on Pornography, (1986), 834, 840, 841
AUAM, *see* American Union Against Militarism
Auerbach, Jerold S., 217, 286

Baird, Bill, *see Bellotti v. Baird*
Baker, Liva, 609
Balch, Emily G., 1401
Baldwin, Roger Nash, 83, 112, 127, 136, 155, 198, 199, 202, 254, 256, 271, 280, 309, 326, 355, 357, 436, 453, 466, 467, 1078–1222, 1247, 1402, 1403, 1411, 1429, 1446
  and anarchism, 1116, 1117
  awards, 1089
  books and articles about, 83, 127, 155, 198, 199, 357, 436, 466 1078–1090, 1212–1222, 1429
  books and articles by, *see* Baldwin, speeches, writings
  and Communism, 1119, 1120, 1133, 1139, 1202, 1210
  FBI file, 1403
  Garland Fund (American Fund for Public Service), 136, 245, 1446
  and international human rights, 1170, 1173, 1188, 1190, 1192–1196, 1205, 1207
  international travels, 1113, 1114, 1118–1120, 1124, 1157, 1170 1189, 1200
  and Japan, post-war U.S. occupation of, 1170, 1189, 1200
  personal papers, 1402
  Roger Baldwin Foundation, 467, 1247
  and Scopes trial, 1183
  social work as profession, 1093, 1094, 1096, 1097, 1099–1103 1106, 1107, 1109, 1115, 1134
  and the Soviet Union, 1119, 1120

Name Index

speeches, 112, 254, 256, 271, 280
writings, 202, 280, 326, 355, 1091–1207
Balter, Michael, 898
Bannan, John F., 717
Bannan, Rosemary S., 717
Barcher, Ann, 67
Barker-Benfield, G.J., 1228
Barnhart, Edward N., 363
Barnum, David, 1066
Barrett, Edward L., 433
Barrister, 680
Basic Pamphlets, 1260
Bates, Ernest Sutherland, 273
Baxandall, Rosalyn Fraad, 1238
Beale, Howard K., 1404
Bean, Barton, 72
Bedau, Hugo Adam, 593, 596
Belknap, Michael, 209, 372
Bende, Paul, 971
Benewick, Robert, 1068
Bennet, James, 796
Benshoof, Janet, 993–995
Benson, Herman, 488
Bentley, Eric, 434
Berger, Vivian, 881–883
Berkman, Alexander, 1117
Berman, Jerry J., 634, 930
Bernard, Mitchell, 60
Bernhard, Edgar, 73
Bertin, Joan E., 996
Berube, Maurice R., 578
Better America Federation, The, 147
Bigelow, Herbert S., 114
Bill of Rights Journal, 461
Bill of Rights Review, 325
Bingham, Richard D., 679, 1405
BioLaw, 996
Birch Society, *see* John Birch Society
Bishop, Joseph W., 529, 530, 718

Black, Jonathan, 533, 556
Blakeley, Mary Kay, 835
Blank, Susan, 1006
Blum, V.C., 493
Blumberg, Richard E., 64
Blumner, Robyn, 884
Boggan, E. Carrington, 37
Bohn, Ted, 863
Bollinger, Lee, 675
Bontecou, Elizabeth, 426
Borchard, Edwin M., 1406
Bork, Robert H., 92, 805–807
Borosage, Robert L., 634
Bosworth, Allan R., 355, 1186
Bourne, Randolph, 96
Boyer, Paul S., 201
Bozell, L. Brent, 386
Bramson, V.C., 684
Brancato, Gilda, 51
Branch, Taylor, 1267
Brant, Irving, 1023
Breener, Laura, 80
Brill, Alida, 1063
British Journal of Sociology, 1065
Britt, Stuart Henderson, 257
Bromley, Dorothy Dudley, 326
Bronstein, Alvin J., 53, 967–969, 1407
Broun, Heywood, 258
Browder, Earl, 377
Brown, Oliver, *see Brown v. Board of Education*
Brown, Ralph S., 427, 428, 430
Brown, Robert, 47
Bruce, J. Campbell, 458
Bruno, Robert J., 857
Buckley, James, *see Buckley v. Valeo*
Buckley, William F., Jr., 386, 435, 444, 531, 610, 647, 664
Budenz, Louis Francis, 1223
Bullough, Vern L., 976
Burden of Blame, The, 587

Bureau of Investigation, 1355. See also Federal Bureau of Investigation
Burger, Warren, 538
Burstyn, Joseph, see *Burstyn v. Wilson*
Business Week, 655
Byse, Clark, 447

Cade, Julia, 53
Calaway, Jim, 757
California, University of, see University of California
California Historical Society, 77, 1358
California History, 77
Cameron, S.C., 858
Campisano, Mark S., 79
Carliner, David, 27, 28
Carlson, M.B., 798
Carter, Dan T., 244
Carter, Jimmy (James Earl), 527, 545, 554, 1089, 1267
Cary, Eve, 61, 579, 739
Case Western Reserve Law Review, 764
Casper, Jonathan, 387, 532
Cassel, Doug, 899
Castner, Lynn S., 580
Catholic World, 493
Caughey, John W., 388, 389, 581
Caught Looking, 837
Censorship News, 18
Center for National Security Studies (CNSS), 14, 166, 635, 814, 829, 897, 899, 907, 909, 928–932, 938–947, 949, 953, 957, 958, 960, 1294
Center Magazine, 787
Central Intelligence Agency (CIA), 634, 638, 707, 719, 929, 931, 932, 935, 938, 940–941, 943, 946–951, 953–958, 960
Ceplair, Larry, 414
Chafee, Zechariah, Jr., 97, 98, 202, 301, 302, 467, 1408
Chasen, Jerry Simon, 29
Chepesiuk, R., 913
Chevigny, Paul, 612, 613
Christian Century, 337, 466, 470, 498, 557, 577, 671, 687, 714 716, 832, 859, 875–877
Christian Register, 1159
Christianity and Crisis, 833
Christianity Today, 858, 860, 878
CIA, see Central Intelligence Agency
CIA and the Cult of Intelligence, The, 707
Cigler, Allen, 1056
CIO (Congress of Industrial Organizations), 276, 281, 289
CISPES, see Committee in Solidarity with the People of El Salvador
City College of New York, 339, 341, 342
Civil Liberties, 6, 11, 89, 525, 576, 724, 757, 761, 770, 773 779, 788, 794, 805, 812, 815, 869, 884–886, 894, 917, 918, 937, 952, 982, 1006–1008, 1018, 1089, 1221, 1245, 1277, 1280
Civil Liberties Alert, 12
Civil Liberties Bureau, see American Union Against Militarism
Civil Liberties Review, 13, 85, 422, 538, 540, 545, 546, 550, 554 632, 637, 709, 752, 969, 1208, 1210, 1211, 1226, 1274
Clark, Grenville, 219, 220, 1409
Clark, Mary E., 979

Name Index

Clark, Ramsey, 594
Clinton, Catherine, 1228
CNSS, *see* Center for National Security Studies
Coffin, William Sloane, 714, 718, 725
Cohen, Carl, 676
Coleman, McAlister, 179
Collier's, 354
Columbia Human Rights Law Review, 608, 740
Columbia Law Review, 224, 336, 356, 882, 883
Columbia Magazine, 820
Columbia Oral History Collection, 1209, 1242, 1254, 1255, 1285
Columbia University, 228, 1209, 1242, 1254, 1255, 1285, 1416, 1427, 1442, 1445
Commentary, 529
Commission on Human Rights, New York City, 741, 747,
Commission on Law and Social Action, of the American Jewish Congress, 1051
Committee in Solidarity with the People of El Salvador (CISPES) 909
Committee on the Bill of Rights, of American Bar Association, 325 1409
Committee on Public Justice, 621
Commonweal, 401
Common Sense, 1129, 1149, 1150
Communication Education, 817, 846
Communications Lawyer, 1075
Concerning Conscription, 93
Congress of Industrial Organizations, *see* CIO
Conklin, Groff, 334
Conservative Digest, 804

Constitutional Law Clinic, Rutgers University Law School, 608
Consumers for Choices in Childbirth Newsletter, 997
Cook, Blanche Wiesen, 1228, 1229
Cook, H., 859
Cornell, Julien, 352, 353
Cornell University, 72
Cortner, Richard C., 1024, 1025, 1044
Cowan, Ruth, 740
Criley, Richard, 420
Criminal Law Bulletin, 618
Crovitz, L.G., 799
Cruzan, Nancy, *see Cruzan v. Harmon*
Curran, William J., 979
Current, 548, 564, 574, 586, 646, 787
Current History, 726, 1170, 1205
Curti, Merle, 135
Cushman, Robert, 328, 329
Customs Bureau, U.S., 695, 703

Dabney, Virginius, 221
Daniel, Cletus, 287
Dan Smoot Report, 555
Darrow, Clarence, 184–186, 189–192, 194, 1410
Dartmouth College, 842, 1409
Davis, A., 842
Days, Drew S., III, 914
Dembitz, Nanette, 356
democracy, 959
Dennett, Mary Ware, 196, 203, 1224
Dershowitz, Alan M., 719, 1001
DeSilver, Albert, 118, 137–141, 173, 204, 1167
Detroit College of Law Review, 534
Dies, Martin, 250, 251, 252, 257, 267, 268, 1152

Dies Committee, *see* House Un-American Activities Committee
Dilling, Elizabeth, 260
Dissent, 544, 1216
di Suvero, Henry, 533
Docket (of ACLU Reproductive Freedom Project), 986
Donald, Peter G., 1078, 1214
Donner, Frank J., 614, 900
Donohue, William A., 74, 760, 763, 793
Dorsen, Norman, 2, 3, 4, 69, 70, 82, 390, 534, 535, 556, 566, 572, 582, 583, 606, 624, 630, 631, 641, 650, 651, 669, 677, 701, 720, 730, 741, 742, 745, 751, 753–756, 764, 765, 769, 783, 786, 797, 813, 861, 872, 891, 914, 923, 933, 944, 967, 971, 1019, 1027, 1069, 1075, 1215, 1244
Doty, Madeline A., 1411
Downs, Donald Alexander, 678, 836
Drinan, Robert F., 494, 495, 665, 1226
Drinnon, Richard, 357
Duffus, Robert L., 1079
Duke Law Journal, 852, 853
Dunn, Robert W., 1412
Dworkin, Andrea, 922
Dwyer, William L., 390

Eastman, Crystal, 1227–1230
Eastwood, Mary, 746, 1413
Ebony, 1272
ECLC, *see* Emergency Civil Liberties Committee
Editor and Publisher, 524
Eisenberg, Arthur, 30
Eisenberg, Ruth, 40
Ellsberg, Daniel, 728, 731

Emergency Civil Liberties Committee (ECLC), 461, *see also* National Emergency Civil Liberties Committee
Emerson, Thomas I., 813, 1026, 1027
Emery, Richard D., 43
Endo, Mitsuye, *see Endo v. United States*
Englund, Steven, 414
Ennis, Bruce J., 43, 75, 623, 624
Ennis, Edward J., 583, 615
Epstein, Beryl, 76
Epstein, Lee, 749, 1045
Epstein, Sam, 76
Ernst, Morris L., 201, 205–207, 222, 314, 315, 326, 421, 452, 453, 483, 511–513, 1172, 1208, 1231–1236, 1414
Erskine, Hazel G., 1059, 1060
Escobedo, Danny, *see Escobedo v. Illinois*
Esquire, 1267
Estrich, Susan R., 923
Etzioni, Amitai, 766
Evans, Elizabeth Glendower, 1415
Ewing, K.D., 1070

F.A.C.T., *see* Feminist Anti-Censorship Task Force
Fairchild, Erika S., 910
Family Planning Perspectives, 1278
Faux, Marian, 648
FBI, *see* Federal Bureau of Investigation
FCC, *see* Federal Communications Commission
Fechtmeier, Karl, 77
Federal Bar News and Journal, 1016
Federal Bureau of Investigation (FBI), 166–168, 419–425, 454–457, 614, 621, 629, 899, 907, 909, 927, 930, 932, 934,

Name Index

935, 946, 1208, 1354, 1355, 1403
Federal Communications Commission (FCC), 524, 1416
Federal Loyalty Program, 426–429
Feminist Anti-Censorship Task Force (F.A.C.T.), 837
Fennell, William G., 316, 378
Ferlinghetti, Lawrence, 514
Ferman, Irving, 435, 455
Fields, H., 838
First Principles, 14, 166, 814, 829, 897, 899, 907, 928–930, 938–943, 945–947, 953, 957, 960
Fish, Hamilton, Jr., 254, 256, 309
Fish Committee, *see* House Un-American Activites Committee
Fite, Gilbert C., 120
Fitelson, H. William, 384
Flexner, Bernard, 1094
Fly, James L., 456, 1416
Flynn, Elizabeth Gurley, 253, 259, 261, 263, 264, 265, 269, 274 1187, 1237–1241, 1417, 1418
FOIA, *see* Freedom of Information Act
Ford, Henry, 290
Fordham Law Review, 431
Foreign Policy, 635, 949
Forum, 273, 290
Fowler, Albert, 515
Fraenkel, Osmond K., 180, 223, 224, 330, 469, 476, 535–537, 615 1242–1245, 1419, 1420
Frankfurter, Felix, 142, 174, 181, 1246, 1421, 1422
Franklin, R.D., 1064
Free Speech League, 1438
Free Speech Yearbook, 681, 847
Freedom from Censorship, 317
Frieberg, P., 977, 978

Friedman, Leon, 538, 584, 721, 735
Friedman, Paul R., 45
Frontiers of Democracy, 1163, 1171

Galanter, Marc, 863
Gale, Mary Ellen, 843, 844, 924
Garbus, Martin, 1247
Gardiner, Harold C., 516
Gardner, Virginia, 436
Garland Fund, *see* American Fund for Public Service
Gartner, Alan, 539
Gault, Gerald, 535
Gaylin, Willard, 541
Gearty, C.A., 1070
Gellhorn, Walter, 391, 437
George Washington Law Review, 746
Gibson, James L., 679
Gideon, Clarence, 535
Gilkey, Langdon, 862
Gillers, Stephen, 42, 621, 630
Ginger, Ray, 185
Ginsberg, Allen, 514
Ginsburg, Ruth Bader, 743
Gitlow, Benjamin, *see Gitlow v. New York*
Gittel, Marilyn, 578
Glaser, Martha, 175, 295
Glasser, Ira, 5, 6, 539–542, 564, 565, 649, 722, 752, 767–770 797, 800, 885, 886, 915, 934–937, 1248
Glastris, Paul, 771
Gobitis, Lillian, William, *see Gobitis v. Pennsylvania*
Godfrey, E. Drexel, 938
Goldberg, Danny, 815
Goldberger, David, 56, 680
Goldin, Greg, 620
Goldmark, John, 390, 393
Goldstein, Howard, 31
Goodman, Walter, 262
Gora, Joel M., 56, 59, 616

Gostin, Lawrence O., 40, 44, 677, 979, 1071
Gottlieb, Gerald H., 595
Government and Opposition, 1068
Graber, Mark A., 1047
Green, Mark, 1048
Greenawalt, Kent, 650
Greene, Nathan, 174, 288
Greenhouse, Steven, 63
Griffith, Robert, 398
Grodzins, Morton, 358
Gross, Fred, 66
Grossman, George S., 916
Grove City College, Pennsylvania, 921
Grow, James R., 64
Grundman, Adolph, 767
Guardian, The, 762, 823, 825, 1222
Guggenheim, Martin, 36, 48, 68
Guild Practitioner, 689
Gumaer, David Emerson, 543
Gutman, Jeremiah, 863, 972
Guttentag, Lucas, 27, 28, 1015, 1016

Habenstreit, Barbara, 78
Haber, David, 1027
Hackett, G., 801
Hadassah Newsletter, 1194
Haft, Marilyn G., 37
Hagstrom, Warren O., 1065
Hague, Frank, 276, 281, 289
Haiman, Franklyn S., 681, 697, 698, 816, 817, 839, 845–847, 1028 Hale, J.P., 864
Hall, Kermit L., 79, 1029
Halliday, Terence C., 392
Halperin, Morton, 56, 632–636, 728, 939–949
Halpern, Charles R., 1048
Halpern, Stephen C., 1030, 1049
Hamlin, David, 682
Hapgood, Norman, 143

Hardwick, Michael, 81
Harlan, John Marshall, 662
Harper's, 234, 334, 362, 492, 512, 589, 649, 658, 718, 1082
Harrington, James C., 772, 1017
Harrington, Michael, 489
Harris, Reed, 228
Harris, Richard, 723
Hart, Gary, 773
Hart, Merwin K., 1163
Harvard University, 1141, 1408, 1419, 1421
Harvard Civil Rights-Civil Liberties Law Review, 154, 268, 742, 744, 765, 840, 1246
Harvard Journal on Legislation, 873
Harvard Law Review, 213, 437, 993
Harvard Magazine, 1215
Harvard University, 1141, 1408, 1419, 1421
Harvard Women's Law Journal, 925
Haskell, Gordon K., 544, 1216
Hastings Law Journal, 1021, 1076
Hayden, Trudy, 54
Hays, Arthur Garfield, 144, 145, 179, 186, 201, 211, 295, 344 345, 346, 376, 379, 434, 459, 484, 1249–1251, 1423
Hearnce, Paul, 50
Hebrew Union College Monthly, 1142
Helton, Arthur, 27, 28
Henderson, Wade, 27, 28, 1019
Hendricks, Evan, 55
Henkin, Louis A., 1072
Hennessey, Patricia, 36
Hentoff, Nat, 683, 724, 774, 775, 818, 819, 848–850, 887, 888 901–905, 999, 1031
Herndon, Angelo, 145, 246
Hershkoff, Helen, 52
Hewitt, Patricia, 1073
Hewman, Susan, 66

Name Index

Hirabayashi, Gordon, 81
Hirschkop, Philip J., 641, 642
Historian, 267
Hoffman, Daniel, 633, 636
Hoke, Travis, 294, 1081
Holmes, John Haynes, 326, 331, 517, 1252, 1424
Holmes, Oliver Wendell, 121
Honig, Douglas, 80
Hook, Ronald W., 980
Hoover, J. Edgar, 421–424
Horowitz, Harold W., 448
Horowitz, Irving L., 684
House Un-American Activities Committee (HUAC), 250–252, 254, 256, 257, 262, 267, 268, 271, 309, 382, 420, 423, 434–444, 628, 1152, 1255, 1450, 1451
Howl, 514
HUAC, *see* House Un-American Activities Committee
Huebsch, Ben W., 124, 176, 1253, 1254, 1425
Hughes, Charles Evans, 187
Hull, Kent, 50
Humanities Research Center, of University of Texas, 1414
Hunter, Nan, 978, 981
Huston, Tom Charles, 425
Hyde, Henry, 894
Hyman, Harold M., 449, 1061

Ickes, Harold L., 225
If You Are Arrested, 480, 597
I.F. Stone's Weekly, 395, 465
ILD, *see* International Labor Defense
Immigration Reform Act: Employer Sanctions and Discrimination Prohibitions, 1015
Independent, The, 208
Index on Censorship, 851

Inquiry, 1002, 1213
Institute for Contemporary Studies, 488
Intercollegian, 1162
Interior Department, U.S., 225
Internal Revenue Service, U.S., 614
International and Comparative Law Quarterly, 1043
International Juridical Association Bulletin, 307
International Labor Defense (ILD), 1448
International League for the Rights of Man, 482
Industrial Workers of the World (IWW), 113, 116, 156, 159, 1126
In These Times, 802, 842, 1217
IRCA, *see* Immigration Reform and Control Act
Irons, Peter, 81, 359, 360
Irwin, Theodore, 332
Isbell, Florence, 545
IWW, *see* Industrial Workers of the World

Jackson, Gardner, 1255
Jackson, Jesse, 773
Jacobs, James B., 970
Jacobs, Jim, 906
Jacobs, Paul, 393
Jensen, Joan, 102
Jensen, Oliver, 1082
John Birch Society, 390, 393, 543
Johnpoll, Bernard K., 1286
Johnson, Donald, 103
Josephson, Harold, 209
Jost, Kenneth, 890
Joughin, G. Louis, 182
Journal of American History, 150, 167

Journal of Criminal Law and Criminology, 893
Journal of Homosexuality, 976
Journal of Public Law, 708, 1044
Journal of Social Issues, 1058, 1060, 1061, 1067
Journalism Educator, 706
Judges and the Judged, The, 415, 417, 418
Judges' Journal, 789
Judicature, 749, 1054
Judis, John, 802
Jussim, Daniel, 1018

Kairys, David, 1032, 1033, 1217
Kallen, Horace, 342
Kalven, Harry, Jr., 477, 1034
Kamisar, Yale, 617
Kammen, Michael, 1035, 1036
Katz, Barbara, 33
Katz, Jonathan Ned, 982
Katz, Stanley N., 82
Kaufman, Henry R., 29
Kelley, Dean, 546
Kendrick, Alexander, 394
Kenyon, Dorothy, 326, 386, 737, 1256, 1257, 1426
Kerr, Virginia, 923
King, Carol Weiss, 146, 1258
King, Rodney, 896
Kinigstein, Noah A., 34
Kirchwey, Freda, 1230
Kirchwey, George W., 210
Kizer, Benjamin H., 1241
Klanwatch, 823
Kluger, Richard, 245
Korematsu, Fred, 356
Koren, Edward I., 53
Krislov, Samuel, 1046
Kropotkin, Peter Alekseyevich, 1116
Ku Klux Klan, 131, 138, 819, 823, 825

Kunstler, William M., 1259
Kutler, Stanley I., 460

Labor Age, 1121
Labor Law Journal, 1011
La Follette, Marcel Chotkowski, 865
La Follette, Robert M., Jr., 286
La Follette family, 1436
La Follette Committee, of U.S. Senate, *see* Subject Index
Lally, Francis J., 496
La Marche, Gara, 685, 776, 777, 820, 821, 851, 866, 997
Lamont, Corliss, 263, 264, 395, 1141, 1260–1263, 1427
Lamson, Peggy, 83
Landau, David, 789
Lane, Winthrop D., 104, 176, 177
Lapp, John A., 327
Larson, E. Richard, 58
Latimer, Ira, 73
Law and Contemporary Problems, 502, 684
Law and Disorder, 598
Law and Freedom Bulletin, 146
Law Enforcement Intelligence Unit (LEIU), 620
Law in Transition Quarterly, 691, 722
Law, Sylvia, 52, 760, 1278
Lawlessness in Law Enforcement, 302
Lawrence, Charles, 852
Lawrence, Jerome, 189
Lawrence, Thomas, 105
Layton, Edwin, 147
League for Industrial Democracy, 177
League for Mutual Aid, 155
League of Nations, 1114, 1118
Ledbetter, Jim, 803

Name Index

Legal Defense Fund (LDF), of NAACP, 881–883, 921, 1054, 1055
Legal Services Corporation, U.S., 1004
Lee, Robert E., 189
Lee, R.W., 804
Leeds, Jeffrey T., 7
Left Wing Manifesto, The, 151, 152, 213
LEIU, *see* Law Enforcement Intelligence Unit
Leo, John, 778
Levine, Alan, 61
Levine, Ellen, 60
Levy, Howard B., 722, 729
Levy, Rob, 44
Lewin, R., 867
Lewis, Flora, 1083
Libertarian Review, 1078
Library Journal, 560, 696
Library of Congress, 1410, 1422, 1424, 1425, 1433, 1435–1437, 1449
Life, 551, 1236
Lilly, Mark, 1074
Lindey, Alexander, 314, 315
Lipman, Lisa, 34
Lippman, Walter, 190
Lister, Charles, 37
Literary Digest, 1088
Loewenson, Carl H., Jr., 779
Loffredo, Stephen, 52
Loomis, Burdett, 1056
Los Angeles Times, The, 1083
Los Derechos De Gene Indocumentada e Imigrante (The Rights of Immigrants and Undocumented Workers), 1017
Los Derechos De Los Extranjeros, 27, 28
Lowry, Marcia, 36
Lowther, W., 868
Lucas, Roy, 566
Lukas, J. Anthony, 686
Luscomb, Florence, 1428
Lusk Committee, *see* Subject Index
Lusk-Stevenson Report, *see* Lusk Committee
Lyles, J.C., 687
Lynch, Mark H., 953
Lynn, Barry, 840, 869
Lynn, Winfred, 344, 345, 346, 347

Machinists' Monthly Journal, 455
Mack, Raymond W., 1062
Malin, Patrick Murphy, 438, 439, 457, 470, 471, 498, 1264, 1265
Maltby, Lewis, 1011, 1012
Mann, J., 688
Manwaring, David R., 369
Marchand, Roland, 106
Marchetti, Victor, 638, 707
Markmann, Charles Lamm, 84
Markowitz, Deborah L., 743
Marks, John D., 638
Marsh, Dave, 822
Martin, Charles H., 246
Marwick, Christine M., 39, 634
Massachusetts Historical Society, 1373
Masses, 371
Matson, Floyd, 363
Mayer, Milton, 780
MacArthur, Douglas, 1170, 1189, 1200
McAuliffe, Mary S., 398, 399
McCarthy, Joseph R., 228, 386, 1256, 1257. *See also* McCarthyism
McClosky, Herbert, 1063
McCollum, Vashti Cromwell, *see* McCollum case

MacDonald, Dwight, 345, 346, 347, 1084, 1429
McDonald, Laughlin, 58, 585, 913
McGehee, R., 955
McGreivy, Susan, 984
McIlhaney, William H., II, 547
McKean, Dayton David, 289
MacKenzie, Angus, 954
Maclean's, 868
McWilliams, Carey, 265, 378
Meese Commission, *see* Attorney General's Commission on Pornography
Meese, Edwin, 834, 840, 841
Meiklejohn, Alexander, 234, 377, 410, 411, 413, 689, 1186, 1430
Meires, G., 823
Mencken, H. L., 211, 266
Menefee, Selden C., 257
Methodist Church, 1289–1291, 1433
Michigan, University of, *see* University of Michigan
Militant, The, 1219
Millemann, M.A., 642
Miller, Merle, 415, 417, 418
Milner, Lucille B., 107, 296, 333, 334, 499
Minnesota Law Review, 223, 476, 490
"Miracle, The," 519
Miranda, Ernesto, *see Miranda v. Arizona*
Mitchell, Jonathan, 226
Mitford, Jessica, 725
Mnookin, Robert H., 652
Mock, James R., 108
Modenbach, G., 825
Modern Age, 515
Mondale, Walter, 773
Moral Majority, 791
Morgan, Charles, Jr., 577, 1266–1269
Morgan, Edmund M., 182
Morgan, Richard E., 1037
Morland, Howard, 826
Morris, Willie, 1218
Moss, Kary, 925
Mountain States Observer, 17
Ms. Magazine, 835
Muir, William K., 666
Murphy, Paul L., 85, 103, 109, 148–150, 178, 1038, 1039
Murray, Pauli, 744–746, 1431
Murray, Robert K., 110
Murrow, Edward R., 385, 394
Museum of Broadcasting, 385
Myer, Dillon S., 357

NAACP, *see* National Association for the Advancement of Colored People
Nader, Ralph, 1048
Naming Names, 440
Nation, The, 101, 127, 138, 139, 163, 173, 186, 204–206, 212, 227, 265, 269, 270, 296, 345, 347, 349, 376, 379, 381, 396, 424, 428, 439, 459, 501, 594, 620, 662, 676, 736, 803, 821, 855, 906, 908, 934, 935, 948, 950, 951, 954, 955, 1013, 1091, 1113, 1114, 1118, 1120, 1123, 1124, 1141, 1160, 1161, 1173, 1178, 1187, 1189, 1192, 1198, 1230
National Ad Hoc Committee Against Censorship, *see* National Coalition Against Censorship
National Archives, 1355
National Association for the Advancement of Colored People (NAACP),

Name Index

153, 468, 473, 478, 881–883, 921, 1051, 1054, 1055, 1449
National Civil Liberties Bureau, 100, 111–118, 120, 151, 152 1227–1230
National Coalition Against Censorship, 18, 699, 841
National Committee Against Repressive Legislation (NCARL), see National Committee to Abolish the House Un-American Activities Committee
National Committee on Conscientious Objectors (NCCO), 352, 1452
National Committee to Abolish the House Un-American Activities Committee, 420, 432, 442, 443, 1450, 1451
National Conference of Charities and Corrections, 1107
National Conference of Social Work, 1093, 1103
National Council for Civil Liberties (NCCL), 1068–1071, 1074
National Education Association (NEA), 1140
National Emergency Civil Liberties Committee (NECLC), 461
National Labor Relations Board (NLRB), 290
National Law Journal, 759, 776, 890
National Lawyers Guild, 689
National Municipal Review, 1105, 1108, 1164
National Office for Decent Literature (NODL), 508, 509, 515

National Popular Government League, 165
National Press Club, 800
National Prison Project Journal, 15, 640
National Probation Association, 1094, 1097
National Review, 531, 610, 647, 664, 674, 790
National Textbook Company, 579, 585, 616, 659, 668, 697, 739
Navasky, Victor, 440
NBC Radio, 327
NCARL, see National Committee Against Repressive Legislation
NCFC, see National Council on Freedom From Censorship (of ACLU)
NCCL, see National Council for Civil Liberties
NCCO, see National Committee on Conscientious Objectors
NEA, see National Education Association
N.E.A. Journal, 568
Near, Jay, 310
Nearing, Scott, 1148, 1270
Nebraska, University of, see University of Nebraska
NECLC, see National Emergency Civil Liberties Committee
Neier, Aryeh, 422, 548–550, 586, 618, 619, 653, 654, 690, 827 1271, 1432
Neisser, Eric, 781, 782
Nelkin, Dorothy, 870
Nelles, Walter, 118, 146, 151, 152, 212, 226, 258, 291, 333, 1167
Neuborne, Burt, 30, 721, 783, 794
New Jersey History, 175, 295
New Jersey Law Journal, 781

New Leader, The, 384, 417, 418, 452, 1154, 1157, 1181, 1220
New Masses, 261, 377, 436, 1136
New Outlook, 854, 1193
New Republic, The, 142, 156, 226, 258, 291, 333, 393, 397, 438 453, 456, 499, 522, 688, 796, 797, 856, 889, 892, 1165, 1172, 1176, 1190, 1203, 1218
New York Affairs, 685
New York Bureau of Legal First Aid, 1453
New York City Tribune, 793
New York Law Journal, 1244
New York Public Library, 1439, 1440, 1443, 1446, 1448, 1453
New York Times Magazine, 7, 413, 474, 553, 654, 686
New York University, 1412, 1417, 1427, 1453
New York University Journal of International Law and Policy, 994
New York University Review of Law and Social Change, 881, 936
New Yorker, 526, 570, 723, 1084, 1268, 1427
Newsletter on Intellectual Freedom, 694
Newsweek, 801, 831, 895
Nixon, Richard M., 495, 705, 727, 728, 731–736, 1269
NLRB, *see* National Labor Relations Board
NODL, *see* National Office for Decent Literature
North American Review, 1081
North, Oliver, 889, 931
Northrup, Herbert, 348, 349
Northwestern University Law Review, 698
Norton, Eleanor Holmes, 747, 917, 1272–1274

Norwick, Kenneth P., 29, 828, 926, 983, 995
Notre Dame Lawyer, 700
Novack, George, 1219
Novick, Jack, 5
NRA, *see* National Recovery Administration
NYU Law, 1225

O'Connor, Harvey, 73
O'Connor, Karen, 748, 749
Ohio State Law Journal, 631, 656, 875
Olds, William, 588
O'Meara, Dean Joseph, Jr., 500
O'Neill, Robert, 38, 57
O'Neill, William, 416
Opportunity, 1146
O'Reilly, Kenneth, 423
Our Endangered Rights, 69, 82, 769, 783, 786, 813, 872, 891, 914 923, 944, 967, 971, 1019
Outen, Wayne N., 34
Oxnam, G. Bromley, 434, 441, 501, 1433

Pacific Historical Review, 147, 159
Pacific Northwest Quarterly, 1241
Palmer, A. Mitchell, 110, 140, 165
Peck, Keenen, 956
Pell, Eve, 784
Pemberton, John de Jarnette, Jr., 568, 700, 701, 726
Pentagon Papers, 728, 731
Penton, M. James, 380
Peratis, Kathleen Willert, 739
Pertschuk, Michael, 807
Peterson, H.C., 120
Peterson, Owen, 816
Peterzell, Jay, 897, 907, 957, 959
Pevar, Stephen L., 41
Pfeffer, Leo, 502, 503, 668, 669, 1276

Name Index

Phi Delta Kappan, 565, 1064
Pickens, William, 153
Pilpel, Harriet Fleischel, 656–658, 702, 1277, 1278
Pitzele, Merlyn S., 415, 417, 418
Playboy, 528
Polebaum, Elliot E., 51
Polenberg, Richard, 121, 267
Policy Review, 792
Policy Studies Journal, 1049
Politics, 344, 346
Pollak, Louis H., 154
Pollak, Walter, 154, 302, 1279
Pollitt, Daniel H., 589
Polovchak, Walter, 1001, 1002
Popeo, Daniel J., 86
Post Office, U.S., 137, 196, 203, 366, 369, 459
Powell, John, 58
Powledge, Fred, 551, 704, 705, 727, 1268
President's Committee on Civil Rights (1947), 475, 1159
Presser, Stefan, 60
Preston, William, Jr., 122, 335
Price, Janet, 61
Princeton University, 1352, 1402, 1420, 1423
Prisoners' Assistance Directory, The, 964
Progressive, The, 780, 818, 826, 898, 913, 956, 1158, 1175, 1177, 1200
Protestants and Other Americans United for Separation of Church and State, 501
Public Opinion Quarterly, 257, 332, 1059
Publishers Weekly, 695, 702, 703, 707, 838, 1253

Quakers, *see* American Friends Service Committee; Swarthmore College

Rabin, Robert L., 65, 1050
Radcliffe College, 1413, 1415, 1428, 1431
Raloff, J., 871
Randall, Clarence B., 1133
Rauh, Joseph L., 1246
Rauschenbush, Winifred, 350
Raymond, Allen, 520
Reader's Digest, 290, 421, 458, 1170
Reagan, Ronald W., 770, 784, 911, 930, 939, 945, 957, 958
Reason, 626
Redlich, Norman, 872, 1051
Reitman, Alan, 8, 87, 148, 217, 335, 389, 472, 489, 552, 569, 615, 1067, 1280
Remmers, H.H., 106
Research Annual, 1066
Responsive Community, The, 766, 843
Revolutionary Radicalism, 119
Rezneck, Daniel A., 753
Ribuffo, Leo, 378
Rice, Elmer, 521–523, 1281, 1434
RICO, *see* Racketeer Influenced and Corrupt Organizations Act
Rights, 443, 1186
Rights of Americans, The, 70, 566, 572, 583, 606, 624, 641, 650, 651, 669, 701, 730, 745, 751, 753–756
Riis, Roger W., 290, 1435
Rivkin, Robert, 46
Robeson, Paul, 383
Robertson, John A., 32
Robinson, Martin, 1069, 1077
Robison, Joseph, 473
Rocah, David, 918, 1007–1008

Roche, John P., 88, 1220
Rodell, Fred, 1236
Roe, Gilbert, 1436
Roger Baldwin Foundation, 467, 1247
Rolling Stone, 1214
Roman Catholic Church, see Catholic Church
Roosevelt, Franklin Delano, 226, 260, 267, 378, 1143, 1236
Rosenberg, James N., 376, 379
Rosengart, Oliver, 62
Rosenthal, John, 1280
Ross, Susan Deller, 67, 742
Rossett, Barney, 514
Rostow, Eugene V., 361, 362
ROTC (Reserve Officer Training Corps), 562
Rothman, David J., 625
Rothman, Sheila M., 625
Rothman, Stuart, 490
Rubenstein, Len, 44
Rubenstein, William, 40, 821
Rubin, David, 63
Rudovsky, David, 53, 720, 891
Rupp, John P., 37
Russell, Bertrand, 339, 341, 342
Rutgers University, 608

Sacco, Nicola, see Sacco and Vanzetti case
St. John's Law Review, 844
Salerno, Steve, 785
Salisbury, Harrison, 424
Samuels, Dorothy, 774
Samuels, Gertrude, 553
Sanger, Margaret, 1437
Sarton, May, 400
Saturday Evening Post, 799, 1086
Saturday Review, The, 517, 1182, 1185, 1188, 1191, 1204, 1206
Sayre, John Nevin, 123
Scalia, Antonin, 768

Schaetzel, Wendy, 807
Schlesinger Library, of Radcliffe College, 1413, 1415, 1428, 1431
Schmalhausen, Samuel D., 1145
Schomburg Library, of NY Public Library, 1448
School and Society, 561
Schrag, Peter, 728
Schrag, Philip G., 754
Schroeder, Theodore, 1438
Schuchman, Herman, 972
Schwartz, Alan U., 513
Schwartz, Bernard, 1040
Schwartz, Herman, 454, 649
Schwartz, Louis B., 892
Schwarzschild, Henry, 596
Science, 563, 867
Science Digest, 866
Science News, 871
Scopes, John Thomas, 191. See also Scopes trial
Seagle, William, 207
"See It Now," 385, 394
Seidenberg, Faith, 750
Selvin, Hanan C., 1065
Senior Scholastic, 573
Senate, U.S., see Congress, U.S.
Seven Arts, 96
Seymour, Whitney North, 1282, 1439
Shack, Barbara, 926
Shapiro, Steven R., 1019
Shattuck, John H.F., 554, 631, 637, 659, 761, 786–789, 893, 959
Sheatsley, Paul B., 1061
Sheehy, Gail, 1090
Shelley, Mr. and Mrs. J.D., 478
Sherrill, Robert, 729
Siegel, Loren, 884, 894
Siegel, Richard L., 1060
Simmons, Jerold, 268, 442
Simon, Rita J., 1066

Name Index

Sinclair, Upton, 156, 159
Slaff, George, 1013
Smith College, 1411, 1426, 1441
Smith, G.L., 671
Smith, Robert Ellis, 660
Smoot, Dan, 555
Snepp, Frank, 960
Soble, Richard, 906
Sobran, Joseph, 790
Social Frontier, 1137
Social Problems, 1062
Social Service Review, 136
Social Work Today, 1134
Social Work Yearbook, 1111, 1130–1132, 1156
Socialist Review, 123, 1110, 1126
Socialist Workers Party, 373
Society, 760, 766
Souraf, Frank, 504
Southern California Law Review, 595
Southern Illinois University, 1438
Soviet Russia Today, 1139
Sparer, Edward V., 755
Specter, The, 398
Spenkelink, John A., 594
Spivak, John L., 1283
Spock, Benjamin, 714, 718, 725
Staggenborg, Suzanne, 998
Stalin, Joseph, 1119, 1120
Stanford Law Review, 448, 607, 1050
Stanford University, 719
Stark, James, 31
State Department, U.S., 456
Stecich, Marianne, 60
Stern, Carl, 302
Stern, Gary M., 56, 909, 939
Stevens, John D., 706
Stichman, Barton F., 46
Stoddard, Thomas B., 37, 983
Stone, Harlan Fiske, 166
Stone, I.F., 395, 465
Stouffer, Samuel, 402
Strachey, John, 235

Stromberg, Yetta, 305
Strossen, Nadine, 852, 853, 873, 874, 924, 1021, 1076
Strum, Philippa, 854
Student Bill of Rights, A, 340
Summers, Clyde, 65, 756
Survey, The, 95, 100, 104, 126, 155, 157, 484, 523, 1091, 1092 1095–1097, 1099, 1100, 1104, 1106, 1109, 1127
Survey Graphic, 274, 326, 483, 1174, 1179
Sussman, Alan, 48, 68
Swanberg, William A., 1287
Swarthmore College, 1400, 1401, 1447, 1452, 1454
Swomley, John, 832, 833, 875–877, 1284
Szasz, Thomas, 626, 627, 1002

Taft, Clinton J., 90
Taft, Philip, 491
Tamiment Institute, of New York University, 1412, 1417, 1453
tenBroek, Jacobus, 363
Tenney, Jack B., 433
Tenney Committee, *see* Subject Index
Texas Lawyer, 777
Texas Tech Law Review, 772
Texas, University of, *see* University of Texas
Thatcher, Margaret, 1070
Theoharis, Athan, 398, 425
Thomas, Norman, 124–126, 157, 337, 474, 492, 1203, 1204, 1285–1287, 1440
Thornburgh, Richard, 796
Tigar, Michael E., 556, 730
Time, 798
Timmons, Mary Sarazin, 571
Tinker, Mary Beth, 81
Tompkins, Jerry R., 1183

To Secure These Rights, 475, 1159
Trial Magazine, 542
Triandis, Harry C., 1067
Trinkl, J., 1222
True, 1265
Truman, Harry S., 475, 1159
Tulane Lawyer, 3
Twice-a-Year, 1135, 1152, 1153, 1155

U.C.L.A. Historical Journal, 168
U.N. World, 1195
Underwood, Murray, 830
Ungar, Sanford J., 731
United Nations, 481, 1195
Unity, 1151
University of California, 168, 410, 411, 1065, 1359
University of Chicago, 327, 1366
University of Michigan, 855
University of Nebraska, 1403
University of Pennsylvania Law Review, 447
University of Texas, 1414, 1434
Urofsky, Melvin I., 1041
U.S. National Commission on Law Observance and Enforcement (Wickersham Commission), 302
U.S. News and World Report, 778, 795

Valentino, Linda, 620
Van Alstyne, William W., 572
Van Kleeck, Mary, 280, 1288, 1441
Varady, M., 984
Varney, Harold Lord, 272, 273
Vigilante, Richard, 792
Vigilante, Susan, 792
Viking Press, 176, 1253, 1254, 1425
Village Voice, The, 590, 683, 774, 775, 819, 848–850, 887, 888, 901–905, 999

Villard, Oswald Garrison, 127
Virginia Law Review, 642
Virginia Quarterly Review, 221
Vose, Clement E., 478, 1042

Wagner, S., 707
Wainwright (*Gideon v. Wainwright*), 535
Wald, Lillian, 1442, 1443
Walker, Jerry, 524
Walker, Samuel E., 91, 92, 103, 128, 760, 763, 793, 910, 1403
Wallace, George, 1272
Wallington, Peter, 1069, 1077
Ward, Harry F., 1289–1291
Warren, Charles, 213
Warren, Earl, 387, 617
Wasby, Stephen L., 708, 1053–1056
Washington Legal Foundation, 86
Washington Monthly, The, 771
Watters, Pat, 621
Wayne Law Review, 105
Weatherly, J., 878
Webb, Vincent J., 910
Wechsler, James, 1245
Wechsler, Nancy, 1245
Weglyn, Michi, 364
Weinberg, Arthur, 192
Weinberger, Harry, 1292, 1444
Weiner, Jon, 855
Weisberg, Bernard, 617
Weisbrod, Burton A., 1057
Westin, Alan, 661, 1208, 1211
Weybright, Victor, 274
What Do You Mean, Free Speech?, 1125
Whelton, Clark, 590
Whipple, Leon, 1042
Whitney, Richard M., 158
Why I Am Not a Christian, 341
Why We Defend Free Speech for Nazis, Fascists—and Communists 292, 293

Name Index

Wickersham Commission (U.S. National Commission on Law Observance and Enforcement), 302
Wilkinson, Frank, 404, 420, 442, 443, 1450, 1451
Will, George F., 831, 895
William and Mary Law Review, 582, 861
Williams, C. Dickerman, 431, 444
Williams, Chester S., 291
Williams, David, 166–168
Willowbrook School, New York State, 625
WILPF, *see* Women's International League for Peace and Freedom
Wirin, A. L., 291
Wisconsin Historical Society, 1399, 1404, 1418, 1430, 1450
Wisconsin Law Review, 446

"Wobblies," *see* Industrial Workers of the World
Women's International League for Peace and Freedom, 1411
Women's Rights Laws Reporter, 743
Wood, James E., 1276
Wood, L. Hollingsworth, 1445
World and I, The, 763, 793
World Tomorrow, The, 125, 140, 141, 151, 1080, 1091, 1102, 1112, 1115, 1122, 1128, 1138, 1148
Wulf, Melvin W., 638, 662, 709

Yale Law Journal, 361, 1046, 1051
Yale Journal of Law and Feminism, 922, 924
Yale University, 427, 428, 430, 1405, 1406, 1429, 1444

Zanger, Martin, 159

Subject Index

Note: Entries are indexed by item number, not by page number.

Abortion, 16, 22, 493, 643, 646–648, 651, 656–658, 775, 778, 888, 902, 905, 985–996, 998, 1284. *See also* Reproductive rights
clinics, disruptions and picketing, and free speech, 778, 902, 905, 989
fetal rights, 996
"human life" amendment to Constitution, 985, 991
parental notification laws, 987, 988, 990
Abrams v. United States, 121
"ABSCAM," 880
Academic freedom, 61, 63, 228–234, 338–342, 405–413, 558–573, 813, 842–855, 859, 860, 862, 865, 867, 868, 870, 871, 1042, 1137, 1140, 1148, 1149, 1270, 1404, 1410. *See also* Censorship; Education; Press, freedom of; Speech, freedom of
Access
to communications media, 706, 709
to membership lists, 252, 459
to public buildings, 231, 858, 869, 873, 877

Equal Access Act, 858, 869, 873, 877
to records, governmental, *see* Freedom of Information Act
to records, of juvenile courts, 1109
to records, medical, 972, 979, 987, 988, 990, 999
Access to Justice Project, of ACLU, 1003
ACLU, *see* specific subjects
Advocacy, *see* Attorneys; Public interest groups
Affiliates, of ACLU, 9, 17, 19, 73, 77, 80, 90, 156, 159, 202, 210, 216, 218, 291, 313, 321, 327, 364, 385, 388, 391, 394, 401, 410–412, 447, 448, 478–480, 504, 514, 525, 533, 539, 541, 548, 549, 557, 564, 565, 567, 570, 571, 574, 576–578, 580, 581, 585, 587, 590, 592, 603, 605, 617, 618, 622, 667, 674–690, 696–698, 708, 713, 715, 717, 718, 721–723, 750, 774, 775–777, 779, 780–782, 811, 815, 824, 830, 842–844, 855, 857, 884,

898, 902–905, 912, 916, 980, 984, 1008, 1017, 1018, 1049, 1298–1351, 1352, 1432
   affiliates' addresses, 1293–1351
Affirmative action, 915, 917, 1009. See also Civil rights; Race; Women's rights
African-Americans, see Race
Aged persons, rights of, see Elderly persons
Agnostics, rights of, 861. See also Religion
AIDS, 40, 961, 962, 973–975, 979, 981, 983, 1293. See also Confidentiality; Ill persons, rights of; Medical records
AIDS and Civil Liberties Project, of ACLU, 1293
Air travel, search and seizure, 610
Alabama, 145, 244, 247, 639, 1266, 1272, 1298
Alaska, 1299
Alcohol, 926
Alien and sedition laws, see Sedition
Aliens, immigrants, refugees, rights of, 27, 28, 122, 235–238, 256, 583, 809, 1005, 1014–1019, 1352. See also Human rights
American Civil Liberties Union, see specific subjects
American Union Against Militarism, 93, 94, 100, 1227–1230, 1352, 1442, 1445, 1447, 1454
Amicus curiae briefs, 502, 609, 662, 889, 1043, 1046
Amnesty, 123, 160–163. See also Aliens, immigrants, refugees; Conscientious objectors; Human rights
Annual reports, of ACLU, 23, 24, 129, 214, 216, 320, 321, 462, 525
Anti-riot laws, 711
Anti-trust laws, 510
Anti-war movement, see Conscientious objectors; Draft; Pacifism; Vietnam War
Arizona, 1300, 1356
Arkansas, 859, 860, 862, 865, 867, 868, 870, 871, 878, 1301, 1357
Army, U.S., 104, 608, 614, 722, 1170, 1189. See also Conscientious objectors; Draft; Military personnel; Militias; Surveillance; War
Artists, rights of, 29, 521–523. See also Censorship
Arts, censorship in, 29, 521–523, 815, 822. See also Censorship; Communications media; Expression, freedom of
Assembly, freedom of, 93, 94, 101, 113, 117, 119–122, 130, 133, 148–150, 156, 159, 169, 171, 173, 174, 177–179, 195, 197–199, 208, 231, 233, 311, 316, 340, 385, 394, 561, 673–685, 687, 689, 711, 715, 716, 725, 729, 902, 905, 989. See also First Amendment; Association, freedom of; Surveillance
Association, freedom of, 9, 93, 94, 101, 113, 117, 119–122,

130, 131, 133, 148–150, 156, 159, 169–179, 195, 197, 210, 229, 232, 234, 254–257, 271, 291, 311, 338, 339, 341, 342, 373, 380, 719, 725, 808, 819, 909, 927, 930, 1009, 1010, 1012, 1137, 1149, 1270. *See also* First Amendment; Assembly, freedom of; Surveillance
Asylum, right of, *see* Aliens, immigrants, refugees, rights of
Atheists, rights of, 304, 861. *See also* Religion
Atlanta, Georgia, 602, 1309, 1297
Attitudes about ACLU, *see* Public opinion
Attorneys, 42, 62, 181, 186, 387, 392, 430, 479, 502, 533, 556, 589, 689, 810, 881, 883, 964, 1043–1057, 1292, 1436
  and ACLU, 75, 118, 146, 151, 152, 154, 207, 223, 224, 291, 302, 314, 315, 330, 476, 502, 503, 594, 616, 617, 642, 668, 680, 721, 723, 747, 925, 966, 984, 1043–1057, 1236, 1242–1244, 1247, 1249, 1259, 1272, 1274, 1277, 1279, 1419, 1444
  and clients, 42, 589, 964
  and death penalty, 594, 595, 881, 882
  public interest law, 1043–1057. *See also* Public interest groups, strategies
  right to counsel, 62, 479, 589, 617, 883, 964. *See also* Miranda warning

Austria, 1124, 1157
Authors, rights of, 29, 521–523, 695. *See also* Censorship; Expression, freedom of; Speech, freedom of; Libraries

Bank Secrecy Act of 1970, 655
Baseball, 831
Bellotti v. Baird, 652
Biennial Conferences of ACLU, 8, 21
Bill of Rights, of U.S. Constitution, 5, 22, 223, 325, 331, 455, 463, 471, 551, 565, 783, 1023, 1025, 1030, 1038, 1040, 1062, 1075, 1135, 1409. *See also* individual amendments
Bill of Rights Lobby, of ACLU, 761
Birmingham, Alabama, 1266
Blacklisting, 414–418
Blacks, *see* Race
Bomb design "secret," and *Progressive* magazine, 826
Boston College, 495
"Boston Five," 725
Boston, Massachusetts, 202, 211, 256, 313, 495, 725, 1320
Broadcasting, *see* Communications media; Federal Communications Commission
Brown v. Board of Education, 245, 918
Bryan, William Jennings, 184–186, 189, 192, 194. *See also* Scopes trial
Buckley v. Valeo, 752
Bund, *see* Nazis
Burger Court (U.S. Supreme Court), 538

Burstyn v. Wilson, 519

California, 77, 90, 156, 159, 210, 283, 291, 305, 357, 358, 363, 364, 388, 391, 410, 411, 433, 448, 449, 514, 576, 581, 595, 605, 715, 719, 815, 843, 898, 900, 902, 984, 1018, 1065, 1302–1304, 1358, 1359
   California Historical Society, 77, 1358
   Century City, 715
   criminal syndicalism law, 210, 283
   history, 77, 168, 1358
   Hollywood, *see* Movies
   Japanese-American internment, 357, 358, 363, 364
   labor disputes in, 283, 291
   Los Angeles (city and county), 168, 448, 581, 604, 605, 715, 896, 898, 900, 1303, 1359
      police, 604, 605, 715, 896, 898, 900
      schools, 581
      Watts, 605
   loyalty oaths, 410, 411, 448
   San Diego, 902, 1304
   San Francisco, 514, 1302, 1358
   Stanford University, 719
   state legislature, 433
   Stromberg v. California, 305
   Tenney Committee, 433
   University of California, 168, 410, 411, 1065, 1359
      Berkeley, 1065
      free speech disputes, 410, 411, 1065
      Los Angeles, 168, 1359
California Fact-Finding Committee on Un-American Activities (Tenney Committee), 433
Campaign financing, 752
Canada, 868
Candidates, rights of, 30, 752, 880
Capital punishment, 591–596, 881, 882
Capital Punishment Project, of ACLU, 594, 596
Catholic Church, 493–496, 498, 500, 508, 509, 515, 516, 665, 864, 1226
CBS Television, 385, 394
Censorship, 9, 18, 29, 39, 59, 71, 108, 196, 201–203, 205–207, 211, 307, 308, 312, 314, 317, 334, 377, 378, 365, 370, 493, 496, 505–509, 512–519, 521–523, 559, 560, 638, 692, 694–696, 703, 707, 808–831, 837, 927–929, 932, 934, 935, 939, 945, 948, 950, 960, 993, 994, 1042, 1206, 1224, 1236, 1148, 1270, 1281, 1414, 1434, 1437, 1438. *See also* Academic freedom; Communications media; Freedom of Information Act; Speech, freedom of
   Feminist Anti-Censorship Task Force (F.A.C.T.), 837
Center for National Security Studies (CNSS), 14, 166, 635, 814, 829, 897, 899, 907, 909, 928–932, 938–947, 949, 953, 957, 958, 960, 1294
Central America, 889, 909, 931, 949, 952, 957, 958, 1014

Subject Index

Central Intelligence Agency
(CIA), 634, 638, 707, 719,
929, 931, 932, 935, 938,
940–941, 943, 946–951,
953–958, 960
Chicago, Illinois, 73, 218, 327, 479,
576, 598, 897, 899–901,
1101, 1312, 1366
    Chicago Child Welfare
Exhibition of 1912, 1101
    police, 479, 598, 897, 899–901
    University of Chicago, 327,
1366
Children, *see* Families; Young
people
Children's Rights Project, of
ACLU, 1000, 1293
Christmas celebrations,
commemorations, 664,
672, 856. *See also* Religion
Church and state, *see* Religion
Church-State Committee, of
ACLU, 877
CIA, *see* Central Intelligence
Agency
Cincinnati, Ohio, 114
Citizenship, U.S., 236
Civil liberties, *see* specific name or
subject
    public opinion about, 149, 150,
257, 343, 402, 1058–1067
Civil Liberties Bureau, of
American Union Against
Militarism, 94–96, 99,
100, 120, 139, 152, 1227–
1230, 1355, 1442, 1445,
1447, 1453. *See also*
American Union Against
Militarism; National
Civil Liberties Bureau
CISPES, *see* Committee in
Solidarity with the
People of El Salvador

Civil rights, 22, 71, 88, 71, 239–247,
276, 322, 343–350, 387,
466, 468, 469, 473, 475–
478, 495, 552, 574–590,
911–926, 1054–1056, 1098,
1146, 1156, 1157, 1159,
1196, 1226, 1252, 1259,
1266–1269, 1272–1274,
1284, 1352, 1431. *See also*
Race
Cleveland, Ohio, 603
Clients' rights, with respect to
attorneys, *see* Attorneys
CNSS, *see* Center for National
Security Studies
Coal miners, *see* Labor
Cold War, 71, 263, 264, 381, 382, 388–392,
398, 399, 402, 404, 423, 440, 443,
449, 460, 461, 465, 927, 1177, 1223,
1416, 1439
Colonial U.S., 318
Colorado, 18, 172, 1305, 1360
Comic books, 506
Committee on Indian Rights, of
ACLU, 239, 241, 243
Committee on Labor's Rights, of
ACLU, 288
Communications media, 205, 206,
308, 317, 327, 371, 385,
394, 415, 510, 511, 524,
649, 701, 704, 705, 709,
1416. *See also* Censorship;
Expression, freedom of;
Speech, freedom of
Communism, 86, 99, 119, 139, 158,
195, 209, 213, 234, 246,
248–274, 287, 293, 299,
305, 309, 323, 377, 382–
384, 390, 391, 393, 395,
400, 402–404, 413, 414–
418, 420, 429, 433, 435,
436, 440, 445, 450–453,
522, 543, 547, 589, 1061,

1133, 1139, 1149, 1150,
1152, 1158, 1172–1174,
1177, 1187, 1202, 1210,
1223, 1238–1241, 1255–
1257, 1426, 1450, 1451
and ACLU, 86, 99, 119, 139,
152, 158, 195, 209, 234,
246, 248–254, 256, 258–
266, 268–272, 274, 287,
293, 299, 305, 309, 323,
377, 382–384, 390, 391,
393, 395, 398–400, 403,
404, 414–418, 420, 429,
433, 435, 436, 440–444,
450–453, 522, 543, 547,
1158, 1172, 1177, 1187,
1210, 1223, 1238–1241,
1256, 1257, 1426, 1450,
1451. *See also* Blacklisting; *Dennis v. United States*; Federal Loyalty Program; House Un-American Activities Committee; McCarthyism; Smith Act
Comstock Laws, 196
Confidentiality of records
of juvenile court proceedings, 1109
medical records, 972, 979, 987, 988, 990, 999
of membership lists, 252, 459
Congress, U.S., 12, 24, 25, 30, 140,
142, 414, 419, 430, 596,
629, 736, 752, 786, 849,
880, 911, 937, 949, 958,
959, 1136, 1159
committees, 250–252, 254, 256,
257, 262, 267, 268, 271,
286, 309, 382, 414, 420,
430, 432, 434–444, 628,
889, 942, 953, 1152, 1255–
1257, 1450–1451

legislation, 12, 24, 25, 69, 93,
115, 117, 121, 140, 142,
160, 161, 163, 174, 196,
204, 212, 239, 241, 248,
287, 319, 351, 372, 373,
419, 424, 428, 450–453,
476, 485, 487, 489, 490,
520, 596, 629, 644, 655,
693, 711, 712, 737, 752,
786, 810, 829, 832, 833,
849, 869, 873, 877, 885–
888, 890, 892–894, 911,
932, 934, 935, 937, 942,
946–950, 953–956, 993,
1015, 1016, 1136, 1143,
1158, 1160, 1161, 1172,
1174, 1239, 1354, 1403
members, 12, 30, 228, 256, 386,
752, 849, 880, 1256, 1257
Connecticut, 1306, 1361, 1405,
1406, 1429, 1444
Conscientious objectors, 93, 94,
101, 102, 104, 111, 112,
115, 120, 123–127, 351–
353, 710, 832, 833, 1091,
1113, 1119, 1120, 1153,
1160, 1161, 1355, 1404,
1411, 1440, 1447, 1452,
1454. *See also* Amnesty; Draft; Military personnel; Pacifism; Political prisoners; Selective service; War
Conscription, military, *see* Draft
Conservatism, in U.S., 74, 86, 134,
143, 147, 158, 220, 255,
258, 260, 273, 378, 416,
435, 529, 531, 538, 555,
674, 761, 763, 789–793,
802, 804, 842, 849, 895,
911, 1037, 1045, 1163
Constitution, U.S., 5, 6, 94, 97, 223,
329, 363, 368, 523, 539,

Subject Index

571, 573, 595, 639, 642, 643, 656, 662, 696, 721, 738, 742, 744, 789, 809, 857, 942, 958, 991, 994, 1018, 1023, 1025, 1026, 1028, 1035, 1036, 1038–1041, 1044, 1235, 1243, 1279
Constitutional convention, 643, 985, 991
   "courtstripping," 789
   Equal Rights Amendment, 738, 742, 744
   war powers, 721, 937, 942, 958. See also Bill of Rights; individual amendments
Consumers' rights, 754
Contras, see Iran-Contra scandal
Convicts, see Ex-offenders, rights of; Prisoners' rights
"COP" Report, see Pornography
Corporal punishment, 569
Counsel, right to, see Attorneys
"Courtstripping," 789
Creation science, 859, 860, 862, 865, 867, 868, 870, 871, 878. See also Evolution; Scopes trial
Creationism, see Creation science
Crime victims, rights of, 31
Criminal justice, 31, 468, 619, 879–910, 1094, 1097, 1101, 1106, 1107, 1109, 1112. See also Due process; Juvenile courts; Police
Criminal syndicalism laws, 151, 152, 195, 197, 210, 283
Critically ill, rights of, see Ill persons, rights of
Cruzan v. Harmon, 999
Cults, religious, rights of members, 863, 866

Dayton, Tennessee, see Scopes trial
Death penalty, see Capital punishment
Debt slavery, 153
Delaware, 1307, 1362
Democratic Party Convention of 1968, 598
Dennis v. United States, 451, 452
Denver, Colorado, 17, 1305, 1362
Deportation, see Aliens, rights of
Depression era in U.S., 214–319
Des Moines, Iowa, 81
Desegregation, racial, see Civil rights; Race
Detroit, Michigan, 831, 897, 1321, 1374
Dies Committee, of U.S. House of Representatives, 250, 251, 252, 257, 267, 268, 1152. See also House Un-American Activities Committee
Disabled persons, rights of, 40, 50. See also AIDS; Elderly; Ill persons; Mentally disabled
Discrimination, racial, see Civil rights; Race
Dissent, see Expression, freedom of; Speech, freedom of; Loyalty
Doctors, rights of, 33
Doe v. Bolton, 648
Draft, military, 93, 94, 100–102, 111, 112, 115, 125, 127, 344, 347, 710, 712, 730, 832, 833, 1091, 1153, 1452, 1454. See also Amnesty; Conscientious objectors; Military personnel; Selective service; War

Drugs, 22, 619, 771, 884, 886, 925, 1009
Due process, 9, 62, 405, 407, 479, 480, 567, 571, 606, 616, 617, 771, 842, 879–888, 890–895, 1001, 1002, 1012

East St. Louis, Illinois, 1092
Economic rights, 1000–1008, 1099, 1103. *See also* Homelessness, housing; Poor persons; Welfare
Education, 61, 63, 183, 187, 188, 190, 193, 228, 229–234, 245, 338–342, 368, 369, 405–413, 499, 542, 558–573, 578, 581, 582, 587, 590, 664, 666, 667, 817, 824, 830, 842–855, 857–860, 862, 865, 867–871, 873, 874, 876–878, 915, 917, 918, 921, 940, 1042, 1137, 1140, 1148–1149. *See also* Creation science, Equal Access Act; Scopes trial
  integration, 245, 581, 582, 918
  offensive speech, protected, and college campus codes, 842–855
  prayer in public schools, 497, 666, 789, 876
  private schools, 582, 663, 667, 857
  "released time" law, 497. *See also* Academic freedom; Race; Religion; Sex education; Students' rights
El Salvador, 909, 1014
Elderly persons, rights of, 47. *See also* Disabled persons; Ill persons; Mentally disabled
Employee rights, 22, 34, 38, 57, 65, 71, 410, 411, 426–428, 456, 486, 487, 489, 490, 756, 771, 927, 962, 1009–1013, 1015–1017, 1093, 1121, 1143, 1145, 1164
  employment-at-will concept, 1011
  public employee rights, 38, 57, 410, 411, 426–428, 456, 771, 927, 962, 1164. *See also* Labor
Endo v. United States, 356
England, 1043, 1068–1071, 1074–1075, 1077
English language, 22
Enlisted personnel, rights of, *see* Military personnel
Entertainment industry, 312, 317, 414, 510, 522–524, 1281. *See also* Censorship; Communications media; Movies
Environmental movement, 751
Equal Access Act, 858, 869, 873, 877
Equal protection, 27–70, 213, 567, 571, 911–926, 1025. *See also* Civil rights
Equal Rights Amendment (ERA), to U.S. Constitution, 738, 742, 744. *See also* Women's rights
ERA, *see* Equal Rights Amendment
Escobedo v. Illinois, 617
Espionage, 456, 457, 1174
  espionage laws, 117, 160–163, 204, 212, 1174. *See also* Smith Act

Subject Index

Espionage Act of 1917, 117, 160, 161, 163, 204, 212. *See also* Sedition Act of 1918
Ethnic groups, *see* Race
Europe, 324, 1113, 1114, 1118, 1124
Evacuation of Japanese-American citizens, *see* Japanese-Americans
Evolution, teaching of, 183, 187, 188, 190, 193, 870. *See also* Creation science; Scopes trial
Executive privilege, of U.S. President, 631
Ex-offenders, rights of, 35. *See also* Prisoners' rights
Export control laws, and free speech, 928. *See also* International information exchange; Passports; Travel restrictions; Visas
Expression, freedom of 9, 22, 56, 61, 71, 93, 94, 97, 98, 108, 117, 119–122, 126, 137, 148–150, 159, 200, 234, 292, 293, 305, 317, 339–342, 371, 372, 505–519, 521–523, 561, 586, 673–685, 687, 689, 691, 692, 694–696, 698–701, 705, 708, 709, 727, 762, 814, 815, 818–822, 831, 834–841, 843–855, 1026, 1028, 1430, 1434. *See also* First Amendment; Press, freedom of; Speech, freedom of

F.A.C.T. (Feminist Anti-Censorship Task Force), 837
Families, rights of, 36, 48, 60, 750, 983, 993, 994, 997, 1000–1002, 1106. *See also* Young people
Family planning, *see* Reproductive rights
Farm workers, 153, 285, 1005
Fascism, 292, 293, 296, 376–379. *See also* Nazis; Skokie case
Federal Bureau of Investigation (FBI), 166–168, 419–425, 454–457, 614, 621, 629, 899, 907, 909, 927, 930, 932, 934, 935, 946, 1208, 1354, 1355, 1403
  Special Commission on the FBI Files, of ACLU, 419. *See also* Freedom of Information Act; Surveillance; Wilkinson, Frank
Federal Election Campaign Act of 1971, 752
Feminism, *see* Women's rights
Fetal rights, *see* Reproductive rights
Fifth Amendment, of U.S. Constitution, 430, 431, 889. *See also* Due process
Film, censorship in, *see* Movies
Fingerprinting, 297, 300
First Amendment, of U.S. Constitution, 97, 98, 159, 175, 177–179, 198–200, 202, 234, 246, 420, 467, 477, 519, 567, 571, 586, 607, 675, 678, 683, 689, 704, 719, 752, 775, 808, 813, 816, 819, 825, 836, 839, 843, 844, 846, 847, 850, 866, 905, 909, 959, 993, 1026, 1028, 1047, 1068, 1145, 1186, 1430. *See also* Assembly,

freedom of; Association, freedom of; Press, freedom of; Speech, freedom of; Religion
First Amendment Foundation, 420
"First Freedom" treaty, 483
Fish Committee, of U.S. House of Representatives, 254, 256, 309. *See also* House Un-American Activities Committee
Flag salute controversies, 81, 303, 365–370
Florida, 884, 1005, 1308, 1363
FOIA, *see* Freedom of Information Act
Foreign policy, U.S., 458, 460, 809, 814, 889, 928, 931, 933, 949, 952, 957, 958, 1014–1021, 1170, 1189, 1179. *See also* Aliens, immigrants, refugees; Central Intelligence Agency; Human rights; National security
Fort Jackson, South Carolina, 722, 729
Fort Leavenworth, Kansas, 104
Fourteenth Amendment, of U.S. Constitution, 213, 1025
France, 847, 1075
Freedom from Censorship, 317
Freedom of Information Act (FOIA) of 1966, 419, 420, 422, 424, 520, 693, 810, 829, 932, 934, 935, 948, 953–956, 1354, 1403. *See also* Central Intelligence Agency; Federal Bureau of Investigation; Surveillance

Gastonia, North Carolina, 144, 277

Gault decision (*In re Gault*), 535
Gay rights, *see* Lesbian and Gay Rights Project of ACLU
Geneva, Switzerland, 1114
Georgia, 592, 602, 811, 1297, 1309, 1364
 Atlanta, 602, 1297, 1309, 1364
Germany, 119, 294, 484. *See also* Nazis
Gideon v. Wainwright, 535
Gitlow v. New York, 151, 152, 154, 209, 213
Gobitis v. Pennsylvania, 81, 366
Goldmark case, 390, 393
Government employees, rights of, *see* Employee rights
Government surveillance, *see* Privacy; Surveillance
Grand juries, 601
Griswold v. Connecticut, 650, 656, 662
Grove City College v. Bell, 921

Habeas corpus, 882
Hague v. CIO, 276, 281, 289
Handbooks, ACLU, 27–68
Handicapped persons, rights of, *see* Disabled persons; Ill persons
Hardwick v. Bowers, 81,
Hatch Act of 1939, 428
Hate speech, 372, 842–855
"Hatrack" case, 211
Hawaii, 1310, 1365
Health professionals, 33, 972
"Heckler's veto," 681
Herndon v. Lowry, 145, 246
Hirabayashi v. United States, 81
Hispanic-Americans, 912. *See also* Aliens, immigrants, refugees; Farm workers
 Spanish language publications, 27, 28, 912, 1017

Subject Index

HIV infection, *see* AIDS; Ill persons, rights of
Holland, 1113
Hollywood, *see* Blacklisting; Movies
Homelessness, *see* Housing
Homosexuals, *see* Lesbian and Gay rights Project of ACLU
Hospital patients, rights of, *see* Elderly persons; Ill persons; Mentally disabled
House of Representatives, U.S., *see* Congress, U.S.
House Un-American Activities Committee (HUAC), 250–252, 254, 256, 257, 262, 267, 268, 271, 309, 382, 404, 420, 423, 432, 434–444, 628, 1152, 1255, 1450, 1451. *See also* Communism; Lusk Committee; Tenney Committee; Wilkinson, Frank
Housing, homelessness, 1003, 1006–1008, 1098, 1099
HUAC, *see* House Un-American Activities Committee
Human rights, international, 466, 481–484, 847, 851, 1020–1021, 1068–1077, 1119, 1120, 1157, 1165, 1166, 1170, 1188, 1190, 1192–1196, 1202, 1205, 1207, 1411
Humanism, 1262
Huston Plan, 425
Hydrogen bomb "secret," and *Progressive* magazine, 826

Idaho, 1311

Ill persons, rights of, 32, 40, 43, 44, 49, 961, 962, 972, 979, 999. *See also* AIDS; Disabled persons; Elderly persons; Mentally disabled
Illegal aliens, *see* Aliens
Illinois, 73, 218, 282, 284, 391, 479, 497, 576, 598, 617, 673–690, 716, 897, 899–901, 1001, 1002, 1312, 1366
Immigrants, rights of, *see* Aliens, immigrants, refugees
Immigration and Aliens' Rights Task Force, of ACLU, 1015, 1293
Immigration Reform and Control Act (IRCA) of 1986, 1015
Imperial Valley, California, *see* California, labor disputes in
Imprisonment, *see* Due process; Prisoners' rights
Indiana, 385, 394, 401, 557, 836, 1313, 1367
Indianapolis, 385, 394, 401, 557, 836, 1313, 1367
Indian Reorganization Act of 1934, 239, 241
Indians, North American, *see* Native Americans
Injunctions, 173, 174, 288
Integration, racial, *see* Civil rights; Race
International information exchange, 809, 814, 1179. *See also* Export control laws, and free speech; Passports; Travel restrictions; Visas
Internment camps, *see* Japanese-Americans
Iowa, 81, 1314, 1368

Iran-Contra scandal, 889, 931, 949, 952, 957, 958
IRCA, *see* Immigration Reform and Control Act
Israel, 1066, 1075
IWW, *see* Industrial Workers of the World

Japan, 1170, 1189, 1200
Japanese-Americans, 81, 354–364, 1168, 1169, 1197
Jehovah's Witnesses, 81, 303, 365–370
Jersey City, New Jersey, 276, 281, 289
Jews, 473, 503, 517, 684, 1051, 1142, 1194
Journalism, 59, 228, 1283
Journalists, rights of, 59, 228. *See also* Censorship; Press, freedom of; Publishing
Justice Department, U.S., 164, 165, 356, 359, 620, 834, 840, 841, 1004. *See also* Federal Bureau of Investigation; Privacy; Surveillance
Juvenile courts, 1094, 1101, 1107, 1109

Kansas, 104, 245, 918, 1315, 1369
Kentucky, 278, 1316, 1370
Kenya, 1018
Korea, 1075, 1173, 1454
Korean War, 1454
Korematsu v. United States, 356

Labor, rights of, 65, 113, 116, 122, 130, 144, 145, 149, 156, 159, 169–179, 198, 275–291, 311, 343, 348, 349, 455, 472, 485–492, 578, 587, 590, 756, 1013, 1121, 1126, 1133, 1143, 1145, 1164, 1289, 1352, 1355, 1412, 1441, 1448. *See also* Employee rights
CIO, 276, 281, 289
La Follette Committee, of U.S. Senate, 286
Laird v. Tatum, 608
Landrum-Griffin Act of 1959, 485, 487, 489, 490
Lawyers, *see* Attorneys
Legislation, *see* Congress, U.S.; Public interest groups, strategies; State laws
Lesbian and Gay Rights Project, of ACLU, 23, 821, 973–975, 977, 978, 981, 1293
Libel, 258, 266, 272, 295, 306, 310, 315, 336, 390, 393, 505. *See also* Censorship; Journalism; Speech, freedom of
Libraries, 559, 560, 696, 811, 824, 826, 830. *See also* Censorship
Lie detectors, 22
Litigation, *see* Attorneys; Public interest groups, strategies
Little Rock, Arkansas, 862
Lobbying, *see* Public interest groups, strategies
Los Angeles, California (city and county), 448, 576, 581, 604, 605, 715, 896, 898, 900, 1303
Louisiana, 1317
Loyalty, political, 99, 119, 139, 204, 212, 229, 232, 338, 382, 410, 411, 426–429, 445–449, 573, 728, 1042, 1136, 1137, 1148, 1149, 1239, 1270, 1355

Subject Index

Loyalty oaths, 229, 232, 338, 410, 411, 426, 427, 445–449, 573. *See also* Academic freedom; Federal Loyalty Program; House Un-American Activities Committee; Smith Act
Lusk Committee (Joint Legislative Committee Investigating Seditious Activities, New York state legislature), 99, 119, 139
Lusk-Stevenson Report, *see* Lusk Committee
Lynching, *see* Race; Vigilantism

Maine, 1318, 1371
Maryland, 391, 1319, 1372
Marxism, 1133. *See also* Communism
Massachusetts, 202, 211, 256, 313, 495, 725, 850, 1320, 1373, 1141, 1408, 1411, 1408, 1411, 1413, 1415, 1426, 1428, 1431
"McCarthyism," 228, 386, 389, 398–400, 522, 620, 1256, 1257
McCollum case (*Ill. ex rel. v. Board of Education*), 497
Media access, 701, 709
Medical professionals, *see* Health professionals
Medical records, confidentiality of, 972, 979, 999
Mentally disabled persons, rights of, 43, 44, 45, 70, 542, 550, 622–627. *See also* Disabled persons; Elderly persons; Ill persons
Mentally ill, rights of, *see* Mentally disabled

Mentally retarded, *see* Mentally disabled
Mexican-Americans, 912. *See also* Aliens, immigrants, refugees; Farm workers
Spanish language publications, 27, 28, 912, 1017
Michigan, 195, 391, 622, 831, 855, 897, 1321, 1374
Middle East, 1066, 1075, 1192–1195, 1205
Midwestern U.S., 17, 1298–1351, 1356–1399
Military personnel, rights of, 46, 104, 344–347, 542, 710, 730, 832, 833, 1091. *See also* Draft; Selective service; Veterans' rights
Militias, state, 275
Miners, *see* Labor
Minneapolis, Minnesota, 373, 835, 836, 1322, 1375
Minnesota, 223, 310, 373, 571, 571, 580, 824, 835, 836, 857, 916, 980, 1322, 1375
Minorities, racial, *see* Race
Minority political parties, 249, 323
Minors, rights of, *see* Young people; Families
"Miracle, The," 519
Miranda v. Arizona, 609
Miranda warning, 609. *See also* Due process; Police
Mississippi, 1259, 1323
Missouri, 830, 1095, 1098, 1095, 1099, 1104, 1105, 1108, 1324, 1325, 1377, 1378
"Monkey Trial," *see* Scopes trial
Monopolies, 510, 511
Montana, 1326, 1379
Mountain States Regional Office, of ACLU, 17, 1296
Mountain States Observer, 17

Movies
  blacklisting, 414
  censorship in, 312, 317, 519
Music, censorship in, 815, 822

NAACP, *see* National Association for the Advancement of Colored People
National Association for the Advancement of Colored People (NAACP), 153, 468, 473, 478, 881–883, 921, 1051, 1054, 1055, 1449
  Legal Defense Fund (LDF), 881–883, 921, 1054, 1055
National Capital Area, office of ACLU, 713, 1327, 1380
National Council on Freedom from Censorship (NCFC), of ACLU, 317, 518, 519
National office, of ACLU, 1293, 1354
National Prison Project, of ACLU, 15, 639, 640, 642, 961–970, 1295, 1407
National Prison Project Journal, 15, 640
National Recovery Administration (NRA), National Industrial Recovery Act of 1933, 1143
National security, 14, 438, 628–638, 728, 731, 927–960, 1018, 1226, 1284, 1294. *See also* Center for National Security Studies
National Security Litigation Project, of ACLU, 1294
Native Americans, 41, 239, 241, 242, 243, 580, 916

Navy, U.S., 588
Nazis, 292–296, 326, 327, 336, 673–690, 1138
NBC Radio, 327
NCARL, *see* National Committee Against Repressive Legislation
NCFC, *see* National Council on Freedom from Censorship
NCCL, *see* National Council for Civil Liberties
NCCO, *see* National Committee on Conscientious Objectors
NEA, *see* National Education Association
Near v. Minnesota, 310
Nebraska, 1328, 1381, 1403
NECLC, *see* National Emergency Civil Liberties Committee
Netherlands, 1113
Nevada, 1329, 1382
"New Deal," 224, 226, 260, 280, 286, 1143
New Hampshire, 842, 1330, 1383, 1409
  Dartmouth College, 842, 1409
New Jersey, 144, 175, 179, 198, 199, 276, 281, 289, 295, 304, 576, 608, 781, 782, 1331, 1352, 1384, 1402, 1420, 1423
New Mexico, 1332, 1385
New York City, 101, 208, 299, 339, 341, 342, 480, 533, 541, 549, 564, 565, 567, 570, 574, 578, 587, 590, 599, 611–613, 618, 667, 696, 721–723, 741, 747, 750, 752, 774, 775, 864, 897, 900, 901, 903, 904, 1008,

Subject Index

1333, 1386, 1432, 1439, 1440, 1443, 1446
City College, 339, 341, 342
Commission on Human Rights, 741, 747, 750
homeless persons, rights of, 1003, 1008
police, 299, 599, 611–613, 897, 900, 901, 903, 904
Police Practices Project, of New York Civil Liberties Union, 611–613
Public Library, 1439, 1440, 1443, 1446, 1448, 1453
schools, 208, 564, 567, 578, 587, 590, 696
Student Rights Project, of New York Civil Liberties Union, 564, 567
teachers' strike of 1968, 578, 587, 590
New York state, 99, 119, 139, 151, 209, 213, 312, 383, 391, 533, 541, 549, 564, 565, 567, 570, 574, 587, 590, 618, 625, 667, 721–723, 750, 752, 774, 775, 864, 1008, 1333, 1386, 1412, 1432
Criminal Anarchy Act of 1902, 151, 152, 209, 213
Gitlow v. New York, 151, 152, 154, 209, 213
Lusk Committee, 99, 119, 139
Lusk-Stevenson Report, *see* New York State, Lusk Committee
state legislature, 99, 119, 139
Willowbrook School, 625
New Zealand, 1075
Newark, New Jersey, 576, 1331, 1384
Nicaragua, 952

NLRB, *see* National Labor Relations Board
NODL, *see* National Office for Decent Literature
Norris-LaGuardia Act of 1932, 174
North Carolina, 144, 277, 1334, 1387
North Dakota, 1335
NRA, *see* National Recovery Administration
Nuclear energy, 907, 936
Nurses, rights of, 33

Oaths, *see* Loyalty oaths
Obscenity, 196, 203, 207, 375, 508, 509, 514, 692, 694, 708, 1224. *See also* Censorship; Pornography; Sexuality
Offensive speech, protected, and college campus codes, 842–855
Ohio, 114, 603, 1336, 1388
Oklahoma, 1337, 1389
Older persons, *see* Elderly persons
Omaha, Nebraska, 1403
Opinions, about civil liberties, *see* Public opinion
Oregon, 708, 1338, 1390

Pacifism, 93, 94, 96, 97, 100, 101, 102, 106, 117, 120, 123, 124, 236, 714, 717, 725, 832, 833, 1091, 1113, 1122, 1252, 1262, 1284, 1285–1287, 1355, 1447, 1452, 1454, 1404, 1411, 1440, 1447, 1452, 1454. *See also* Conscientious objectors; Draft; Military personnel; Political prisoners
Palestine, 1018, 1205
Palmer Raids, 110, 140, 165

Parents, rights of, 36, 48. *See also* Families
Passaic, New Jersey, strike, of 1926, 178
Passports, visas, 458, 460, 809, 814, 1179. *See also* Export control laws, and free speech; International information exchange; Travel restrictions
Paterson, New Jersey, strike, of 1924, 175, 198, 199
Patients, rights of, *see* AIDS; Elderly persons; Ill persons; Mentally disabled
Pawtucket, Rhode Island, 856
Peace movement, *see* Pacifism
Peekskill, New York, 383
Pennsylvania, 144, 170, 171, 412, 447, 900, 921, 1339
    Loyalty Oath, 447
Penology, *see* Prisons
Pentagon Papers, 728, 731
Philadelphia, Pennsylvania, 412, 447, 900, 1339
Physicians, *see* Doctors
Pierce v. Society of Sisters, 142
Planned Parenthood, 657, 1277, 1278
Poe v. Ullman, 662
Police, 51, 71, 130, 133, 171, 297–302, 319, 479, 480, 598, 599, 602–607, 609, 611–613, 615, 617, 618, 620, 713, 715, 716, 775, 879, 894–910
    private security forces, 907. *See also* Vigilantes
    review boards, 599, 618
    rights of, 51. *See also* Criminal justice; Due process; *Miranda* warning; Suspects' rights
Police Practices Project, of New York Civil Liberties Union, 611–613
Political campaigning, 30, 752, 773, 796–804
Political prisoners, 104, 123, 160, 161, 162, 163. *See also* Amnesty; Human rights
"Politically correct" speech, expression, 842–855
Polygraph, *see* Lie detector
Poor people, rights of, 52, 479, 549, 550, 1109, 1100
Pornography, 375, 508, 509, 692, 694, 708, 834, 840, 841.
    See also Censorship; Obscenity; Sexuality
    Attorney General's Commission on, 694, 834, 840, 841
    feminist anti-pornography movement, 835–837, 839
Portland, Oregon, 708, 1338
Poverty, 52, 479, 549, 550, 1099, 1100
Prejudice, racial, *see* Race
President, U.S.:
    campaign for presidency, 1988, 92, 796–804
    executive orders, 939
    executive privilege, 631
    political campaigning, 752, 796–804
    war powers of, 721, 937, 942, 958
Press, freedom of 59, 71, 137, 196, 201–203, 207, 211, 228, 307, 310, 317, 371, 372, 374, 375, 380, 483, 505–517, 518, 521–523, 691, 692, 694–696, 699, 700,

Subject Index

702, 703, 706, 708, 728, 731, 808–809, 811, 818, 820–822, 824, 826, 834–841, 870, 888, 927–929, 950, 1026, 1028, 1075, 1179, 1224, 1236, 1430, 1434. *See also* Censorship; First Amendment
Preventive detention, 600
Prisoners, political, *see* Political prisoners
Prisoners' rights, 15, 35, 53, 70, 160–163, 542, 549, 639–642, 961–970, 1295, 1407
  capital punishment, 591–596, 881, 882
Prisons, imprisonment, 15, 53, 70, 104, 112, 123, 127, 160–163, 542, 549, 639–642, 961–970, 1102, 1112, 1117, 1122, 1239, 1295, 1407
Privacy, 9, 39, 54, 55, 71, 164, 166, 252, 319, 454–457, 459, 610, 632, 634, 637, 643–662, 698, 810, 927, 971–999, 1009, 1012. *See also* Freedom of Information Act; Reproductive rights; Surveillance
Privacy Act of 1976, 644, 810
Privacy Project, of ACLU, 645, 660
Privacy Report, 645
Private police, security forces, guards, *see* Police
Probation, 1094, 1097. *See also* Criminal justice
Pro-choice movement, *see* Abortion; Reproductive rights
Progressive magazine, and bomb design "secret" controversy, 826
Project on Political Surveillance, of ACLU, 614, 900
Project on Technology and Civil Liberties, of ACLU, 1294
Protected classes of persons, and free speech, 842–855
Protest, right to, *see* Expression, freedom of; Speech, freedom of
Protestants, 441, 501, 1252, 1289–1291, 1433
Public assembly, *see* Assembly, freedom of
Public attitudes, *see* Public opinion
Public employees, rights of, *see* Employee rights
Public interest groups, advocacy, 179, 245, 279, 473, 502, 533, 549, 581, 594, 642, 663, 740, 748, 749, 769, 786, 966, 968, 1043–1057, 1068, 1069
  strategies, tactics, 12, 69, 142, 179, 245, 279, 442, 451, 502, 504, 533, 549, 581, 594, 617, 642, 663, 708, 740, 748, 749, 769, 776, 786, 810, 828, 836, 915, 926, 966, 968, 970, 983, 989, 995, 1044, 1046, 1049, 1050, 1052, 1054–1056, 1278. *See also* Social movements; specific subject, e.g., Civil rights; Women's rights
Public opinion:
  about ACLU, 257, 758, 1067
  about civil liberties, 149, 150, 257, 343, 402, 758, 1058–1067
Publishing industry, 176, 380, 510, 827, 1253, 1254, 1425

"underground" press, 827. See also Censorship
"Purity," see Censorship; Obscenity
"Purity," racial, see Race

Quakers, see American Friends Service Committee; Swarthmore College

Race, 22, 58, 69, 71, 88, 131, 138, 153, 239–247, 306, 343–350, 354–364, 380, 475–478, 505, 550, 574–578, 580–582, 584–590, 592, 603, 605, 673, 744, 780, 842–855, 911–918, 1092, 1098, 1146, 1191, 1266, 1268, 1269, 1272
  affirmative action, 915, 917
  racist speech, protected, and college campus codes, 842–855. See also Civil rights
Racketeer Influenced and Corrupt Organizations Act (RICO) of 1970, 887, 888, 890
Radio, 205, 206, 308, 317, 327, 385, 415, 510, 511, 524
  blacklisting in, 415
  censorship in, 205, 206, 308, 317, 524
  monopoly control of, 510, 511
Records, and privacy, see Access; Confidentiality
"Red Scare," see Communism
"Red squads," see Police, misconduct; Surveillance
Refugees, rights of, see Aliens, immigrants, refugees
Registration:
  of aliens, see Aliens

draft, see Selective service
of members of dissident organizations, 252, 459
"Released time" law, see Religion, and schools
Religion, 9, 22, 71, 121, 142, 183, 188, 193, 303, 304, 306, 365–370, 468, 493–505, 508, 663–672, 789, 856–878, 856–878, 994, 1119, 1120, 1141, 1142, 1144, 1226, 1252, 1276, 1284, 1289–1291, 1433. See also Scopes trial; Speech, freedom of; Names of individual denominations, e.g., Catholics, Jehovah's Witnesses, Jews
  cults, rights of members, 863, 866
  and schools, 183, 187, 188, 190, 193, 582, 663, 667, 857–860, 862, 865, 867–871, 873, 874, 876–878
  Creation science, 183, 187, 188, 190, 193, 859, 860, 862, 865, 867, 868, 870, 871, 874, 878
  equal access law, 858, 869, 873, 877
  prayer in public schools, 497, 666, 789, 876
  private schools, 582, 663, 667, 857
  "released time" law, 497
  social gospel, 1289, 1291
Relocation camps, see Japanese-Americans
Reporters, rights of, see Journalists, rights of
Reproductive freedom, see Reproductive rights

Subject Index

Reproductive Freedom Project, of ACLU, 16, 24, 986–995, 998, 1293
    Docket, 986
    Reproductive Rights Update, 16
Reproductive rights, 16, 22, 24, 493, 496, 643, 646–648, 651, 652, 656–658, 775, 778, 888, 902, 905, 985–998, 1277, 1278, 1284, 1414, 1437. *See also* Privacy; Sexuality; Women's rights
    "chastity act" (federal legislation), 993
    fetal rights, 996
    "human life" amendment to Constitution, 985, 991
    parental notification laws, 987, 988, 990
    Roe v. Wade, 648, 650
    women's health clinics, disruptions and picketing, 778, 902, 905, 989
Research, university, government-sponsored, 563, 940. *See also* Academic freedom
Retardation, retarded persons, *see* Mentally disabled
Rhode Island, 856, 1340, 1392
RICO, *see* Racketeer Influenced and Corrupt Organizations Act
Right to die, 999
Rights, *see* name of individual group or subject matter; e.g., Artists; Civil rights; Gay rights; Women's rights
Right-wing groups, politics, *see* Conservatism;
Roe v. Wade, 648, 650

Roman Catholic Church, *see* Catholic Church
Russia, 1116, 1117, 1119, 1120, 1139. *See also* Soviet Union

Sacco and Vanzetti case, 144, 180–182, 1151, 1255
St. Louis, Missouri, 1098, 1099, 1104, 1105, 1108
San Diego, California, 902
San Francisco, California, 514
Schools, *see* Academic freedom; Education; Teachers' rights
Scopes trial, 144, 183–194, 1183, 1410
Scottsboro case, 145, 244, 247
Search and seizure, 9, 62, 610, 695, 703, 771, 895, 1009, 1012. *See also* Due process; Police; Privacy
Seattle, Washington, 910, 1096
Security, and loyalty, *see* Federal Loyalty Program; Loyalty; National security
Security, national, *see* National security
Security forces, guards, private, *see* Police
Sedition, 119, 140, 197, 204, 248, 282, 373, 378, 380. *See also* Loyalty; Smith Act; Speech, freedom of
Sedition Act of 1918, 121, 204. *See also* Espionage Act of 1917
Segregation, racial, *see* Civil rights; Race
Selective service laws, 93, 111, 115, 125, 351, 710, 712, 832, 833, 1160, 1161. *See also*

Conscientious objectors;
Draft; Military
personnel; War Self-
incrimination, *see* Fifth
Amendment
Senate, U.S., *see* Congress, U.S.
Separation of church and state, *see*
Religion
Servicemen's rights, *see* Military
personnel
Sexuality, 16, 22, 23, 24, 22, 196,
203, 657, 658, 834–841,
971–984, 1224. *See also*
Lesbian and Gay Rights
Project of ACLU;
Obscenity; Pornography;
Privacy; Reproductive
rights; Women's rights
sex education, 196, 203, 1224
Sexist speech, protected, and
college campus codes,
842–855
Shelley v. Kraemer, 478
Single persons, rights of, 60
Sioux Falls, South Dakota, 671
"Sit-ins," 575
Skokie case, 673–690, 759, 1063
Slander, *see* Libel
Smith Act of 1940, 248, 373, 1136,
1158, 1172, 1174, 1239.
See also Communism
Social change, *see* Public interest
groups; Social
movements
Social movements, 106, 128, 158,
540–542, 549, 550, 792,
1024, 1036, 1037, 1045,
1048, 1050–1052, 1093,
1100, 1103, 1198, 1199,
1262, 1289–1291. *See also*
Public advocacy; specific
subject, e.g., Civil Rights;
Women's rights

Socialism, 137, 234, 249, 323, 373,
402, 1124, 1203, 1204,
1262, 1285–1287, 1440
South Carolina, 722, 729, 1341,
1393
South Dakota, 671, 1342
South Korea, 1075, 1173, 1454
Southern Regional Office, of
ACLU, 577, 585, 1266–
1269, 1297
Soviet Union, 456, 1001, 1002,
1117, 1119, 1120, 1139,
1202
Spanish language publications, 27,
28, 912, 1017
Special Commission on the FBI
Files, of ACLU, 419
Speech, freedom of, 56, 59, 61, 71,
93, 94, 97, 98, 101, 108,
117, 120, 121, 126, 132,
133, 137, 148–150, 159,
169, 171, 173, 175, 177–
179, 195–200, 202–204,
207, 208, 228–234, 258,
271, 290, 292, 293, 306–
309, 317, 333–336, 338,
340, 351–353, 371, 372,
374, 376–380, 464, 483,
505, 508–513, 516–519,
561, 586, 673–685, 687,
689, 697–701, 705, 718,
719–721, 723, 727, 729,
762, 778, 808–809, 812–
817, 819–821, 823, 831,
834–855, 887, 888, 902,
905, 909, 927–929, 989,
1009, 1010, 1012, 1026,
1028, 1031, 1032, 1034,
1059, 1075, 1125, 1136–
1138, 1149, 1178, 1179,
1207, 1224, 1236, 1270,
1272, 1430, 1434, 1438
"heckler's veto," 681

Subject Index

"politically correct" speech, 842–855
symbolic speech, 586
 at women's health clinics, 778, 902, 905, 989. *See also* First Amendment; Skokie case
Speech codes (racist, sexist expression), 842–855
Spies, spying, *see* Espionage; Surveillance
State laws, 69, 151, 152, 183–195, 197, 210, 249, 275, 282, 283, 288, 295, 367, 391, 445, 447, 497, 737, 750, 772, 779, 980, 1106
 anti-Communist, 391, 445, 447
 and child welfare, 1106
 criminal syndicalism, 151, 152, 195, 197, 210, 283. *See also* State laws, sedition
 on education, 183, 497, 857
  teaching "Creationism" and evolution, in public schools, 144, 183, 185, 187, 188, 193, 860, 862, 865, 867, 868, 870, 871, 874, 878. *See also* Scopes trial
 on juries, 737
 on labor, 275, 282, 283, 288
 on libel, 295
 on loyalty, 445, 447
 on religion, 367, 497. *See also* State laws, education
 on sedition, 197, 282. *See also* State laws, criminal syndicalism
 on sexuality, 980
 on voting, 249. *See also* Civil rights
State legislatures, 99, 119, 139, 390, 393, 430, 433, 1095

State militias, 275
State supreme courts, 199, 295, 779
Strategies for social change, *see* Public interest groups, strategies
Strikes, *see* Labor
Stromberg v. California, 305
Student publications, 228. *See also* Censorship; Education; Press, freedom of
Student Rights Project, of New York Civil Liberties Union, 564, 567
Students' rights, 61, 228, 233, 234, 340, 368, 369, 405, 408, 409, 542, 558–562, 564–571, 868, 869, 873, 877. *See also* Academic freedom; Education; Speech, freedom of
 corporal punishment and, 569
 Equal Access Act, 858, 869, 873, 877
Supreme Court, U.S., 92, 105, 142, 181, 209, 213, 219, 223, 224, 244, 245, 246, 276, 281, 305, 310, 330, 356, 359, 361, 362, 363, 378, 366, 387, 451, 452, 468, 469, 475–477, 502, 519, 535, 537, 538, 597, 608, 609, 648, 665, 666, 735, 743, 749, 779, 783, 805–807, 918, 959, 960, 999, 1022, 1024, 1025, 1242–1244, 1409, 1419
 Bork nomination, 92, 805–807
 Burger Court, 538
 Warren Court, 387
Surveillance, by government, 39, 164, 166–168, 319, 419, 420, 425, 454–457, 607, 608, 614, 620, 621, 629,

630, 632, 634, 637, 649, 653, 654, 659–661, 728, 826, 827, 887, 888, 890, 897–901, 903, 904, 906–910, 927, 929, 930, 946, 1174, 1354, 1355, 1403. *See also* Central Intelligence Agency; Federal Bureau of Investigation; Freedom of Information Act; Police; Privacy
Suspects' rights, 9, 62, 479, 480, 600, 601, 606, 609, 620, 879–880, 884–895. *See also* Due process; Miranda warning; Police
Switzerland, 1114
Syndicalism, *see* Criminal syndicalism laws

Task Force on Civil Liberties in the Workplace, of ACLU, 1011, 1012
Teachers' rights, 63, 229, 232, 233, 234, 405–407, 409, 410, 411, 413, 558–560, 572, 573, 578, 817, 1042, 1137, 1140, 1148, 1149. *See also* Academic freedom; Education; Loyalty
Teaching, *see* Academic freedom; Education; Teachers' rights
Television, 385, 394, 701, 704, 705
Tenant farmers, 153, 285
Tenants' rights, 64, 1003
Tennessee, 183, 187, 188, 193, 194, 1183, 1343, 1394
Tenney Committee (California Fact-Finding Committee on Un-American Activities), 433

Texas, 772, 776, 777, 912, 1017, 1344, 1395, 1414, 1434
Tinker v. Des Moines, 81
Topeka, Kansas, 245, 918
Topeka Board of Education, *see Brown v. Board of Education*
Travel restrictions, 458, 460, 809, 814, 1014–1019, 1108, 1179. *See also* Aliens, immigrants, refugees, rights of; Export control laws; International information exchange; Passports; Visas
Trial, right to, 691, 700
Tribal rights, *see* Native Americans

Un-American activities, *see* House Un-American Activities Committee; Lusk Committee; Tenney Committee
Undocumented aliens, undocumented workers, *see* Aliens, immigrants, refugees, rights of; Employee rights
Unions, *see* Employee rights; Labor
United States v. McWilliams, 378
USSR, *see* Soviet Union
Utah, 1345, 1396

Vermont, 1346, 1397
Veterans' rights, 66. *See also* Military personnel; War
Vice societies, *see* Censorship
Victims' rights, 31
Vienna, Austria, 1124

Subject Index

Vietnam War, 495, 508, 530, 544, 549, 551, 710–731, 1226, 1259, 1269, 1454
Vigilantes, 102, 114, 131, 153, 291, 366
Violence, right to advocate, 200
Virginia, 221, 1347, 1398
Visas, passports, 458, 460, 809, 814, 1179. *See also* Aliens, immigrants, refugees, rights of; Export control laws; International information exchange; Travel restrictions
Voters' rights, 30, 249, 323. *See also* Civil rights
Voting Rights Project, of ACLU, 913

Wagner Act of 1935, 287
War, 93, 94, 96, 100–103, 105, 114, 120, 123, 124, 204, 212, 322, 324, 329, 333–335, 351, 374, 365, 508, 530, 544, 549, 551, 721, 780, 937, 942, 958, 1152, 1178, 1181, 1355. *See also* Conscientious objectors; Military personnel; Korean War; Vietnam War; World War I; World War II
war powers, as delegated by Constitution, 721, 937, 942, 958
War Memorial Auditorium controversy, *see* Indianapolis
War Powers Act of 1971, 937, 942
Warren Court (U.S. Supreme court), 387, 617

Washington, D.C., 1354, 1354, 1410, 1422, 1424, 1425, 1433, 1435–1437
National Capital Area office of ACLU, 713, 1327, 1380
Washington office of ACLU, 12, 25, 435, 455, 554, 631, 632, 637, 659, 728, 761, 786–788, 840, 941, 943, 944, 959, 1266–1269, 1294, 1354
Washington state, 80, 390, 393, 391, 910, 1096, 1348
Watergate scandal, 495, 732–736, 959, 1226, 1226, 1269
Watts, Los Angeles, California, 605
Welfare recipients, rights of, 755. *See also* Economic rights; Housing; Poverty
Welfare state, 540, 541
West Virginia, 144, 1121, 1349
Willowbrook School, New York State, 625
WILPF, *see* Women's International League for Peace and Freedom
Wiretapping, 454–457, 632, 649. *See also* Federal Bureau of Investigation; Surveillance
Wisconsin, 1350, 1399, 1404, 1418, 1430, 1450
Wisconsin Historical Society, 1399, 1404, 1418, 1430, 1450
Women's rights, 26, 67, 550, 579, 737–750, 835–837, 839, 842–855, 917, 919–926, 985–998, 1119, 1120, 1198, 1199, 1400, 1401, 1411, 1426, 1428, 1431, 1437
affirmative action, 917

childbirth and pregnancy, 16, 22, 493, 643, 646–648, 651, 656–658, 657, 775, 778, 888, 902, 905, 925, 985–998, 1437
Equal Rights Amendment, 738, 742, 744
feminist anti-pornography movement, 835–837, 839
reproductive rights, 16, 22, 24, 493, 496, 643, 646–648, 651, 652, 656–658, 657, 775, 778, 888, 902, 905, 985–998, 1437
sexist speech, protected, and college campus codes, 842–855
Women's Rights Project, of ACLU, 26, 740, 748, 749, 919, 920, 925, 996, 1293
Workers' rights, *see* Employee rights; Labor
World War I, 93–97, 99, 100–105, 108, 109, 114, 118, 120, 122–126, 160, 161, 162, 163, 333, 1042, 1092, 1148, 1270, 1292, 1355, 1436, 1444, 1454
World War II, 107, 108, 322, 324, 326–329, 332–337, 344–347, 351–365, 374, 376–380, 1153, 1160–1162, 1166, 1167–1171, 1175, 1176, 1178, 1181, 1189, 1200, 1439, 1454
Wyoming, 1351

Yale University, 427, 428, 430, 1405, 1406, 1429, 1444
Young people. *See also* Education; Students' rights:
publications for, 22, 76, 78, 340, 567
rights of, 22, 68, 76, 652, 753, 987, 988, 990, 1000–1002, 1094, 1101, 1106, 1107, 1109
parental notification laws concerning reproductive rights, 987, 988, 990

LIBRARY USE ONLY
DOES NOT CIRCULATE